GW00374951

Ashraf's Blessings of

MARRIAGE©

Ashraf's Amānat

An Imprint of

Amānah Studio ~ Dewsbury ~ UK

ഇൻൽ

Shaykh Abul Hasan 'Ali Nadwee 🌸 *commented, '...A close study of the life of Prophet Muhammad* 🌸 *will reveal such respect, consideration, justice, appreciation and perception for the natural inclinations of the weaker gender, which are not found in the lives of other great personalities or even other Prophets* 🌸*. The informality with his wives; participation in their lawful interests and forethought for their inclinations is incomparable. This mild and affable approach was not restricted to the womenfolk but encompassed the children also...'* (The Rank of Ladies in Islām)

Dr. Annie Besant (a British Theosophist) wrote: 'But do you mean to tell me that the man who in the full flush of youthful vigour, a young man of four and twenty (24 years), married a woman much his senior, and remained faithful to her for six and twenty years (26 years), at fifty years of age when the passions are dying married for lust and sexual passion? Not thus are men's lives to be judged. And you look at the women whom he married, you will find that by every one of them an alliance was made for his people, or something was gained for his followers, or the woman was in sore need of protection.'

(The Life and Teachings of Muhammad, Madras, 1932)

Ashraf's Blessings of

MARRIAGE©

Based Upon the Teachings

of

Shaykh Ashraf 'Ali Thãnwi ◈,

Shaykh-ul-Hadeeth Ibrãheem Palanpoori ◈,

Shaykh Maseehullah Khãn ◈,

Shaykh-ul-Hadeeth Zakariyyã ◈,

Shaykh Mufti Muhammad Shafee ◈,

Shaykh Mufti 'Abdur Raheem Lajpoori ◈,

Shaykh Mufti 'Ãshiq 'Ellahi Madanee ◈,

Shaykh Abul Hasan 'Ali Nadwee ◈

Shaykh Dr. Abdul Hayy Ãrifee ◈,

Shaykh Abrãr-ul-Haqq Hardoi ◈,

Shaykh Hakeem Muhammad Akhtar,

Shaykh Mufti Taqee 'Uthmãni,

Shaykh Muhammad Saleem Dhorat et al

Editorial Board

Maulãnã Qãri Yousuf, Maulana Maseehullah *&*

Hafiz Muhammad 'Abdullah

Series Editor

Hãfiz Aslam Patel

BA (Hons) Arch. Dip. Arch.

ASHRAF'S AMÃNAT

Amãnah Studio, PO Box 12, Dewsbury, UK, WF12 9YX

Tel: 01924 488929

Copyright Notice

Ashraf's Blessings of Marriage©
ISBN-978-1-902627-01-4 (Hardback)
First Edition 1420 AH/1999CE, Reprinted: 1421 (2000), 1422 (2001), 1423 (2002 & 2003), Enlarged Second Edition: 1424AH/ 2003 CE Reprinted as Softback 1425AH/ 2004 CE.
This Revised & Enlarged Fourth Edition Published 1429/2008
Prepared & Published by M. Aslam Patel of Ashraf's Amānat©,
PO Box 12, Dewsbury, West Yorkshire, U.K., WF12 9YX

Copyright ©2008/1429 M. Aslam Patel of Ashraf's Amānat©
The right of M. Aslam Patel to be identified as author of this work, pursuant to s.77 of the Copyright, Designs & Patents Act 1988, is hereby inserted. All rights reserved. No part of this work may be reproduced in any material form (including photocopying or storing it in any medium by electronic means) without the WRITTEN permissions of the copyright owner and publisher, except in accordance with the provisions of the Copyright, Designs and Patents Act 1988. Any unauthorised act in this respect may lead to legal proceedings.

United Kingdom
British Library Cataloguing-in-Publication Data. A catalogue record for this book is available from the British Library. Copies of this publication have been deposited with The Agent for the Copyright Libraries, London.

United States of America
This book has been registered with The Copyright Office, Library of Congress, 101 Independence Avenue, S.E., Washington, D.C. 20559-6000, U.S.A.

South Africa
A Copy of this book has been deposited with The Legal Deposit Office, National Library of South Africa

India
A Copy of this book has been deposited with the Director, Government of India National Library Belverdere, Calcutta 700027, India

Australia
Under the Australian Copyright Act 1968, a copy of this publication has been deposited with the Copyright Advisor at the Australian Library and the Australian Copyright Council

Canada
A Copy of this book has been deposited with The Legal Deposit Office, National Library of Canada, 395 Wellington Street, Ottawa, Ontario

France
A Copy of this book has been deposited at the Bibliothèque Nationale de France, France

Pakistan
A Copy of this book has been deposited with the National Library of Pakistan

New Zealand
A Copy of this book has been deposited with The Legal Deposit Office, National Library of New Zealand, PO Box 12-340, Wellington

Malaysia
A Copy of this book has been deposited with the Director, National Library of Malaysia

Recommended Retail Price in UK: £10.00
Buy Direct @ Discounted Online Price from:
www.amanahstudio.org
All proceeds received by Amanah Studio fund new works.

Ashraf's Amānat & Copyright

Shaykh Mufti 'Abdur Raheem Lajpoori ﷺ writes in *Fatāwā Raheemeeyah (Vol. 3)*…

'Any book comes into existence after the toil and labour of the writer, accordingly the foremost right of publishing it belongs to him alone. Moreover, besides the intention of propagating Knowledge of Deen, the author has the right to derive profit from his writings. Accordingly, until the author's interest is connected with the book, nobody else has the right to publish it. Other people who publish a popular book without (written permission from the author) do so only out of selfish commercial interest. Their argument of propagating the Knowledge of Deen (and being of benefit to Muslims) is baseless because if this was a true intention of theirs then what prevents them from buying the Kitāb in large quantities from the author and distributing it for the purpose of thawāb? Similarly, although everybody has the right to adopt a particular title for his (Jamā'at), nevertheless when a certain person has adopted a title for his activity and his finances are bound with the said title...then no one else has the right to use this very title for his business…'

Ashraf's Amānat© is an imprint of Amanah Studio. Through Tawfeeq from Allah ﷻ, we attempt to present authentic Teachings of Pious Scholars in Light of the Qur'ān and Hadeeth for the benefit of western educated Muslims. Our work is ongoing; new titles are under preparation and would be assisted by your support & du'aa's. If you wish to order our books or support our work please write or send Lillah donations to:

Amānah Studio

PO Box 12, Dewsbury, UK, WF12 9YX

Tel: 01924 488929

www.amanahstudio.org

v

Contents

* *Chapter One*

The Importance of Marriage in Islãm

* *Chapter Two*

Consequence of Adultery & Binge Culture

* *Chapter Six*

Performing Nikãh

* *Chapter Seven*

Shab-ê-Zufãf & Ãdabs of Sexual Behaviour

* *Chapter Eight*

The Sunnah Waleemah

* *Chapter Nine*

Advice for the Muslim Couple

* *Chapter Ten*

Common Sexual Problems & Remedies

Common Sexual Problems for Men............ 164

Common Sexual Problems for Ladies

* *Chapter Thirteen*

Marriage & The Importance of Family Ties

Modern Day Extremisms in Family Ties

* *Chapter Fourteen*

Harms of Talāq (Divorce)...............................278

* _Chapter Fifteen_

Pregnancy, Childbirth & Infant Care

* *Chapter Sixteen*

Tarbiyyah (Training) of Muslim Children

* *Chapter Seventeen*

Muslim Children & Importance of Makatib

Foreword

Shaykh Muhammad Saleem Dhorat
Principal Lecturer in Hadeeth, Jāmeah Riyādul-Uloom, Leicester

slām is a code of life which encompasses every aspect of human existence. This includes all facets of the relationship between husband and wife. *Māshā'Allah*, my respected students Maulana Maseehullah Patel, Hafiz Abdullah and associates Maulana Yousuf & Aslam Patel have prepared one of the most comprehensive books on this subject which outline principles for husband and wife right from before engagement to *tarbiyyah* of their children-to-be. It is only through the *Fadhl* of Allah ﷻ this work has been granted wide acceptance and *alhamdulillah* the fourth edition of this very beneficial work is available. Readers will find herein fragrances of many flowers.

In books of hadeeth and fiqh clear guidance on conjugal behaviour is explained in detail. Adhering to these teachings will not only be a means of acquiring a blissful marriage but it will also help in safeguarding one's health. Nowadays, the subject of sex has been overexposed, degraded and misrepresented through channels of mass education and the media (especially on TV and internet). Accordingly it is important to guide our youth in order to save them from sexual deviance. May Allah ﷻ accept this work and make it a means of safeguarding the youth and a means of salvation in the Hereafter. It is an honour for this humble one to be associated with Amānah Studio.

Salãt & Salãms upon our Beloved Nabee ﷺ

Permission & Du'aa's

Shaykh Mufti
Muhammad Taqee 'Uthmãni

Member Shar'eeat Appellate Bench
Supreme Court of Pakistan
Deputy Chairman, Islãmic Fiqh Academy (OIC) Jeddah
Vice-President, Darul Uloom Karachi

Assalamu Alaikum,

Editor,

Ashraf's Amãnat

8th Zil Hijjah 1420

(14th March 2000)

$\mathcal{I}$ am pleased to give you permission for translating some of my discourses in *Islãhi Khutbaat...*If you undertake a new translation, you are permitted from my side.

May Allah ﷻ approve your efforts and make them beneficial for the Ummah.

Ãmeen,

Was-salãm,

(Shaykh Mufti)

Muhammad Taqee 'Uthmãni

﷽

Salāt & Salāms upon our beloved Nabee ﷺ

Preface

Shaykh Yusuf A. Darwan

Senior Lecturer in Hadeeth, Dewsbury, UK

Success in both this world and the Ãkhirah is attainable only through adherence to Deen. For a person to follow Deen: knowledge is conditional and is the first step to success; action and propagation of Deen are the next two steps.

There is a scarcity of well-written, informative and understandable Islãmic literature available in the English language. Muslim youth are highly vulnerable to outside influences. It is therefore imperative to present them with the true teachings of Islãm. Through the infinite Mercy & Grace of Allah ﷻ, Ashraf's Amãnat have published a series of beneficial Islãmic books. May Allah ﷻ grant them Tawfeeq to progress in this noble and rewarding endeavour and bless them with continuous ikhlaas & steadfastness. May Allah ﷻ make these publications beneficial and informative especially for our younger Muslim brothers/ sisters and grant all readers the Tawfeeq to appreciate, learn and practice thereupon.

We hope and pray to Allah ﷻ that this latest publication is just one of many more topics to be covered by brother Aslam Patel of Ashraf's Amãnat. Ãmeen.

(Shaykh) Yusuf A. Darwan

What other Senior Scholars & Mashã-ikh have said about Ashraf's Amãnat₀...

Shaykh 'Abdullah Kapodrawi of Canada...

'These publications contain the works of our akãbir (pious predecessors & elders) upon which we have full confidence. May Allah ﷻ grant greater barakat.'

Shaykh 'Abdul Hameed Isaac of South Africa...

'I am sure and, it is my du'aa, that by this great work Muslims living in western countries or whose mother tongue has become English, will be able to appreciate the great treasures of Islãmic Knowledge...'

Shaykh Mufti Rafee 'Uthmãni...

'Mashã'Allah! Excellent set of publications...'

Shaykh 'Abdur Ra'oof Lajpoori of UK...

'May Allah ﷻ grant ikhlaas and accept your services.'

Shaykh Mufti Zubayr Bhayat of South Africa...

'Mashã'Allah! The work being undertaken is very good & much needed.'

Shaykh Ahmad Sadiq Desai of South Africa...

'May Allah ﷻ accept your service & increase your Deeni activities.'

Shaykh Dr. Ismã'eel Mangera of South Africa...

'May Allah ﷻ fulfil your wishes to serve the Ummah. May your publications be a means of spreading the teachings of our akãbir to others, young and old.'

Shaykh Dr. Muhammad Sãbir ﷺ...

'Shaykh Ashraf 'Ali Thãnwi ﷺ narrated, 'After 50 years, my works will be translated and published on a large scale.' We are today witnessing this event...Mashã'Allah...the heart is pleased...this work is undoubtedly due to the sincerity of our cherished predecessors...'

Shaykh Mufti 'Abdur Rahmãn Mangera of USA...

'Bringing into English the spirit of the work of our pious predecessors is a very noble deed. May Allah ﷻ accept it.'

Shaykh Mufti Saiful Islam of UK...

'Alhamdulillah! The work being produced is very good!'

Salat & Salams Upon The Final Messenger ﷺ

Introduction

$\mathcal{A}$llah ﷻ mentions in the Glorious Qur'ān:

> *'O believers! Fear Allah* ﷻ *and join the company of the truthful (as-saadiqeen).'*

Arabic Proverb,

> *'These are my ancestors whom I am proud of; can you present to me somebody like them?'*

From the inauguration of Islām to today, in every era, for welfare of Servants of Allah ﷻ and for reformation of their character, the gatherings of 'Ulamā and Mashā-ikh have been established. In every age, Allah ﷻ selects a certain from amongst His servants and endows them with outstanding wisdom. From the tongue of these Pious Scholars, such panaceas in the Light of Glorious Qur'ān and Hadeeth emerge instinctively which fulfil the needs of the time and appear Divinely Inspired.

We, at Amanah Studio in Dewsbury, are fortunate to assist in the compilation of such aphorisms of our contemporary scholars and pray that Allah ﷻ grants all of us the *tawfeeq* to derive benefit and may He accept this humble effort now entering its fourth edition, Ameen.

Maulana Qāri Yousuf, Maulana Maseehullah & Hāfiz Muhammad 'Abdullah

References

- **Ma'āriful Qur'ān** (Urdu)
Shaykh Muhammad Shafee' ﷺ .... Darul Ishā'at

- **The Noble Qur'ān** (Arabic with English translation)
Shaykh Dr. M. Taqi-ud-Din & Dr. M. Muhsin Khan............................ Maktaba Dar-us-Salām

- **Mazāhir Haqq** (Urdu)
Shaykh Muhammad Qutbuddeen Khān Dehlwi ﷺ .... Darul Ishā'at

- **Ma'āriful Hadeeth** (Urdu)
Shaykh Manzoor Nu'maani ﷺ .... Darul Ishā'at

- **Saheeh Bukhari** (Arabic)
Imām Muhammad ibn Isma'eel Bukhari .... Darul Kutub al-Ilmiy'yah

- **Saheeh Muslim** (Arabic)
Imām Muslim ibn Hajjaj .... Darul Kutub al-Ilmiy'yah

- **Jāmi' Tirmidhi** (Arabic)
Imām Abu Eesa Tirmidhi .... Darul Kutub al-Ilmiy'yah

- **Sunan Abu Dawood** (Arabic)
Imām Sulayman ibn Ash'ath Sijistani.. Darul Kutub al-Ilmiy'yah

- **Sunan Ibn Majah** (Arabic)
Imām Muhammad ibn Yazeed al-Qizweeni....................................... Darul Kutub al-Ilmiy'yah

- **Sunan Na'sa'ee** (Arabic)
Imām Na'sa'ee... Darul Kutub al-Ilmiy'yah

- **Riyadus Sāliheen** (Urdu)
Shaykh Muhyuddeen Abee Zakariyya ﷺ .... Darul Ishā'at

- **Al-Hidāyah** (Arabic)
Shaykh-ul-Islām Burhanuddeen ﷺ .... Makatab Shirkatul 'Ilm

- **Fatāwā Raheemiyah** (Urdu)
Shaykh Mufti 'Abdur-Raheem Lajpoori ﷺ ....Maktab Rahmāneeyah

- **Heavenly Ornaments** (Urdu)
Shaykh Ashraf 'Ali Thānwi ﷺ .... Darul Ishā'at

- **Lectures of Hakeemul Ummah** (Urdu)
Shaykh Ashraf 'Ali Thānwi ﷺ .... Idārah Taleefāt Ashrafeeyah

- **Lectures of 'Ali Mia** (Urdu, Compiled by Maulana Ramadhan Mia)
Shaykh 'Ali Mia Nadwee ﷺ .... Darul Ishā'at

- **Lectures of Ihtishaam** (Urdu)
Shaykh Ihtishaam-ul-Haqq Thānwi ﷺ .... Idārah Taleefāt Ashrafeeyah

- **Riyādul Jannah** (English)
Shaykh Muhammad Saleem Dhorat .... Islāmic Da'wah Academy

- **Sawtul Haqq** (Urdu ~ Audio/CD)
Shaykh Muhammad Saleem Dhorat .... Da'wah Book Centre

XX

- **Islāmic Weddings/Upbringing of Children**
(Compiled by Mufti Muhammad Zayd)
Shaykh Ashraf 'Ali Thānwi ﷺ .... Darul Ishā'at

- **Gift of Nikah** (Urdu)
Shaykh-ul-Hadeeth Ibrāheem Palanpoori ﷺ .... Shaykh Sayyid Ahmad

- **The Rank of Ladies in Islām** (Urdu)
Shaykh Abul Hasan 'Ali Nadwee ﷺ .... Majlis Nasriyat Islām

- **Majālis** (Urdu ~ Book & Audio)
Shaykh Maseehullah Khān ﷺ .... Jāmea Miftāhul Uloom

- **Islāhi Discourses** (Urdu, 15 Vols.)
Shaykh Mufti Taqee Uthmāni .... Mayman Islāmic Publishers

- **Islāhi Lectures** (Urdu 4 vols.)
Shaykh Mufti 'Abdur Ra'oof Sakharwee .... Mayman Islāmic Publishers

- **Uswa Rasool Akram** ﷺ (Urdu)
Shaykh Dr. 'Abdul Hayy 'Ārifee .... Darul Ishā'at

- **Statements of Pious Elders** ﷺ (Urdu)
Shaykh Mufti Taqee Uthmāni .... Idārah Tāleefat Ashrafeeyah

- **The Pious Wife & The Pious Husband** (English)
Shaykh Ahmad Sādiq Desai .... Majlisul Ulamā of South Africa

- **Munājat Maqbool** (Urdu)
Shaykh Ashraf 'Ali Thānwi ﷺ .... Darul Ishā'at

- **Virtues of Du'aa** (Urdu)
Shaykh Mufti 'Ashiq Ellahi ﷺ .... Idārah Ishā'at Deeniyat

- **Al Hisnul Haseen** (Urdu)
Allamah Muhammad Al-Jazri ﷺ .... Darul Ishā'at

- **Tahzeeb Akhlaq** ﷺ (Compiled by Shaykh Muhammad Iqbal Qurayshi)
Shaykh Ashraf 'Ali Thānwi ﷺ .... Idārah Tāleefat Ashrafeeyah

- **Ādāb-ul-Jimā' & Mubāsharat** (Urdu)
Shaykh Marghoob Ahmad Lajpoori .... Jameat-ul-Qiraat

- **Ādāb Mubāsharat** (Urdu)
Dr. Aftab Ahmad Shāh .... Tabeeb Academy

- **The Rights of Women & Blissful Marital Life** (Urdu)
Shaykh Hakeem Muhammad Akhtar .... Kutub Khana Mazharee

- **Sadaee Dil** (Original)
Shaykh 'Abdullah Kapodrawi .... Majlis Ma'arif Kapodra

- **Successful Student of Deen** (Original)
Roohullah Naqshbandi .... Darul Huda

*Certain advises are those heard from the lectures/company of Scholars, Mashā-
ikh, Huffaz & Muslim Medical Doctors.*

*S*haykh Ihtishāmul-Haqq Thānwi 🌸 related,

'A young intelligent maiden was once walking through town, when some unscrupulous male cast an evil gaze and became enchanted upon her beauty. He followed her out of town some way. Sensing mischief, the young lady abruptly turned around and confronted this man behind her, demanding sternly, 'Why are you following me?' 'I have fallen in love with your enchanting beauty!' replied the male. The wise maiden commented, 'No big deal, a human falls in love with another human, but I shall tell you a small secret...look yonder, comes my sister; younger and more pretty than me, if you were to fall in love with her, that really would be something!' The fool turned around to have a look, whereupon the lady gave him a big kick up the backside... 'Scoundrel! So is this upon what you claim love? The first news of somebody more attractive than me...and you are willing to goggle and incline towards her!' Walking away, she left the idiot to sulk at his stupidity.'

Nowadays everybody claims love, yet very few people possess true love, for if we did, one would never raise a deliberate gaze towards any non-mahram. Shaykh Maseehullah Khān 🌸 commented, 'By truly loving and looking at only one's spouse, one becomes the Friend (Walee) of Allah 🌸.'

Chapter One

The Importance of Marriage in Islām

Based upon the Teachings of

Shaykh Abul Hasan 'Ali Nadwee 🌸 &

Shaykh Mufti 'Abdur Raheem Lajpoori 🌸

Although marriage is an act of continuous worship the health benefits of marriage appear to be strong for men, women and children.

A bachelor in his early thirties is one and a half times more likely to die than a married man of the same age.

Married women are less likely to suffer long term illness than spinsters.

Children of married couples are more likely to stay on in education after 16 and are much less likely to suffer long term illness if they live with both their natural parents.

(Figures from ONS Focus on Families, 2007)

*R*asoolullah ﷺ commented, 'It is better for you that a metal rod be plunged into your head than you touching a female who is not lawful for you.'

(Targeeb, Bayhaqi, Tabrani)

*Q*uestion: 'What is the importance of nikāh in Islām? Many people consider it merely an institution wherein is fulfilment of one's desires. Please elaborate in the Light of the Glorious Qur'ān and Hadeeth and kindly inform us of the Islāmic huqooq (rights) of the wife and husband...just how should a husband behave towards his wife and how should a wife behave with her husband...?'

*S*haykh Mufti 'Abdur-Raheem Lajpoori ﷺ replies in *Fatāwā Raheemeeyah (Vol. 8)*...

*A*nswer: 'Nikāh is a great nemat (bounty) of Allah ﷻ wherein the lady who was prohibited to even view: because of nikāh now not only becomes halāl (permissible) for her husband but also his *rafeeq-e-hayāt* (partner in life). She illuminates her husbands' home; they share each other's joys and sorrows and become the means through their children of future generations. There are numerous deeni and worldly benefits of nikāh, the foremost of which is it being the Sunnah of Rasoolullah ﷺ and the Prophets ﷺ. In a hadeeth related by Anas ﷺ,

'Three Sahābāh ✤, in order to ascertain the mode of worship of Rasoolullah ﷺ, sought the views of the Mothers of the Believers ✤. Thereafter, these Companions ✤ commented, 'What is the rank of Rasoolullah ﷺ and what is our significance? His past and future misjudgements have been forgiven, accordingly he does not need to worship in abundance.' Whereupon, one of them commented, 'I shall always pray salāh throughout the night!' The second commented, 'I shall fast continuously and not make iftaar.' The third commented, 'I shall never marry (and thereby save myself from the responsibilities of a family so that I may spend my entire time in worship).'

Just then, Rasoolullah ﷺ entered and spoke, 'You were saying such-and-such; listen well! By Oath of Allah! I am the most Allah-Fearing amongst you and the most pious, however, (my sunnah) is that I fast and make iftaar; I pray tahajjud, yet also rest: I perform nikāh with women (this is my Sunnah). Whomsoever forgoes my Sunnah is not mine.'

(Muslim 1401, Bukhāri quoted in Vol. 8, p320, Fatāwā Raheemeeyah)

In another hadeeth related by Abu Ayoob ✤, Rasoolullah ﷺ commented,

'Four matters are from amongst the Sunnah of the Prophets ﷺ: 1) to have hayā (modesty and chastity, elsewhere circumcision is related); 2) to apply it'r (perfume); 3) to use a miswāk; 4) to perform nikāh.'

(Tirmidhi p206, 44, ibid.)

Marriage is an Ibãdah of Twenty-Four Hours

Understand well, marital life is an *ibãdah* for which tremendous *thawãb* (reward) is earned. It appears in a hadeeth wherein Rasoolullah ﷺ commented,

> *'Fulfil your nafsãni (carnal) desires (in a halãl way), this too is sadaqah (worship).' Upon this the Sahãbãh ؓ inquired,*

> *'O Rasoolullah ﷺ! How may this be sadaqah? If a person is fulfilling his desires why should he receive reward?'*

> *Rasoolullah ﷺ replied, 'If a human fulfils his desires at a harãm place he is sinful; accordingly, when he enacts his desires in a halãl manner then (undoubtedly) he receives reward.'* (Muslim 1006, ibid.)

To spend upon one's wife, children and family with the *niyyat* of *thawãb* is also *sadaqah*. Related Rasoolullah ﷺ,

> *'Whenever a Muslim spends upon his family (whatever amount) with the intention and hope of thawãb, then for him (this is) sadaqah.'*

> (Muslim 1002, ibid.)

From these narrations, it is obvious that *nikãh* is an unique *ibãdah* but what is not often appreciated is the everlasting nature: whether one is sleeping, awake, standing, sitting, silent, conversing, whether it be night or day, at all times a married person is in *ibãdah*. Other forms of worship such as salãh, saum, hajj, zakãt are all specific to time and location...during their performance a person is in *ibãdah*, however, upon completion the *ibãdah* ends.

Husband & Wife are Clothes For One Another

Accordingly, upon acquiring this *nemat* we should appreciate its true worth and be grateful to Allah ﷻ. Nikāh is not mere amusement but an institution which occupies a lofty rank in Islām and which gives rise to an extremely strong and powerful bond. Allah ﷻ says in the Glorious Qur'ān:

> '...*They are libās (covering) for you and you are libās for them...*' (2:187)

In the way clothes cover and hide a person's privacy, similarly the married couple act as a covering for each other: from revelation of defects and a medium of saviour from sins. Just as clothes grant a person rest, tranquillity and protection from many harms and the elements: in the same way, nikāh provides peace and succour of the heart (*qalbi sukoon*). Like a person is closely attached to his clothes (both mentally and physically), similarly is the bond between husband and wife...especially at the time of lovemaking, when their bodies are enjoined as if clothes enwrapped one to another. Allah ﷻ mentions in the Glorious Qur'ān:

> '*And amongst His signs is that He created for you wives from amongst yourselves, that you may find repose in them and, He has created between you affection and mercy. Indeed, herein are signs for people who reflect.*' (30:21)

It is apparent that *nikāh* is also a feature of the *qudrat* (power) of Allah ﷻ.

An Unmarried Person is Dependent & Helpless

*R*asoolullah ﷺ has mentioned about the unmarried person,

'Dependent is he...helpless is the male who has no wife!' When people inquired, 'What, even if he is very wealthy, is he still dependent?' Nabee ﷺ replied, 'Yes, even though he may be extremely wealthy.'

Thereafter, Nabee ﷺ commented, 'Dependent is she...helpless is the lady who has no husband!' When people inquired, 'What if she is very wealthy, is she still dependent?' Nabee ﷺ replied, 'Yes, even though she may be extremely wealthy.' (Mishkhāt)

'There is nothing better than either the (shadow) of her husband or the grave for a lady.'

'Everything of the world is worthy of benefit and the most beneficial medium of this world is a pious lady.' (Muslim, 1467)

*R*esearchers have found that married men and women, *'...tend to be in better health than their single counterparts. This is partly because of the 'social support' of having a wife or husband - and perhaps because both single men and women have a worse lifestyle - and no-one to look out for their well-being... The health benefits of being married are so large that single men are at greater risk of dying than smokers...and one in four men and women were miserable when single...it is as clear as day from the data that marriage, rather than money, is what keeps people alive.'* (Professor Andrew Oswald, courtesy of www.bbc.news)

Marriage: A Contract or Sunnah of Nabee ﷺ?

Shaykh Aboo Ãmir Zãhid ar-Rãshidee *dãmat barakãtuhum* comments, 'Nabee ﷺ described marriage as his Sunnah and people who abstain from it as being detached from him. Nikãh is a natural demand for a human and the agency for the preservation of mankind.

This is why when certain Sahãbah ؓ vouched to remain single, Nabee ﷺ displayed his disapproval and commented that Nikãh was his Sunnah and that of the previous Prophets ﷺ. Moreover, not only is nikãh a desired Sharee' ideal, but its proper and lifelong fulfilment has been stressed and its breakdown, i.e. divorce, denounced and discouraged until there is an absolute and genuine need.

In various ahadeeth, Nabee ﷺ has described expenditure upon one's wife... to the extent of even lovingly placing a morsel of food into her mouth as a medium for the husband acquiring the Pleasure of Allah ﷻ. Similarly, (Sharee') obedience and service to the husband has been described as a pathway to Paradise for the wife.

In Islãm nikãh has been elevated to the rank of 'compulsory acts,' because it ensures spiritual purity and gives rise to the 'family unit' which is the bedrock of a healthy society. Despite all our failings, weaknesses and shortcomings as an Ummah, the Muslim family unit is still the strongest and this is why, the whole effort of outsiders is to destroy this 'centre.' Ironically, these very champions of 'free society' are looking enviously at this Muslim family unit because they have realised the benefits notwithstanding their mad clamour to detach marriage from religion and replace it with a 'social contract' in order to pacify the call for 'equality' and 'liberation.'

Should all this appear as the prejudiced religious bigotry of Muslim Scholars, then consider the view of President Mikhail Gorbachev, the person accredited with modernising the former USSR in the 1980/90's. In his famous book, *Perestroika* (Reconstruction) he devotes a chapter to the 'Status of Women,' wherein he comments,

> *'In western societies, women have been brought out of their homes...no doubt there are some (economic) advantages to this arrangement such as increased productivity...however, a necessary consequence has been the destruction of our family system...because of which, we have had to face such disasters which outweigh the (economic) benefits. Accordingly, I have initiated a program by the name of Perestroika, in which one of my biggest aims is to address the issue of how to bring back into the home environment those women who have gone out...just how do we bring them back? We shall have to consider ways, otherwise just as our family system has disintegrated, similarly will our whole nation be annihilated.'* (p149, Islaahi Lectures)

Even today, if our society truly starts to view nikāh as a Sunnah of Nabee ﷺ and an *ibaadah* instead of a 'social contract and agreement between equals,' then the ills which are besetting our social fabric will *inshā'Allah* end.

The Reality of Nikāh

*S*haykh Abul Hasan 'Ali Nadwee ۞ comments, 'Our whole life is one of continuous and perfect questioning. Trade, authority, teaching, all are a form of questioning wherein one party seeks (*sa'il*) and another is liable (*mas'ool*). Moreover, every seeker is liable and every responsible one is a seeker. In our society, we are connected to even the lowest ranking human; because the needs of one are interdependent upon others and no group of people may save themselves from this. It is a feature of civilised human existence.

What is marriage (aqd) and nikāh? This too is a dignified and blessed form of questioning. One noble family approaches another honourable family and requests them for a life companion for their darling in order to fulfil and complete his life. The other family happily accept and fulfil this plea. Taking the Glorious Name of Allah ۞ both now become so enjoined; whereby two individuals who previously until yesterday were strangers, unknown and detached are now so attached and coupled that no other relationship is even remotely comparable. The fate of one is henceforth attached to the other and the happiness and pleasure of each become entwined.

All these features are the result of taking the Glorious Name of Allah ۞, Who has converted harām into halāl; impermissible into permissible; negligence and sin into obedience and *ibādah*. A total, complete and epic revolution in life. This is why in the nikāh sermon, Allah ۞

is exhorting us to honour His Glorious Name, otherwise it would be an act of great selfishness, that you take His Glorious Name to fulfil your objectives and desires but thereafter forget His Blessed Name and Commands throughout your life ...

'...And fear Allah through Whom you demand (your mutual rights) and (do not cut the relations of) the womb (kinship). Surely Allah is Ever an All-Watcher over you.' (Glorious Qur'ān, 4:1)

Today, We are gifting you a new bond, however you are also being reminded of your obligations and rights towards the existing (*qadeem*) relationships. Events should not transpire whereby in fulfilling rights you only remember your wife and forget your mother; in aiding your in-laws you forget and turn away from your father. Lest somebody questions the validity 'that who is there to question me on such matters?' Allah ﷻ states, 'Surely Allah is Ever an All-Watcher over you.' No matter how occupied, affluent, enjoyable and long a life we live, the thought must remain of our death in accordance to the Commands of Allah ﷻ and in the state of Imān. Finally, just before the bridegroom makes the long-awaited statement 'I have accepted,' for which all have gathered, the Glorious Qur'ān is forewarning a message, 'O you who believe! Keep your duty to Allah and fear him, and speak the truth (always)...' The newly wed are being advised to ponder upon the huge responsibilities and repercussions of their acceptance. Should anybody adopt this habit of pondering and reflecting before speaking, they will automatically create an awareness of the demands and behaviour expected from them on all occasions. Their entire life and behaviour will be formulated (in accordance to the Sharee'ah) and transformed into an exemplary role model for whom the Forgiveness and Pleasure of Allah 🕮 are assured...

'...And whomsoever obeys Allah and His Messenger (🕮), he has indeed achieved a great achievement (i.e. he will be saved from Hell-fire and will be admitted to Paradise).' (33:71)

Domestic Life ~ An Ibãdah

In Islãm, domestic life is not viewed upon merely as a necessity but has been elevated to the status of *ibãdah* and a medium through which a person gains the proximity of Allah 🕮. This is why Nabee 🕮 gave it practical expression...

'From amongst you the finest is he who is the best for his household...and for my family I am the best for them from amongst all of you.' (p158, The Rank of Ladies...)

Accordingly, a close study of the Seerah of Rasoolullah 🕮 will reveal such respect, consideration, justice, appreciation and perception for the natural inclinations of the weaker gender, which are not found in the lives of other great personalities or even other Prophets 🕮. The informality with his wives; participation in their lawful interests; forethought for their inclinations is incomparable. This mild and affable approach was not restricted to the womenfolk but encompassed the children also. Even when engaged in such a sublime and beloved activity as Salãh...he would shorten it upon hearing the cry of a child, so that its mother would be saved from anguish. This is the exemplary role model available to humanity and the standard expected when husband and wife come together with the Blessed Name of Allah ﷻ.

The Dilemma & Fate Facing Western Society

Living in western society, we Muslims have not only to present the beliefs of Islām but we need to also display the true family-structure, domestic and social life of Islām. Western culture is rapidly degenerating, everybody is aware of this; this is nothing new or controversial. One of the foremost reasons for this is the breakdown of the family-unit. The love, trust and confidence between husband and wife is decreasing and deteriorating day-by-day. The same fate that befell the ancient Greek, Persian and Roman civilisations, I am afraid, appears to be the lot of the west...Western intellectuals and 'think-tanks' are publishing papers and books to resolve this growing social problem. Despite having overpowered many other cultures and harnessed the resources of this world to reach outer space, they are unable to acquire succour of the heart and convert their homes into parables of Paradise. In complete contrast, even today in the east, many Muslim couples for whom a basic daily meal is difficult, nevertheless are experiencing the joy of Paradise...the bond between the couple should be of such a nature that even poverty, destitution and hunger is tolerated and overcome.'

'There is no doubt that it is around the family and the home that all the greatest virtues, the most dominating virtues of human society, are created, strengthened and maintained.' (Churchill, Family Education Trust)

Consequences of Adultery & The Binge Culture

Rasoolullah ﷺ commented:

'*O group of youths, whosoever amongst you has the means of getting married, should do so because it lowers the gaze and protects the private parts; and whosoever does not have the ability, should fast, for indeed, it is a protection for him.*' *(Bukhāri)*

'*Whomsoever gives me the guarantee of safeguarding his tongue and his private parts, I give him the guarantee of Paradise.*' *(Bukhāri)*

'*Whenever the habit of depravity increases in a nation, to the extent they openly practise promiscuity, then amongst these people plagues and such illnesses become widespread; which were not present during the time of their forefathers.*' *(Ibn Majah)*

Allah ﷻ says in the Glorious Qur'ān:

'O you who believe! Intoxicants (of all kind)...are an abomination of Shaytan's handiwork. So avoid (strictly all) such (abomination) in order that you may be successful.' (5:90)

'Do not come near to adultery, indeed it is a shameful deed and an evil way.' (17:32)

Rasoolullah ﷺ commented:

'There will be people of my Ummah who will seek to make lawful; fornication, wine-drinking and the use of ma`aazif (musical instruments).' (Bukhāri)

'O Assembly of Muslims! Beware of adultery, for indeed, it is accompanied by six evil consequences: three in this world and three in the Hereafter. The three in this world are:

1) Loss of radiance (of Imān) from the face.

2) Reduction in life span.

3) Continuous poverty.

The three misfortunes in the Hereafter are:

1) The Wrath of Allah ﷻ.

2) A dreadful reckoning.

3) Punishment of Hell-Fire.'   (Baihaqi, Al Kabaair, p53)

'A fornicator, at the time he is committing illicit sexual intercourse is not a believer; and a person, at the time of drinking alcohol is not a believer...'

(Bukhāri)

'From amongst the portents of the Final Hour are the following: general ignorance (in religious affairs) will prevail; religious knowledge will decrease; illegal sexual intercourse will prevail; alcoholic drinks will be drunk (in abundance)...'

(Bukhāri)

Current Trends

Allah ﷻ says in the Glorious Qur'ān:

'When We decide to destroy a place (i.e. the community therein), We command its affluent ones. They then perpetrate transgression. The Decree (of Punishment) becomes confirmed. Thus, We utterly destroy it (the town along with its people).' (17:16)

Arabic Proverb,

'Through good character do nations rise,

moreover, through bad character do nations fall.'

It is estimated that a growing number of our Muslim youth lose their virginity before marriage. Shaykh Maseehullah Khan ﷻ used to say, 'Nowadays what first night? What first and only true love, wherein Angels arrive and salute the Mu'min...' Figures released by Genitourinary Medicine Clinics (GUM) who deal with sexually transmitted diseases (STIs) in the UK reveal, an inner-city clinic serving one of the largest community of Muslims in the UK, stating that almost 4500 people of Indian, Pakistani & Bangladeshi origin visited their centre for treatment in 2006. Referrals for abortion amongst Asian patients was double the clinic figure for other ethnic groups. Treatment for sexually transmitted diseases was not far behind. A similar gloomy picture emerges from other Clinics in the UK with high Muslim populations. Such findings reinforces the views of those Muslim Scholars and Doctors involved in welfare work. There is overwhelming socio-scientific evidence to show the harms of adultery and its detrimental effects on personal health, families and society.

According to official figures for the UK released in early 2003, children as young as 11 years of age are now being treated for sexually transmitted diseases and for binge drinking. What of the health consequences? The number of youngsters visiting GUM Clinics in the UK in 2005 was 1.8 million, more than double the number recorded in 2002. The pressure on GUM services was highlighted in a House of Commons Health Committee Third Report of Session 2002-03. They said that:

> *'England is currently witnessing a rapid decline in its sexual health... Sexual health services appear ill-equipped to deal with the crisis that confronts them. Median waiting times to services are currently around 10-12 days and some services are turning hundreds of people away each week.'*
>
> (House of Commons Health Committee, 2003)

> *'The increase in sexually transmitted infections (STIs) and the high levels of teenage pregnancy in the United Kingdom are disturbing. That alcohol and drugs are used to enhance sexual activity is in no doubt. But why is it happening, and what are the risks and the implications for our young people...?'*

'The recently published Unicef report records that out of 21 countries, the UK is at the bottom of the league table for child well-being. And that specifically children in the UK had the highest incidence of risk taking behaviour: more have had sexual intercourse by the age of 15 than in any other country, more have been drunk two or more times aged 11, 13 and 15 than in any other country, and they are the third highest users of cannabis... As adults, are we reneging on our responsibilities?'

(Independent Advisory Group)

Sexually Transmitted Infections (STIs)

AIDS ~ The disease which literally knocks out the body's defence system and leaves it vulnerable and susceptible to even the most minor of infections. 'As yet, no cure has been found for this disease. It is contracted and spread by various means, but the original cause has been unanimously accepted as perverted sexual acts like adultery and homosexuality.'

Adulterous Diseases	Recent Rises	Rise Over 2005
HIV/Aids	10% every year	17%
Syphilis	2,054% since 1996	23%
Genital Chlamydia	207% since 1996	5%
Gonorrhoea	54% since 1997	-13%
Genital Warts	26% since 1996	1%

Gonorrhoea ~ The second most common sexually transmitted disease in the UK causing inflammation of the testicles, blockage of the urethra, inflammation of the joints and sterility.

Genital Ulcers ~ This disease causes inflammation of the lymphatic glands. It also gives rise to chronic festering of tumours, inflammation of the urethra, severe pain in the joints and swelling of the limbs.

Syphilis ~ This is a type of venereal disease commonly known amongst the Arabs as 'The English Disease' since its origin lies in European societies where free intermingling of the sexes and immorality is rife. It results in insanity, paralysis, blindness and other nerve disorders. It can also lead to blood vessel damage and death.

Hepatitis B ~ Its symptoms include fever, fatigue, nausea and jaundice. It results in chronic hepatitis or liver cancer.

(IDA booklet, Homosexuality ~ The Islāmic Viewpoint)

Genital Chlamydia ~ This is the most common sexually transmitted bacterial disease affecting not only the genitals of both men and women but also a cause of infection of the rectum, throat and eyes. The majority of people infected are unaware of its presence, accordingly it is an extremely dangerous 'silent' disease.

Consequently, the risk of infertility, ectopic pregnancy (a pregnancy outside the womb), cervical cancer in women is increased. Male fertility may also be impaired as a result of infection. According to recent studies, it is estimated that 1 person in every 8 in the UK is carrying the disease.

Champions of Freedom Are Themselves Tyrants

Shaykh Abul Hasan 'Ali Nadwee ﷺ commented, 'Despite so many universities and such technological progress, man has degenerated to animal extinct and living. The educated one's; who supposedly are suave, have culture, sophistication and codes of conduct behave in such bestial ways towards other humans which even an animal would be ashamed of...in the final analysis, have they lost their brains? Despite knowing so much, the lust for wealth, land and pleasures overwhelms them. They have forgotten the norms of human behaviour and resorted to acts of primitivism and ignorance. Championing the cause and rights of humanity to the world, they themselves are trampling the norms of chivalrous and civilised behaviour. All this because of failure to acknowledge the reality of one day having to stand before the Supreme Creator and answer for one's misdeeds...'

New Age of Raunch or Return To Era of Ignorance?

Why do Muslim youngsters loose their natural modesty (*tab'ee haya*) and adopt raunch values and risky sexual behaviour?

One reason is in adopting and learning the language of non-Muslim cultures, our youth inevitably adopt their ideologies, values and outlook.

What role do ogling at non-mahram, bad company, alcohol and drugs play in such sexual misdemeanour? With rising levels of alcohol consumption, it is estimated that 1 in 10 people in the UK are dependent on alcohol. Twice as many as are hooked on all other drugs (estimated to be 1 in 25). In the UK, 17% of men and 7% of women are considered binge drinkers. Alcohol is being described as the 'fuel' for adultery; it is a bigger danger to our youth than is commonly understood and, it is not just Muslim males who are falling prey to alcohol and raunch behaviour.

Whilst Muslim teenage girls are outperforming their male counterparts in academic achievements and grades at schools and universities, paradoxically, they are out dressing them as well (indigenous girls are also officially bigger binge drinkers). In a recent UK survey of 1,000 girls aged 15 to 19 years, 63 per cent considered their ideal profession to be 'glamour model;' posing nude or seminude.

Whilst this is assumed to be an indication of the immorality of non-Muslims girls, nevertheless the number of screaming female Muslim attendees and their mode of dress at the June 2007 Bollywood Oscars in Sheffield, UK (viewed by an estimated half a billion audience worldwide) testifies and gives some indication into the direction which an alarming number of Muslim girls are also taking and was undoubtedly the cause of the ensuing worst floods for over 150 years. Sonia Gandhi commented,

> *The (Bolly/Hollywood) film industries have inflicted destruction to the foundation of (Muslim society). Our media have won such a war which was not possible with conventional weapons. Today, the Muslim child is a plaything of (Bolly/Hollywood).'*

(Al-Balagh, Vol. 46, Issue 12, p 48)

We Are What We Eat, Drink, View, Hear & Wear

Although many Muslim girls and boys attend Makãtib in Islãmic wear; underneath a fair percentage are wearing jeans, tee-shirts and hairstyles to match their non-Muslim peers. When the wearing of non-Muslim clothing was suggested to Umar ﷺ, he replied, 'We are a nation who have been granted respect by Allah ﷻ through Islãm.' Rasoolullah ﷺ has warned us, 'Whomsoever imitates a nation becomes of them.'

Physically and spiritually we are what we earn; what we eat and drink; what we hear and see; what we wear; what we read; what we view and with whom we associate. Many youngsters are fed unwholesome (not necessarily haram) food which originate from unreliable sources. They view and hear futility via mass advertising tools; TV, Internet and mobile technology which are now more than simple instruments of communication and advertisement; they relate features of major cultures.

The subliminal message is always unfettered freedom; immediate gratification; live for now; instant credit; the latest must have; alcohol; drugs and adultery. All the root causes which lead unto depravity are subconsciously accepted. One only needs to study the effects on our body organs and faculties of having either consumed unwholesome food; worn the clothing, read the literature or listened and viewed programs associated with a non-Muslim culture. There is immediate spiritual lethargy; apathy towards the Hereafter; drop in modesty; lack of inclination towards good deeds and an urge to sin.

Why Is Adultery Haram in Islãm?

haykh Hakeem Muhammad Akhtar *hafizahullah* relates, 'I was once asked by a person, 'Why is adultery forbidden in Islãm?' I replied, 'So that you do not become illegitimate; for Allah ﷻ Wishes His servants to remain halãl!' Imãm Shãfee' ﷺ would recite a couplet:

عِفُّوْا تَعِفَّ نِسَاؤُكُمْ فِى الْمَحْرَمِ   وَ تَجَنَّبُوْا مَا لَا يَلِيْقُ بِمُسْلِمِ

'Be chaste and the ladies in your household will stay chaste – Refrain from that which does not suit a Muslim.

اِنَّ الزِّنَا دَيْنٌ فَاِنْ اَقْرَضْتَهُ   كَانَ الْوَفَا مِنْ اَهْلِ بَيْتِكَ فَاعْلَمِ

Adultery is a loan, if you give it to someone, then remember it will be repaid from within your family.

يَا هَاتِكًا حُرَمَ الرِّجَالِ وَ قَاطِعًا   سُبُلَ الْمَوَدَّةِ عِشْتَ غَيْرَ مُكَرَّمِ

O you who severs the dignity of noble people and, devours the paths of love and harmony; may you live void of any respect.

لَوْ كُنْتَ حُرًّا مِنْ سُلَالَةِ مَاجِدٍ   مَا كُنْتَ هَتَّاكًا لِحُرْمَةِ مُسْلِمِ

If you were a noble person from a respected family, you would not cause any disgrace to your fellow Muslim.

مَنْ يَزْنِ يُزْنَ بِهِ وَلَوْ بِجِدَارِهِ   اِنْ كُنْتَ يَا هٰذَا لَبِيْبًا فَافْهَمِ

Remember! Whosoever fornicates will have to suffer the same, even if the act was to be repeated with his wall. If you are a man of understanding then take heed.'

$\mathcal{OS}$haykh Mufti Taqee Uthmāni *hafizahullah* narrates, 'Once a young man arrived in *Madeenah Al-Munawwarah* and requested Rasoolullah 🌸, 'Please grant me permission to commit adultery.' The Companions 🌸, sitting nearby, became enraged at this impudent statement. However, Rasoolullah 🌸 responded, 'Come near to me. Would you like anyone to commit adultery with your mother?' The young man replied, 'No, not at all.' Rasoolullah 🌸 responded, 'Then other people will also never tolerate such a shameful act with their mothers.' Rasoolullah 🌸 asked him the same question regarding his sister, aunt, etc., and the youth answered each time in the negative. Thereafter, Rasoolullah 🌸 placed his noble hand upon the chest of this young visitor and prayed, 'O Allah! Purify his heart, forgive his sins and guard him against adultery.' The young man commented, 'Thereafter, nothing was more odious to me than adultery.' *(Majma'al Zawaid)*

Adultery is a crime against all of society and is regarded as amongst the worst of sins by all the heavenly religions. It is highly inappropriate for any grandchild of Prophet Adam 🌸 to be unfaithful. Islām, the complete, perfect and final religion has shown mankind how to save itself from infidelity by banning all avenues leading unto fornication. Rasoolullah 🌸 commented,

'The adultery of the eyes is evil looks. The adultery of the feet is to walk towards the sin. The adultery of the tongue is lustful talk. The adultery of the heart is evil desire and in the end the sexual organs testify to all this or deny it.' *(Bukhāri)*

Root Cause Of Boy/Girl Friend Amongst Muslims

R asoolullah ﷺ commented,

'It is better for you that a metal rod be plunged into your head then you touching a female who is not lawful for you.'

'He who places his hand with lust on a female who was not lawful for him...will arise on the Day of Qiyamah with his hand bound to his neck. If he had kissed her, his lips will be cut in the Fire...'

(Hadeeth quoted in The Majlis, Vol 7, No. 8 & Vol 13, No. 9)

The constant bombardment of images and messages that it is progressive and acceptable to engage in relationships before and outside of nikah has wrecked moral havoc. Consequently, a Muslim teenager without a girl or boy friend is viewed by his peers as a 'freak.' Why? Because the nominal quest for 'equal rights' and 'freedom' has brought along in its wake 'equal wrong' and 'servitude.' Muslim parents and elders fail to constantly remind themselves and their juniors of the need to lower our gaze; pivotal in saving oneself from adultery and immorality. Allah ﷻ promises us through a statement of Rasoolullah ﷺ,

'Verily the evil gaze is an arrow from amongst the poisoned arrows of Shaytaan, whosoever forgoes it for My sake I shall grant such power in his Imãn that he shall experience it's sweetness in his heart.'

(Kanzul Um'mãl)

'Allamah Ibn Qayyum Jawzee ﷺ commented, 'Whomsoever saves his gaze from (non-mahram) beauties has sacrificed the sweetness of his vision unto Allah ﷻ. In return Allah ﷻ grants him sweetness of the heart and because Allah ﷻ is Everlasting, this sweetness is also everlasting.'

In complete contrast, ogling at (non-mahram) beauties only adds to the agitation of one's heart. A scholar once wrote, 'Shaykh, although I have control over focussing my gaze I do not have the strength to remove my gaze.' Shaykh Ashraf 'Ali Thānwi ﷻ replied, 'Despite being so educated and learned in philosophy, you are talking in this manner? Control applies to matters over which one has choice, whether to enact or not...when you have the power to focus your gaze, then of a surety you have the power to remove your gaze.' Another letter arrived, 'When I save my gaze, a great pain is felt by the heart; regret and sorrow arises, 'Wow, what beauty she must possess, what eyes, nose, etc...a wound is felt by the heart.'

Shaykh Ashraf 'Ali Thānwi ﷻ answered by posing a question, 'Tell me, in not ogling how long does the heart feel agitated and for how long is the heart perturbed when you do view non-mahram?'

The Scholar replied, 'When I do not ogle, the regret is felt for a few minutes and thereafter sweetness is experienced; but when I do look, for three days and night I imagine her features and my heart remains in turmoil.'

Shaykh Ashraf 'Ali Thānwi ﷻ answered, 'You yourself should conclude whether it is better to experience the pain of a minute or that of a few days!' The Scholar replied, 'Shaykh, I repent, I have understood.'

(p20, Manazil of Self-Reformation)

The Spiritual Solution For Hedonism

*A*llah ﷻ mentions in the Glorious Qur'ān:

'Has not the time come for the hearts of Believers to be affected by Allah's Reminder...?' (57:15)

*S*haykh Ashraf 'Ali Thānwi ﷫ narrated,

'In this era I consider the company of the pious scholars to be compulsory (fardh-e-'ain) and issue a decree (fatwa) accordingly. What doubt is there in the religious compulsion of establishing a correct relationship with the pious in this day and age? Experience shows that nowadays the well-being of our faith (iman) is only possible in the company of the pious...and after establishing a correct relationship with them; through the Fadhl of Allah ﷻ no wizardry can effect one.' (Al-Ifaadāt Yawmeeyah)

*S*haykh Dr. Abdul Hayy 'Arifee ﷫ used to say, 'There is only one road to meet Him. Link up with those close to Him.' When Allah ﷻ Wishes to guide a servant, then every atom of such a person begins to hear His Call...'We are yours, you are ours. From both sides a pledge flowers.' The first sign of guidance is the urge to meet pious people. Whomsoever desires to reform, receives the tawfeeq to link up with a guide.

*S*haykh Ashraf 'Ali Thānwi ﷫ advised a person who had written and sought to end an adulterous relationship... 'Firstly, you should understand that without courage even the easiest of task is impossible. Observe, how for physical ailments one needs to take bitter medicine:

because the objective is good health one undertakes it with courage. For spiritual ailments there is a need for greater valour, when this reality is understood then pay heed and follow the following course of proven treatment with courage; *Inshā'Allah* perfect cure will be achieved.

1. Firstly, totally cut off all relationship and contact with the person. Neither meet, view, listen, speak, write, (text or phone) her...even if a third person tries to mention her then bring the conversation to an abrupt end. In fact, under any pretext, without any formality or excuse, speak negatively about her to the extent you do not incline towards or hope ever to meet each other again. Remain so distanced from her, that there remains no possibility of even accidentally viewing her. There must be total and complete separation.

2. Secondly, fix a regular time in solitude; take a bath, don clean clothes and *it'r*. Face the *qiblah* and incline towards Allah ﷻ: first pray two rakats Salat Tawbah, repent, making du'aa in abundance seeking His help in being saved from this misfortune. Thereafter, recite *La'Illaha Ill'Allah* between 500-1000 times repeatedly in such a way that with each *La'Illaha* ponder, 'I have emptied everybody except Allah ﷻ from my heart,' and with each *Ill'Allah* ponder, 'I have grounded the Love of Allah ﷻ in my heart.'

3. Thirdly, with whichever Shaykh or pious scholar you have greater acquaintance, ponder about him in your heart, that he is sitting nearby and supervising the purity of your heart.

4. Frequently study a book of Hadeeth, authentic commentary or kitab wherein the Wrath of Allah ﷻ, Hell and Punishment for disobedience are related.

5. Fix a time when you sit in solitude and contemplate standing in the Presence of Allah ﷻ on the Day of Judgement wherein He is addressing you, 'O Shameful one! Are you not abashed in forgoing Us and inclining towards a piece of carrion; is this what We created you for? Was this Our due? You employed My bounties: eyes, heart, hands and organs in Our disobedience, are you not ashamed! Remain submerged and occupied in this reflection for a long time.

Although this prescription is difficult on one's self (*nafs*), nevertheless it should be persevered with courageously, Allah ﷻ is Supreme.'   *(Tarbiyatus Sālik, Vol. 1, p 278)*

Shaykh Hakeem Akhtar *hafizahullah* relates, Shāh 'Abdul 'Ghanee Phoolpoori ﷫ used to say:

'Even if a person, because of weakness of deeds, does not become a Friend of Allah ﷻ immediately, nevertheless through the blessings of establishing a relationship with the pious, Allah ﷻ will endow such a person with His Muhabbat before death.'

'There was a famous poet by the name of Hafeez in Jaunpoor, addicted to alcohol. When he observed Shaykh Dr. 'Abdul Hayy 'Arifee ﷫, he commented, 'Shaykh! You are a university post-graduate so how did you acquire this hat (*topee*) and lengthy *kurta*...whereby great, great scholars are inclining and learning Deen from you? From where did you acquire this life?' Dr. 'Arifee ۞ replied, 'I stayed in the company of Shaykh Ashraf 'Ali Thānwi ۞ through whom Allah ۞ blessed us with the bounty of Divine Love (*muhabbat*).' Hafeez Jaunpoori inquired, 'Can we also go there?' Dr. 'Arifee ۞ replied, 'Yes, of course, you should go to the *Khānqāh*...a spiritual hospital; it is there precisely for sinners and people who have erred, for patient's arrive at a hospital not the healthy ones.'

Hafeez Jaunpoori departed for the *Khānqāh* with a beard growth of a few days. Upon arrival, he summoned the barber and clean-shaved his stubble and thereafter presented himself and requested Shaykh Thānwi ۞ to accept his allegiance of reformation (*bay'at*). Shaykh Thānwi ۞ inquired, 'Hafeez! I know you are poet 'laureate' (of All-India), but tell me, whatever you had you've shaved that off also, why is *this* the way to repent (*tawbah*)?' Hafeez replied, 'Shaykh! You are Hakeemul Ummat whilst I am Mareedhul Ummat...and the patient should present his true state so that the doctor may cure him. From today, *Inshā'Allah* no blade will touch this face.' After pledging allegiance he departed. A year later, it so happened that Shaykh Thānwi ۞ travelled to Jaunpoor, he observed an old-man with a long beard approaching him and inquired, 'Who is this?' Associates replied, 'this is the very Hafeez who came to meet you last year.' Another example is that of Jighar Murādabadee, a life-long alcoholic. When Allah ۞ granted him tawfeeq to repent, he approached Khawajah 'Azeez-ul-Hasan Majzoob ۞, 'I wish to stop drinking and become pious...but how?' 'The same way we did!' replied the latter, 'We are a tax and revenue inspector, but look at our *kurta* and *izar*, our *salah* and *sawm*. You too go to Thãna Bhãwan!' Jighar confided, 'Yes, I shall go but I am an alcoholic so I shall have to drink there also.' Khawajah Majzoob ﷺ related this predicament to Shaykh Thãnwi ﷺ who replied, 'Khawajah, go tell him, I will not let him drink in the Khãnqah! However, I shall make him a guest in my home because when Rasoolullah ﷺ hosted non-muslims in his house, then I may host a sinful Muslim.' Upon hearing this reply, Jighar began to weep, 'I always thought these pious Saints would hold a sinner in loathing and contempt, today I have realised there is no one more affectionate than them.' Thereafter, he requested four du'aa's from Shaykh Thãnwi ﷺ: to stop drinking alcohol; to grow a full Sharee' beard; to perform Hajj; his death be upon Imãn. Shaykh Thãnwi ﷺ raised his hands and made du'aa. Jighar stopped drinking completely. He suffered withdrawal symptoms and fell dangerously ill. The doctors advised he drink a little...to which he replied, 'If I keep drinking I may live a few years longer but in the Wrath of Allah ﷻ, however if I die having stopped drinking I will greet death whilst in His Mercy.' He recovered, departed for Hajj and returned with a Sharee' beard. The company of Saints is so effective in giving up vices of the highest order.

'If your heart be hard as stone and lacking capacity for good, but you be fortunate to keep the company of the pious, you will undoubtedly become a pearl.'

Masturbation & Homosexuality

According to the Health Protection Agency, between 1999 and 2004 there was a steady increase of 30% in 'diagnosis' rates in the UK among men who had sex with men. Islām has uprooted the root of immorality. Although other cultures may approve and deny the physical and spiritual harms, in Islām it is forbidden to masturbate, practise homosexuality or lesbianism. Allah ﷻ says:

'And (remember Prophet) Lût, when he said to his people: 'Do you commit the worst sin such as none proceeding you has committed in the Ãlamîn (mankind and jinn)? Indeed, you practice your lusts on men instead of women. Nay but you are a people transgressing beyond bounds.'

...And We rained down upon them a rain (of stones). Then see what was the end of the criminals and transgressors.' (Glorious Qur'ān, 7:80-83)

*R*asoolullah ﷺ commented:

'Whomsoever commits an unnatural act with any male or female...Allah Ta'ālā will not even look upon them!' (Ma'āriful Hadeeth, p36, Vol. 7)

Once a young man attended the lecture of the great Sahābee 'Abdullah Ibn Abbas ؓ and stayed behind to ask a question, 'I am a young person with no wife, I often masturbate with my hand, is it sinful?' Ibn Abbas ؓ turned his face away (to show disapproval) and advised, 'It would be better for you to marry the most (inferior woman) than commit this (despicable sin and) act!'

The Benefits of Taqwā

'What is Taqwā? Taqwā is the name of the spiritual veil which saves one from the disobedience of Allah ﷻ.'   *(Sawtul Haq)*

r. Muhammad Sābir ؓ related an episode narrated by Shaykh Maseehullah Khān ؒ, 'A group of merchants were voyaging across the ocean, when a Saint on-board the ship made an announcement, 'Who will purchase this Verse of the Glorious Qur'ān from me?' The amount being asked was quite substantial and none of the travellers had the required amount... except one young man named 'Abdullah who mustered up courage and approached the Saint with his entire wealth. Before revealing the specific Āyah, the elderly Shaykh made 'Abdullah throw overboard the entire 'asking price,' coin by coin, to cleanse his heart from love of the world. Thereafter he recited the Verse:

$$\text{وَ مَنْ يَّتَّقِ اللهَ يَجْعَلْ لَّهُ مَخْرَجًا ★ وَ يَرْزُقْهُ مِنْ حَيْثُ لَا}$$
$$\text{يَحْتَسِبُ ۽ وَ مَنْ يَّتَوَكَّلْ عَلَى اللهِ فَهُوَ حَسْبُهُ ۽ اِنَّ اللهَ بَالِغُ اَمْرِهِ ۽}$$
$$\text{قَدْ جَعَلَ اللهُ لِكُلِّ شَيْءٍ قَدْرًا ★}$$

'...And whosoever fears Allah and keeps his duty unto Him. He will make a way out for him (from every difficulty). And He will provide him from (sources) one could never imagine. And whomsoever places his trust in Allah, then He will suffice for him. Verily, Allah will accomplish his purpose. Indeed Allah has set a measure for all things.' (65:2-3)

The Saint thereafter instructed 'Abdullah to recite this Verse whenever faced with any need or difficulty. Some time later during the voyage, the ship became caught in a horrific storm and capsized. All on-board drowned except for 'Abdullah, who whilst reciting this Verse found refuge on a plank...which eventually drifted towards and landed on an island.

Hauling himself ashore, 'Abdullah was shocked to observe the tropical beach scattered with hundreds of skulls. Also present was a terrified young lady...a princess sheltering behind some trees. From afar, 'Abdullah inquired into this dreadful spectacle. The grief-stricken princess informed him that these skulls were the poor souls terrorised and killed by a powerful and wicked jinni who had also abducted her from the Royal Palace on the other side of the island and left her here until his return. It was common knowledge that nobody escaped the villainy of this dreaded jinni.

Unperturbed, 'Abdullah replied, 'Do not fear, I shall recite the Glorious Qur'ān when he appears.' Towards dusk a huge figure bellowing smoke appeared upon the horizon, immediately 'Abdullah began reciting the Verse...as a result of which the jinni burst into flames and was scorched to dust! Thereafter, walking in front so that his gaze would not fall upon the princess, 'Abdullah proceeded through the jungle and requested the princess to give directions from behind. Eventually they came across a troop of soldiers sent out by the King to locate his daughter and both were escorted to the Palace where the princess narrated the whole episode to a relieved King and thereafter requested,

'Beloved father! You shall be giving my hand in marriage one day...why not marry me to this pious young man, who even in the remoteness of the jungle at night, never once looked at me...what better testimony to his piety!'

The wise King after reflecting agreed and married the princess to 'Abdullah, appointing him Governor of a principality and gifting the couple a palace for a residence.'

If this appears far-fetched and exaggerated, reflect upon the episode of Prophet Moosã ﷺ who after emigrating from Egypt to Midian to escape persecution from *Firown* (Pharaoh) aided two ladies (who unknown to him were the respected daughters of Prophet Sho'aib ﷺ) in hauling water for their flock of sheep from a deep well. When these ladies returned home and related this incident of a stranger having helped them, their aged father Prophet Sho'aib ﷺ instructed one of his daughters to invite Prophet Moosã ﷺ to come home and meet him. When Prophet Moosã ﷺ came...he too walked in-front so that his gaze would not fall upon the lady. Later on, he was blessed with the good-fortune of marrying this lady.

Allah ﷻ has promised in the Glorious Qur'ãn (7:128):

$$وَ الْعَاقِبَةُ لِلْمُتَّقِيْنَ$$

'And the ultimate success is for the pious.'

෨০ও

Etiquette's

of

Choosing a

Marriage Partner

Based upon an abridged & edited Lecture

of

Shaykh Muhammad Saleem Dhorat

hafizahullah

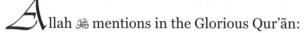

Allah ﷻ mentions in the Glorious Qur'ãn:

'And those who believe and whose offspring follow them in Imãn (faith): to them We shall join their offspring, and We shall not decrease the reward of their deeds in anything. Every person is a pledge for that which he has earned.' (52:21)

Prophet Muhammad ﷺ commented,

'It is also a right of the child (incumbent) upon the father that he selects a good name and teaches (and embellishes the child) with husne adab (noble good manners).'   *(Baihaqee, quoted in Ma'ãriful Hadeeth, Vol. 6, p29)*

Through the auspicious personality, mission and teachings of the Final Messenger Muhammad ﷺ, Allah ﷻ has sent to us a perfect way of life which covers every aspect of human living and existence.

As far as the *tarbiyyah* (upbringing) of children is concerned, comprehensive principles are present and vividly apparent in the teachings of Rasoolullah ﷺ. Our Ulamã have elaborated on each aspect of these guidelines and should one resolutely practice upon these as outlined by Rasoolullah ﷺ, it could be claimed that the majority of the youth of this Ummah would live a life in accordance to the Pleasure of Allah ﷻ.

However, current conditions beg the question, 'how many parents are truly aware of these teachings and guidelines?'

Wherever the Sharee'ah has stipulated the rights of parents upon children, it has also designated the rights of children upon parents. Today, because of the turmoil prevalent within our society, the complaint of, 'my child is not behaving or living in accordance to my wishes!' is heard from the lips of every parent. There are many reasons for this development, the foremost of which is failure to appreciate the reality that although rights of parents become incumbent upon the child when he/she reaches puberty, these very rights and etiquette's need to be taught beforehand. After puberty, these rights will become incumbent and failure to uphold them will result in Divine Retribution.

In complete contrast, the rights of children are compulsory upon parents *before* birth of the child, in actual fact even before the couple marry! The rights of children commence from when both the bride and bridegroom are single. The first right imposed by the Sharee'ah upon the would-be father is to ensure a good and pious mother for his child to be. Bring such a mother into your home who is chaste, pious, God-fearing, religiously inclined, one who will be able to make correct *tarbiyyah* of the children. The mother is the 'first madrasah' for the child; her outlook will govern the development (or otherwise) of the child.

Today, it is our gross misfortune, that the deeni efforts and resources which are being utilised in the *tarbiyyah* of our boys...a fraction of this is being expanded for the benefit of our daughters. This is a grave shortcoming which needs to be addressed urgently: we must consult, formulate and enact. Why? Because the first impressions upon the child will be that of the mother, not of the father. Yet paradoxically, we expand almost all our resources upon the father to-be with little, if any, efforts upon our daughters.

It is related about the famous Shaykh Fareeduddeen Shakarghanch 🌺 (569-664 AH ~ 1173-1265 CE)...a saint to whom people from all over the world, including great scholars, inclined for their spiritual development. One day whilst sitting in front of his mother, he mentioned this reality to his mother and asked her whether she was happy upon this achievement by her son? The mother replied, 'Darling! This is not your excellence but my achievement!' Her son Fareeduddeen replied, 'But mother, it is I who, through the Grace of Allah 🌺, has made all the struggles and spiritual exercises, performed tahajjud, zikr, etc., then how may you claim that it is your achievement?'

His mother 🌺 replied, 'Darling, it is undoubtedly due to my achievement, because I breast-fed you in the state of wudhu after performing *tahajjud*...all this is the result of my *tarbiyyah,* precautions and efforts.'

Now reflect upon how much effort we expand upon our boys and, thereafter ponder how little we do for our daughters, whereas it is the mother who will be shaping and formulating the future of the child. If the infant child was incapable of being influenced, the Sharee'ah would not have instructed us to give *Azān* and *Iqāmah* into the newborn child's ears.

The Sharee' Criteria's for Selecting one's Partner

Rasoolullah ﷺ commented,

'A lady is married upon one of four reasons: wealth; pedigree (family rank & standing); beauty; piety; you should marry a pious lady and achieve success.'

(Muslim, 1466)

Today, our society has become so corrupted that we have applied our own criteria's which have no significant Sharee' basis. Even when the father is convinced (in his heart) that in marrying my daughter to such-and-such a pious boy lies her deeni and worldly success, nevertheless out of ethnic pride he refuses to marry her.

Contrast this with the behaviour of the Sahābāh ﷺ. Umar Fāruq ﷺ, the second Ameerul Mu'mineen was travelling through Madeenah at night to check upon the state of his subjects. Returning towards Masjid-An-Nabawee ﷺ for Fajr Salāh, 'Umar Fāruq ﷺ felt very tired and rested against the wall of a house to regain his breath; when suddenly he heard the voice of a mother awakening her daughter and saying...

'Beloved wake up its Fajr time; hurry milk the animals and pour some water into the milk; so that we may earn more money for our needs. It is still quite dark outside; quickly pour some water...nobody will see you!'

The honest young maiden ﷺ replied,

'Dear mother, do you not remember what 'Umar ﷺ said yesterday in his lecture about deceiving people?'

The mother commented,

> *'Get up and pour the water, there is neither 'Umar or anybody else around here to see what we are doing!'*

The young maiden 🕮 replied,

> *'But mother, it just is not possible for me to obey Ameerul Mu'mineen when he is present and disobey him behind his back. Moreover, even if nobody is watching us, Allah 🕮 the All-Seer is always watching us!'*

When 'Umar Fãruq 🕮 overheard this conversation, he was so impressed by this young lady's piety...living in a mud hut on the outskirts of Madeenah, that he immediately told his servant to make a careful note of the house. Later that morning, 'Umar Fãruq 🕮 summoned his slave and asked him to find out the credentials of these people whom they had overheard and find out whether the young maiden was married. He returned with news that mother and her unmarried daughter were poor members of the Bani Hilal tribe. Hearing this, 'Umar Fãruq 🕮 summoned his son 'Ãsim 🕮 and advised,

> *'Dear son accept my advice, I know of a young lady to whom I shall send a marriage proposal on your behalf, for she is so pious I have hope that Inshã'Allah a pious son will be born who will raise the flag of Islãm.'*

Both parents and children of previous era's were pious... unlike parents and children of today...who only have time for their own selfish interests and desires. 'Ãsim 🕮 accepted his father's suggestion and requested him to send a proposal on his behalf. 'Umar Fãruq ﷺ invited both mother and daughter to attend...she was indeed beautiful, both in character and appearance. 'Umar Fãruq ﷺ addressed her...

'Islãm needs daughters like you and as a Caliph of Islãm it is my duty to acknowledge your pious qualities. I would consider it a honour if you will accept my son's marriage proposal and become my daughter-in-law.'

The milkmaid with the advice and consent of her mother accepted and married 'Ãsim ﷺ. From this union a daughter was born whose name was Umme 'Ãsim ﷺ. She was a pious and intelligent girl who learnt Deeni 'Ilm from her grandfather and who became the mother of the great Umar bin 'Abdul-Azeez ﷺ (63-101 AH/686-724 CE) ~ labelled the 'fifth' Khulafãh-e-Rãshideen because of his piety.

Modern Day Criteria's

Compare this behaviour with the criteria which we have established. Even when we are certain of the appropriateness of a marriage proposal, we apply our ethnic prejudices and bigotry. As a consequence, in the modern-day environment of unbridled freedom, children who are unable to tolerate such pressures will run-away from home and eventually from Deen. Parents should reflect upon their 'desires' when the very Imãn of their children is at stake. Living in the west, both parents and children have to come to terms with the fact that it is best to marry the child in accordance to his/her wishes.

Appeal to Children

Nevertheless, to children we appeal, although you should marry a person of your choice...this too should be in conjunction with the choice of your parents. Should you disapprove of your parents choice, inform them politely but clearly. The parents should then seek another match and within the confines of the Sharee'ah, accept the choice of their daughters/sons.

Notwithstanding, youngsters should understand well, pedigree too has an effect on children-to-be to a certain extent, therefore do not just select any girl as your spouse. Children also commit dramatic blunders in this field, sometimes falling head-over-heels over girls whose very Imãn is questionable. What long-term benefit, peace and succour may one expect from such a girl? Your entire life will be destroyed.

It is therefore my plea to parents, girls and boys to decide their marriage always with a gaze on their deeni and worldly future. Children should also appreciate that the decisions of their parents, although incomprehensible at this stage, will be for your betterment. I have so many friends, who married in conflict to the choice of their parents and, now say, 'Shaykh! It was a grave mistake, I now wish I had listened to my mother and father...she is quite unbearable to live with!'

Remember and understand well, if you become difficult for your parents now, he/she whom you have chosen will prove difficult for you later.

Respect, Wealth & Beauty are Fleeting Entities

Once an allegorical meeting took place between three wayfarers: ilm (deeni knowledge), ibaadah (worship) and respect. After conversing for a while, they bid farewell and began to depart their own ways...

Ilm: I have developed a bond with you; therefore if you wish to meet me, seek me at the residences of the Ulamā and in madarises.

Ibaadah: I too have to depart and have become fond of you; nevertheless you may seek me in masājids and khanqah's.

Respect stood quietly, whereupon the other two inquired, 'why do you not tell us of your whereabouts?' Respect replied, 'Whenever I leave once, I never return!'

Take care of respect...which too is a great bounty of Allah ﷻ and is achieved after much toil. However one act of misbehaviour and it disappears in seconds. Therefore, recognise Allah ﷻ and live a life of taqwā, *Inshā'Allah,* whatever assault is made on one's respect will then prove ineffective. However, the person who is rebellious towards Allah ﷻ and His Rasool ﷺ...then when Allah ﷻ decides to disgrace him, no power upon earth is able to save him. Misbehaviour by even a distant family member will pour water over any respect your clan enjoys within hours.

Wealth is also very fickle; the *ghanee* (rich) of the previous evening is reduced to a penniless pauper by morning. Similarly, one single illness or accident (Allah ﷻ Forbid) could remove the beauty of the most handsome person.

Piety and Deen are the only entities (which as long as one considers them to be the Favours of Allah ﷻ and not the result of one's own achievement) are everlasting and present with one: in this world; in the grave; on the Day of Qiyãmah and upon the Pûl (Bridge) over Hell. Remember, beauty is for a few days and years, 30-40-50 years, then when she becomes old, your gaze will wander hither-thither...

>   *'Husne soorat (external beauty) is for days a few,*
>   *husne seerat (spiritual beauty) is forever to view.*
>   *Whilst husne soorat will the eyes please,*
>   *it is husne seerat wherein lies the heart's peace.'*

Never make the blunder of making beauty the sole reason for choosing a marriage partner...for this will be a very shaky foundation. In complete contrast, *seerat* (spiritual beauty and character) is such an entity which increases with age and becomes more captivating, appealing and infatuating. Therefore, make *seerat* the foremost criteria and, should such a person also be wealthy, handsome and of noble birth...or all three, then all the better and your good fortune. May Allah ﷻ grant all of us correct Tawfeeq. Ãmeen, Was-salãm.

Shaykh Muhammad Saleem Dhorat

dãmat barakãtuhum

ৡ১৫৩

Chapter Four

When Should A Muslim Marry?

With notes from the Teachings of

Shaykh Ashraf 'Ali Thānwi 🕮 &

Shaykh-ul-Hadeeth Ibrāheem Palanpoori 🕮

exual promiscuity can have serious health consequences and confining sexual intimacy to a committed, faithful, lifelong, monogamous relationship (i.e. marriage) is the surest way of eliminating the risk of STIs. Today, in view of the horrific increases in sexual diseases, even medical experts are encouraging youngsters to abstain from sex until they marry. Dr. T. Stammers (BSc, FRCGP) a tutor in general practice states, '...research shows that early intercourse carried greater risks and often led to subsequent regret. Sexually active teenagers are also more likely to be emotionally hurt and have an increased risk of depression and suicide. The discipline of abstinence in teenage years is a good preparation for fulfilling sex in later life...'

(Family Education Trust)

Beginning of Maturity

Shaykh-ul-Hadeeth Ibrãheem Palanpoori ﷺ relates, 'According to the Sharee'ah of Islãm, females are classified as *buloogh* (mature) when their periods (menses) commence or when they experience 'wet-dreams.' Should any of these signs not be present, then when the child reaches 15 years of age, the Sharee'ah classifies her as mature.

Similarly, for males the discharge of *manee* (semen) heralds the start of *buloogh*. Again, should this sign not be present, then when the child reaches 15 years of age, the Sharee'ah classifies him as mature. Immediately, upon reaching *buloogh,* all the Commands of the Sharee'ah become compulsory upon one. For example, performance of salãh, saum, zakãt, etc. Now, should this person fail to uphold any *farã'idh* and *wãjib* (compulsory) acts, they will be sinful and liable to punishment unless they make *taubah* (repentance) and *qadhã* (compensate)...' (p8, Nikãh) Incidentally, although the doctors define *buloogh* as someone from whom *manee* comes out, our *Awliya* (Friends of Allah ﷻ) define spiritual buloogh as the stage whereby one comes out from *manee*. This means one no longer suffers from *takkabur* (pride). Shaykh Maseehullah ﷺ commented, 'You will find many a Muslim who does not drink alcohol, but you will rarely find one who does not have *takkabur*.' This disease of *takkabur* is the root of all evil and almost all marital problems. Therefore, both husband and wife should rid themselves of pride because *tawãdhu* (Islãmic humility) is the key to marital bliss.

Adolescence

'Adolescence is a branch of madness.'

(Arabic Proverb)

As soon as a young person nears buloogh...the teenager experiences various 'new' urges and becomes aware of events around. This is a delicate phase. Parents should be extra vigilant when their child reaches this stage, ensuring the youngster keeps only the company of pious persons whilst staying far, far away from people who are lewd or amoral. Remember: 'A man is known by the company he keeps...and by the books he reads!'

Nowadays, exposure to TV, pornographic material and mingling with people of the opposite gender from a young age has destroyed the Muslim's *tab'ee* (natural) shame and modesty. Rasoolullah ﷺ commented:

'Every religion has a distinguishing feature (khulq): our prominent khulq is modesty and shame (hayã).'

'Whenever Allah Ta'ālā wishes to destroy a person He snatches hayã away from him. Now bereft of shame (this person) becomes disgraced and wretched in the eyes of people...'

(Both Hadeeth quoted from *Uswa Rasool Akram* ﷺ)

All Humans possess two traits: carnal desires and the yearning for love, friendship and affection. With the commencement of adolescence, these features erupt. To complicate matters, at this early stage of life, intelligence is still defective. Consequently, the very real danger exists of these traits being employed incorrectly. Elders should therefore note:

- Always keep an 'eye' upon youngsters and occupy them in some beneficial activity (either deeni or worldly). Remember, 'The devil makes use of idle hands.'

- Ensure our children always associate with people of pious and noble character. Shaykh Ashraf 'Ali Thãnwi 🌸 often used to comment, 'Even if a person is not very pious, if he/she is at least *shareef* (Islãmically cultured and well-mannered) they will be saved from many a fitnah.'

- Exposure to harãm 'indecent' material (whether in novels, magazine, TV, video or multimedia format) erupts 'carnal desires' in a wrong manner with detrimental physical and mental effects. Censor what your child reads, even religious books; ask some pious Ãlim (scholar).

- Intermingling and staring at the opposite gender as well as listening to music is totally poisonous.

- Discuss and explain to children what is Islãmically acceptable as far as the internet, chat lines, mobile phones and emails are concerned. These mediums are not a blank license to do as one pleases...their usage is governed by the Sharee'ah.

- When the child appears 'understanding' (usually at seven years of age), separate beds, even between brothers and sisters.

When to Marry?

'O (Muslim) youth! Whomsoever is able to fulfil the responsibilities of nikāh should perform nikāh: because it lowers (saves) one's gaze and safeguards one's private organs...'   (Muslim, 1400)

*U*pon maturity, although thoughts and enthusiasm for marriage commence, nevertheless, nikāh at an early age, when physical body parts are still developing is harmful. At this young stage, organ growth has not peaked and, a drain in *manee* (semen) because of irresponsible behaviour is detrimental. Understand well, *manee* although classified as impure in matters of *tahārat* (purity) by the Sharee'ah, is viewed as a very precious commodity. It takes eight drops of blood, which in turn is the result of much nourishment to produce just one drop of this life-making substance. Should large amounts of *manee* be wasted at an early stage, vital body organs will be deprived of their nourishment; health suffers and growth is stunted: with dire consequences later in life. However, should youngsters protect their youth, chastity, health and *manee* from misuse: then upon full maturity and marriage; they will experience indescribable sweetness, ecstasy and peace. This is why it is good practice to nurture a 'suitable' match (but only with the consent of one's child ~ around 16 years of age for girls and for boys 18 years) so that natural desires and thoughts are focussed towards their future partner, though do remember before nikāh they remain *harām* to each other: be it viewing, meeting, touching or speaking.

Islãmic Commands

Allah ﷻ states in the Glorious Qur'ãn:

'And marry those amongst you who are single and also the Sãlihun (pious)...

If they be poor, Allah will enrich them out of His Bounty. And Allah is All-Sufficient for His creatures' needs, All-Knowing.' (24:32)

Rasoolullah ﷺ advised 'Ali ؓ:

'O Ali! Do not delay in three matters: firstly, salãh when its time arrives; secondly, (burial of the) janãzãh, when it is ready; thirdly, in the marriage of a single boy or girl when a (suitable) match is found.' (Tirmizi, p. 38, Islãmic Weddings)

In another hadeeth,

'Whomsoever has a child (girl or boy) should select a good (proper Islãmic) name; endow him/her with tãleem and tarbiyyah; and when he/she reaches buloogh wed (the child).

If after buloogh, you do not wed the child and he/she becomes involved in some misdemeanour, then the father will be sinful.' (Mishkhãt, ibid.)

Shaykh Ashraf 'Ali Thãnwi ﷻ comments, 'From such Verses of the Glorious Qur'ãn and ahadeeth the following are apparent:

Wājib Nikāh

When there is a need, i.e. the urge (to make love) is present in one's *nafs* (self) and one possesses the means (even if it be a minimum income) to (support a wife) then under such circumstances to marry is *wājib*. Moreover, refraining (from nikah under such circumstances will be sinful).

Farāidh Nikāh

If together with means, one has such a pressing urge that the danger and possibility exists of falling into some harām act, then under such circumstances to get married is *fardh* (compulsory). By harām act is (also) implied staring at harām and masturbation.   (p36, ibid.)

Impermissible

However, if there is the (real) fear of being unable to fulfil the *haqq* of one's (spouse), whether it be a physical or material *haqq*, then undoubtedly it is *mamnû* (prohibited) for such a person to wed.'   (ibid.)

Marriage with Non-Muslims & the Ahl-e-Kitab

haykh Mufti Abdur-Raheem Lajpoori ﷺ comments in *Fatāwā Raheemeeyah* (Vol. 2, p. 102), '...In this day and age, upon Sharee' reasons, it is neither permissible to marry nor correlate with Jewish or Christian women (or men). This is especially applicable in *Darul Harb* (non-muslim countries) wherein such association and an evil environment gives rise to firstly the corruption of one's own and secondly the children's *aqaaid* (beliefs). Allah ﷻ states in the Glorious Qur'ān:

'And incline not towards those who do wrong, lest the Fire (of Hell) touches you...' (11:113)

During the time of *Ameerul Mu'mineen* 'Umar ﷺ, the condition of Muslims was one of extreme piety and purity; wherein the general populace was inclined towards Deen. Nevertheless, 'Umar ﷺ forbade Muslims from marrying the women of the Ahl-e-Kitab (Christians and Jews). He stated, 'Although I am not decreeing halāl as harām; for undoubtedly Allah ﷻ has granted permission to marry Ahl-e-Kitab women; nevertheless, the general welfare of the Ummah demands that Muslims be forbidden from acting upon this leeway.' Remember, this was at a time when Christian women were sincere and acting upon their kitabs, in complete contrast to this era wherein they have no true kitab or religion; only a holy cover for atheism and science. Therefore, it is all the more important to act upon the decree of 'Umar ﷺ and not marry such women...for the ladies of Europe nowadays cannot be termed Christians.'

Shaykh Ashraf 'Ali Thānwi ﷺ had decreed a *Fatwā*, 'Nowadays, those people who are termed Christians; the majority of them are classified thus only because of topography; religiously they are atheist and scientologists. The leeway and permission to marry (Christian and Jewish women) does not apply to these people.' The famous Darul Uloom of Deoband had also issued a *Fatwā*, 'Nowadays, of those people who are termed Jews, the majority are atheist and non-believers of any religion or even in the existence of a Creator. Although politically they are classified as Jews, nevertheless the Sharee'ah does not classify them as Ahl-e-Kitab.' (p103, ibid.)

Etiquette's of Nikah

haykh Ashraf 'Ali Thãnwi ❁ states: 'It is well established from the Glorious Qur'ãn that the purpose behind nikãh is to:

- Protect honour, chastity, health and descendants...this is the true purpose of nikãh...not merely to fulfil one's desires like animals.

- Humans require friendship and love, this is our natural need. Accordingly, women were created for this purpose (although Adam ﷺ was presented with everything in Jannah, he was alone and requested a wife Hawwã ﷺ). Ladies possess this unique quality of offering friendship and love, nobody else may comfort and soothe a man.

- Whilst females are physically 'weaker,' nevertheless they possess an altogether unique and brilliant ability to manage affairs of the household and up bring children.

- The carnal desires present in a man find 'true' fulfilment only in his wife. Allah ﷻ has created the wife as a field in which the farmer (husband) plants his seed and reaps his crop (pious children).

- Through nikãh, humans become conscientious and responsible, fearing the results of rash behaviour. He/she now loves faithfulness and chastity, living contently, both saving themselves from numerous calamities. There is no greater social institution for human and national progress. It saves individuals and society from numerous calamities, misfortunes and diseases, both physical and social.   (p, 28, Islãmic Weddings)

Specific Intentions

haykh-ul-Hadeeth Ibrãheem Palanpoori ☸ narrates, 'Amongst the etiquette's of marriage the most important is to ensure correct *niyyat* (Intention), because keeping one's motive correct in even 'worldly' activities results in *thawãb* (reward):

1) Perform nikãh because it is a Sunnah of Nabee ☸ who commented, *'To perform nikãh is my Sunnah and whomsoever refuses to act upon my Sunnah is not (from amongst us).'* (p 23, Tuhfatun Nikah)

2) Perform nikãh because it saves one from evil ways and maintains one's *nafs* (self) under control. In addition, one's heart is saved from many *wasãwis* (stray and evil thoughts) as is the eye from staring at non-mahrãm.

3) Through the blessings of nikãh, Allah ☸ bestows pious children; whatever good deeds and du'aa's they perform will earn their parents' tremendous rewards.

4) A person with spouse and children receives more reward for good deeds than a single person...therefore do make this niyyah also.

5) All children born will form part of the Ummah of Rasoolullah ☸ who will take pride in this greater number. Whichever child participates in *da'wah illallah* (propagation), both the Ummah and their parents will benefit.

6) The death of a child becomes a means for parents achieving saviour from Hell-Fire and entry into Jannah.

Ãdãb of Choosing a Partner

R asoolullah ﷺ commented:
'*Do not marry women (merely) on account of their beauty...for it is possible that this very beauty may become the cause of her destruction. Neither marry women because of their wealth...for it is possible this may be a cause for her rebellion and mischief. Rather marry women because of their religious (piety). (Remember!) A dark complexion slave-girl graced with piety and noble character is infinitely superior to a beautiful high class women of poor character.*' (Ibn Mãjah)

Persian couplet:

'*Should the builder lay the foundation incorrectly,*

Will arise the wall, even it be as high as to the heavens crookedly!'

When a person reaches the age of marriage, his/her wishes and choice should always be sought. If due to shyness or modesty, no clear answer is given, their thoughts and desires could be gauged from close friends by parents and responsible elders.

When parents become aware of their child's preference, they should sincerely reflect upon the proposed partners' piety, suitability and, family background. Ponder whether these two will be compatible or not. At this stage, always bear in mind, it is foolish to act in total contradiction to the boy (or girls) wishes or behind his/her back in arranging a suitable match. Why? Because it is the couple who will be living together life-long, otherwise, the very real possibility exists of unhappiness and *talãq* (divorce). Therefore, always, always bear in mind the wishes of the couple. Of course, should either of them be so irresponsible and foolish as to ignore a 'good' (pious) choice of their parents and insist on marrying some *fãsiq* (sinful person) then resort to du'aa (for Allah ﷻ has full control over the hearts of people), couple this with gentle, loving and tact persuasion. Never resort to hysteria, force or threats, this is totally counter-productive. Relating the benefits of marrying a 'good' person in an amicable 'light' way is the parents responsibility and will, *inshã'Allah*, reap rewards. Moreover, it will ensure no hatred arises in the parents' heart.

Importance & Limits of Viewing A Prospective Partner

Both partners should always take a 'look' at each other with the consent of parents...but not in private as is becoming the norm for this is harãm. Just what prevents a father/mahram to be present when allowing his 'prospective' son-in-law from viewing his daughter?

This 'one' look is encouraged by Rasoolullah ﷺ as it initiates greater love and affection for each other. One wisdom behind this act is that on many occasions, what each person has heard of the other is based on hearsay and second-hand reports. Each individual's taste, inclinations and perception differs, therefore a physical view allows both to decide for themselves, saving the possibility of disagreement and rancour later. However, this 'one look' should not be used as a license for daily dating, going-out, love talk and text messaging over the mobile phone as is becoming quite common amongst western engaged Muslim 'couples.' Why not? Because before nikāh, each is harām for the other...it is nikāh not engagement which makes each halāl for the other.

Some further points to remember when considering an 'ideal' match:

- The girls' age should preferably be two to four years younger than the boys. For a young bachelor, a virgin girl is more appropriate...the Hadeeth encourages this as there is greater love, compatibility and enthusiasm.

- It is vital to consider the prospective partners piety, character and in the case of girls; also their ability to manage domestic affairs and duties. The same applies to choosing a husband. Girls and parents should consider a boy's piety (above all else) before marrying. In this regard, the statement of Hasan Basree ﷦ of Iraq is most appropriate, 'Marry your daughter to some pious person; for if nothing else, at least on account of his bond with Allah ﷻ he will not abuse her nor fail to fulfil her rights.'

Shaykh Maseehullah Khān ﷦ stated, 'Although piety is the foremost criteria when choosing a husband/son-in-law, ensure he is also mild-hearted, mild-natured and cultured so that your daughter remains happy and is not oppressed.' Today parents seek a boy who is well educated and wealthy thinking 'he will keep my daughter materially happy.' Reality is, of course, quite different:

*S*haykh Ashraf 'Ali Thãnwi ◈ relates, 'Today I have received a letter from a good pious noble lady who has been writing to me (and seeking Deeni advice for the past 40 years). She mentions her husband's tyranny, injustice and infidelity...reading it causes me great pain and sorrow. She mentions the great oppression upon women...this poor soul complains that constant crying has weakened her eyesight...she sometimes feels like committing suicide...however, because this is totally against the Sharee'ah she refrains there from.

She has been married 17 years, in which time she has faithfully served her husband. No doubt when he married her, she must have been pretty and youthful, for her husband married with great enthusiasm and joy, asking many to forward his proposal. Now, in old age, this idiot does not even look at her. When she mentions her years of love, devotion, service and faithfulness...he jibes back, 'What service have you rendered?'

How low may a person sink! Heaven knows what 'list of service' the fool had in mind, which this poor soul has been unable to fulfil...what ingratitude! Husbands especially should remember, it appears in Hadeeth, that Allah ﷻ is the Supporter of those who have no helper. When the *mazloom* (oppressed) makes a du'aa...Allah ﷻ replies...'Of a surety, I shall aid you even though it may appear after some time!' Therefore, fear Allah ﷻ and never commit oppression upon juniors...for one will have to pay its price here in dunyã...for He has full power to engulf one in some calamity.'

Four Reasons for Choosing

*N*abee ﷺ commented:

'*Women are married because of four reasons: Wealth, Family Rank, Beauty and Piety. You should marry a pious lady and achieve success.*'

(Bukhārī, Muslim)

Let us briefly study each reason.

*B*eauty ~ Our elders have related a very wise criteria, 'Your partner should be pleasing and not displeasing to view.' Beauty whilst being a blessing, desirable and heart pleasing nevertheless is not everlasting. Heaven forbid, an accident or illness could soon end it. Moreover, beauty is a guest of short duration; natural aging and childbirth takes its toil...the attractiveness of youth soon begins to disappear: 'Those long, glistening hair which seem ever so enchanting today, will appear more revolting than a donkey's tail when she becomes old.'

Another point to bear in mind is that whilst you have chosen this person only because of her/his attractiveness...do remember, they too will have 'airs' on account of their beauty, therefore ponder, will you be able to tolerate and fulfil her tantrums? Also, she too will be desiring an equally beautiful person as her match...do you possess such qualities, otherwise, although in nikāh you will be desirous of her and willing to sacrifice your all...she will consider you as her inferior and incline elsewhere. What pleasure may there be in such a relationship? In addition, others too, like you, will have their eyes and heart upon this beautiful person, events should not take such a turn whereby, although she is in your nikāh, her other admirers will be desiring and scheming your 'removal' from the scene. This is why it is never wise to forgo piety and marry someone merely because of his or her beauty. However, should beauty be present with piety then *Nuruun alla Nur*. In this case, one should not be suspicious of this pious beautiful lady, whom Allah ﷻ has blessed you as a *nemat* (bounty).

Wealth intoxicates the mind of some people and determines their reason for choosing a marriage partner. But remember, wealth is even more fickle than beauty: 'Wealthy at night, pauper by morning.' You should also reflect that although the girls family maybe rich, when she arrives into your nikāh, generally, she will not be bringing any wealth with her and should she receive this wealth, why, does your manhood and sense of honour accept 'sponging' off your wife's wealth? In addition, even if she is from a wealthy background...her tastes, desires and requirements too will be expensive. Do you possess the means and ability to fulfil these? 'An elephant requires a massive diet'...do you think a wealthy girl will be satisfied with your comparatively small income? You will be constrained to daily plead with such a person (or nowadays, allow her to go out to work to finance her tastes)...the sum result of which will be you having to live 'under her thumb.' The wise have said: 'Ideally, in wealth, the bride should be from a less wealthy background, so that she remains grateful and contented.'

*F**amily** background.* Some people search for a person from a socially higher class considering this will give them greater fame, respect and superiority over others. Like previous two reasons, this too is not a sensible basis for choosing a marriage partner.

*P**iety** according* to the Sharee'ah determines a persons rank and worth. Beauty, wealth and family background are all fickle and flimsy...especially as far as girls are concerned...for their most precious commodity is honour and chastity. 'Ali ☙ narrates, 'We were present with Rasoolullah ﷺ when He asked us: 'Inform me, what is best for ladies?' All the Sahābāh ☙ present maintained silence. 'Ali ☙ relates 'I returned and asked Fātimah ☙, 'What is best for ladies?' She replied 'She should not look at any non -mahram male nor should any male look at her.' 'Ali ☙ related this reply to Rasoolullah ﷺ who commented: 'Fātimah is a portion of my heart (therefore, she understood)." This is why both parents and the person marrying should very carefully consider their prospective partners':

1) Aqaaid (beliefs) ~ Remember, many a western educated person suffers from queer beliefs regarding the Ākhirah. Find out their exact views.

2) Ibaadah (worship) ~ Is the person punctual in Salāh, Saum, Zakat, etc? These are not insignificant acts.

3) Akhlāq (good character) ~ Ask sensible people about the person's habits, traits, manner of speaking, etc.

4) Muãmalāt (transactions) ~ Try to ascertain the person's

financial dealings, honesty and integrity.

5) Muãsharat (social intercourse) ~ Does the person know how to conduct themselves in society and within the family circle?

6) Health ~ This too is important; do they suffer from any illnesses?

7) Relationship ~ Generally, though not always, there is greater compatibility between people of the same family and ethnicity.

8) Temperament ~ Ideally both the boy and girl should enjoy the same outlook...otherwise if one is quite positive, enthusiastic, lively and an extrovert whilst the other be subdued and a simpleton...then obviously life could be problematic.

9) Education ~ Both should have received a sensible level of Deeni Tãleem and basic education and not be a complete ignoramus.

10) Housekeeping Skills & Profession ~ It is important the girl be competent in all aspects of domestic duties whilst the boy be one who behaves like our Nabee ﷺ...always willing to lend a hand in household chores. The boy should also possess some trade, profession or skill (either Deeni or worldly) so he may maintain his wife and family and not be dependent on others.

11) Modern day habits ~ Nowadays, it is also necessary to find out whether the boy or girl suffers from a drug or alcohol problem or is addicted to the TV.

Du'aa (Supplication)

Allah ﷻ says in the Glorious Qur'ān:

'Make du'aa to Me, I shall accept!'

Rasoolullah ﷺ commented:

'Whomsoever has received the Tawfeeq (ability) to make du'aa...for him (or her) the doors of acceptance (Jannah and Rahmat) are opened.'

'Only du'aa is able to alter qadhā (fate).'

(Quoted from Islāmic Weddings, p. 110)

Shaykh Ashraf 'Ali Thānwi ﷺ suggests, 'Du'aa (supplication) is such a wonderful bounty that it contains benefits for both Ākhirah and dunyā. If at every stage of one's marital life, du'aa is made in abundance, tremendous blessings will follow. Remember, each and every du'aa of a Mu'min is assured acceptance, 'Raising hands in the Court of Allah ﷻ always brings some benefit.' This maybe in one of three forms:

1) That which was specifically requested is received.

2) A greater alternative is reserved for one in the Ākhirah.

3) Some misfortune or calamity coming one's way is diverted.

However, a common misconception is to only regard the raising of hands and supplicating as du'aa and to forgo physical effort, whereas there are two forms of supplication: oral du'aa and physical du'aa (the adoption of halāl means).

Etiquette's of Du'aa

*T*he girl, boy and their parents' should note the following etiquette's of du'aa:

1) Du'aa means our asking, with the permission of Allah ﷻ for what we assume to be good for us. If in the Knowledge of Allah ﷻ, it be beneficial for us, then we desire it, otherwise not; because we are contented with His decree under all circumstances.

2) We are unaware of *taqdeer* (Divine predestination), therefore; we ask of Allah ﷻ what is best for us...and thereafter happily resign ourselves to His Choice.

3) Whilst making du'aa, we must also adopt all sensible avenues, means and ways allowed by the Sharee'ah.

Beautiful Comprehensive Du'aa's

رَبَّنَا هَبْ لَنَا مِنْ اَزْوَاجِنَا وَ ذُرِّيَّاتِنَا قُرَّةَ اَعْيُنٍ

وَّ اجْعَلْنَا لِلْمُتَّقِيْنَ اِمَامًا

'O Allah! Bestow on us from our wives and children the comfort of our eyes, and make us leaders of the Mut'taqeen (pious).'   (Glorious Qur'ān, 25:74)

اَللّٰهُمَّ اِنِّیْ اَسْئَلُکَ الْعَفْوَ وَ الْعَافِیَةَ

فِیْ دِیْنِیْ وَ دُنْیَایَ وَ اَهْلِیْ وَ مَالِیْ

'O Allah! I ask of You forgiveness and peace in the matter of my religion, dunya, family and wealth.'

اَللّٰهُمَّ اِنِّیْ اَسْئَلُکَ مِنْ صَالِحِ مَا تُؤْتِی النَّاسَ

مِنَ الْاَهْلِ وَ الْوَلَدِ غَیْرَ ضَالٍّ وَّ لَا مُضِلٍّ

'O Allah! I ask of you good noble things which you bestow to people: wealth; wife and children; neither they be astray not be those who lead astray.'

اَللّٰهُمَّ بَارِكْ لَنَا فِىْ اَسْمَاعِنَا وَ اَبْصَارِنَا وَ قُلُوْبِنَا

وَ اَزْوَاجِنَا وَ ذُرِّيَّاتِنَا وَ تُبْ عَلَيْنَا اِنَّكَ اَنْتَ التَّوَّابُ الرَّحِيْمُ

'O Allah! Grant us blessings in our faculties of hearing, seeing and in our heart, wives and children. Moreover, accept our repentance, for undoubtedly only You are the Most forgiving, Most Merciful.'

اَللّٰهُمَّ اِنِّىْ اَعُوْذُ بِكَ مِنِ امْرَأَةٍ تُشِيِّبُنِىْ قَبْلَ الْمَشِيْبِ وَ اَعُوْذُ بِكَ

مِنْ وَلَدٍ يَكُوْنُ عَلَىَّ وَبَالاً وَ اَعُوْذُ بِكَ مِنْ مَالٍ يَكُوْنُ عَلَىَّ عَذَابًا

'O Allah! I seek your protection from such a wife who ages me before old age. I seek your protection from such children who may vex me. Also, I seek your protection from such wealth which is a punishment.'

اَللّٰهُمَّ اِنِّىْ اَعُوْذُ بِكَ مِنْ فِتْنَةِ النِّسَآءِ، اَللّٰهُمَّ اِنِّىْ اَعُوْذُ بِكَ مِنْ

كُلِّ عَمَلٍ يُخْذِيْنِىْ، وَ اَعُوْذُ بِكَ مِنْ كُلِّ صَاحِبٍ يُؤْذِيْنِىْ، وَ

اَعُوْذُ بِكَ مِنْ كُلِّ اَمَلٍ يُلْهِيْنِىْ

'O Allah! I seek your protection from the mischief of women. O Allah! I seek your protection from every such action which may disgrace me. I seek your protection from every such companion who may harm me, and I seek protection from every such a moment which keeps me negligent.' (Maqbool, Du'aa's 65, 139, 162, 195)

The Importance of Counselling & Relevance of Istikhãrah

Allah ﷻ says in the Glorious Qur'ãn:

'...And consult with them in affairs. Then when you have taken a decision, put your trust in Allah, certainly, Allah loves those who put their trust (in Him).' (3:159)

'And those who answer the Call of their Lord and perform Salãh and who (conduct) their affairs by mutual consultation and who spend of what We have bestowed on them.' (42:38)

Jabir ﷺ narrates,

'In the same way Rasoolullah ﷺ imparted upon us the Verses of the Glorious Qur'ãn, he also taught us to perform Istikhãrah in all affairs (of magnitude). He ﷺ commented, 'Whenever an important matter arises, perform two rakãts nafl (salãh) and the du'aa (for Istikhãrah)...' (p430, Riyadus Sãliheen)

Whenever a Muslim decides to enact any important or significant matter, he/she should firstly seek the opinion of a person who is both a *habeeb* (true friend and well-wisher) and *labeeb* (knowledgeable and wherever possible a pious Ãlim). This *mashwarah* (consultation, whether in person, by letter or phone) is extremely important, full of blessings and more beneficial than *only* praying *Salāt Istikhārah.* Moreover, such pious counselling should not be dismissed out rightly if it goes against one's whim and fancy but should be reflected upon with an unbiased mind. It is upon such good advise that *Istikhārah* should be performed.

Nowadays, many youngsters who are not even punctual with their five daily Fardh Salāh, feel that by praying two rakāts *Salāt Istikhārah,* an answer from the Heavens as to their predetermined and established choice of future spouse will be forthcoming. This is mere self-deception, a 'smoke screen' and the distorting of an Sunnah act of worship to soothe one's conscience. It is sometimes used as a convenient cover for not only dismissing the opinions of elders but also to give Deeni 'colour' to one's misbehaviour.

haykh Ashraf 'Ali Thānwi 🌸 narrates, 'Istikhārah is beneficial for the person who maintains an open-mind (in the matter being considered)...otherwise one's pre-conceived choice dominates the heart. This person now considers (after Istikhārah) his thoughts and any dream to justify this previous choice. Remember, it is not at all necessary to perform *Istikhārah* only at night...this has become almost customary...nor is it necessary to go to sleep immediately after. It may be prayed at any time (except the three *makruh* times), for example after Zohar Salāh, perform two rakāts Nafl and then pray Istikhārah du'aa...though do remember, if before Istikhārah one has a partiality then clear this thought or idea from the heart before sitting down and inclining towards one's *qalb* (heart). One may repeat this as many times in one day.'

Du'aa for Istikhãrah

اَللّٰهُمَّ اِنِّیْ اَسْتَخِیْرُکَ بِعِلْمِکَ وَ اَسْتَقْدِرُکَ بِقُدْرَتِکَ وَ اَسْئَلُکَ

مِنْ فَضْلِکَ الْعَظِیْمِ فَاِنَّکَ تَقْدِرُ وَ لَا اَقْدِرُ وَ تَعْلَمُ وَ لَا اَعْلَمُ وَ

اَنْتَ عَلَّامُ الْغُیُوْبِ، اَللّٰهُمَّ اِنْ کُنْتَ تَعْلَمُ اَنَّ هٰذَا الْاَمْرَ خَیْرٌ لِّیْ

فِیْ دِیْنِیْ وَ مَعَاشِیْ وَ عَاقِبَةِ اَمْرِیْ فَاقْدِرْهُ لِیْ وَ یَسِّرْهُ لِیْ ثُمَّ

بَارِکْ لِیْ فِیْهِ، وَ اِنْ کُنْتَ تَعْلَمُ اَنَّ هٰذَا الْاَمْرَ شَرٌّ لِّیْ فِیْ دِیْنِیْ وَ

مَعَاشِیْ وَ عَاقِبَةِ اَمْرِیْ فَاصْرِفْهُ عَنِّیْ وَ اصْرِفْنِیْ عَنْهُ وَ اقْدِرْ لِیَ

الْخَیْرَ حَیْثُ کَانَ ثُمَّ اَرْضِنِیْ بِهِ

'O Allah! I seek good guidance from You through Your Attribute of Knowledge, and I seek strength from You through Your Attribute of Power and I beg You for Your Great Favour. You are all-Powerful, and I am helpless; You are All-Knowing and I am ignorant: You know the unseen. If in your Knowledge this act (at this point think of your purpose) is good for me, for my faith, my dunyã and Ãkhirah, ordain it for me, and make it easy, and bless me in it. Moreover, if in Your Knowledge, this act (again think of your purpose) is harmful for me, for my faith, my dunyã and Ãkhirah, keep me away from it and prevent me from doing it, moreover ordain for me what is good, wherever and whatever undertaking it may be, and then, make me contented with it.'

With Whom Should Consultation Be Made?

 $\mathcal{S}$ haykh Mufti Taqee Uthmãni *dãmat barakãtuhum* narrates, 'When Nabee ﷺ was instructed to make consultation with the Sahãbãh ﷺ, then we people are in greater need of *mashwarah*. However, it is necessary to be aware of certain pertinent issues relating to consultation:

1) Consultation should only be made with such a person who has full insight (baseerat) in the matter. When one enlists the services of such a person, Allah ﷺ will create blessings. However, if one consults a person who is unaware of the matter and lacks foresight, then what is the benefit? At times, in matters of the Deen (and nikãh is half of Imãn), people consult with those who lack true 'Ilm of Deen; as a consequence those who are astray lead others astray. Accordingly, the first quality to look for is (Deeni) knowledge and expertise.

2) The second prerequisite for consultation is to fathom out the true purpose and subject matter. If the topic under scrutiny has already been decreed fardh, wãjib or harãm by Allah ﷺ (for example, it is clearly forbidden to marry a non-muslim), then the question of consultation just does not arise. Why? Because the deed, which is fardh or wãjib, is compulsory anyway...and those matters that have been categorised as harãm are always forbidden.

3) The third condition for *mashwarah* was stipulated by Nabee ﷺ, 'The consultant should be trustworthy.' (p35, V11, Islãhi...) Consulting someone is the same as depositing a trust with them wherein they keep it safe and prevent abuse.

Accordingly, the person being consulted should unambiguously state his inability to advise if he lacks insight in the matter. However, nowadays people will never admit to their lack of expertise and blurt their opinion or wishful thought.

4) The fourth condition for *mashwarah* is for the consultant to only worry about giving his true opinion; irrespective of whether it appeals bitter to the seeker. The purpose is not to please or appease the person asking, but to forward your genuine opinion. For example, when a person asks whether he should propose to a certain individual, then on such occasions one is allowed and should air one's views...even the bad points (to your knowledge) of a person. Whilst normally this would constitute *gheebat* (backbiting), on such occasions, it is not sinful because the person is seeking your benevolent view. In fact, let the seeker know that you are raising this point out of concern and stress upon him not to relate your views to others. This is a mutual demand of *mashwarah*.

5) The fifth prerequisite for consultation is to keep the matter secret. When the person approached you for *mashwarah* and revealed his predicament and feelings, he appointed you as a confidante revealing his inner thoughts...it now becomes incumbent upon you to guard his secret and not reveal it to anyone.

6) The final condition is to realise that when you have forwarded your opinion, it is not at all necessary for the seeker to follow it. He or she is at liberty to accept or reject the advice. The decision is entirely theirs; you should not

feel offended. The purpose was to consult not to become subjugated. On the Day of Qiyāmah, you will not be asked whether he acted upon your advice...

7) These are the etiquettes of *mashwarah* taught to us by the Glorious Qur'ān and the Sunnah of Nabee ﷺ. If we act accordingly, then Allah ﷻ will grant barakat (blessings) therein and no turmoil, friction or enmity will arise.

Finally, one should endeavour to remember the following advice of 'Allamah Shabbir 'Uthmāni ﷺ...

> *'Haqq (true) speech or dialogue, with a haqq niyyat (intention), delivered with haqq method is never without effect and never creates fitnah or fasad (strife and dissension).'*

Three pre-requisites have been formulated: firstly, whatever one is relating must be haqq; secondly, our intention for relating it must be haqq (sincere); finally, the method we employ to deliver must be haqq.

If these three conditions are present, Inshā'Allah, fitnah will not arise. Moreover, whenever in relating any haqq matter, dissension does arise, immediately conclude that one of these conditions is lacking: either the niyyat, dialogue or the method employed is not haqq.

Remember, the Muslim did not arrive in this world as the soldier of Allah ﷻ, our mission is only to constantly relate to others haqq dialogue, with haqq niyyat and haqq method. Never become despondent in doing so, but also do not behave in any way whereby fitnah is initiated.

(Vols. 10, 11, Islaahi Khutabaat)

haykh Ashraf 'Ali Thãnwi ﷺ relates, 'There was a pious person who received many proposals for the marriage of his daughter. One day, he approached his neighbour, who although a Jew, was a gentleman. The Muslim relating his predicament of picking a match for his daughter asked the Jewish neighbour; who advised, 'In reality you should not be asking me because in religion I am your opponent...and how may one fully trust an opponent.' The Muslim replied, 'You although not a Muslim are a gentleman and, Inshã'Allah, will give good counsel.'

The Jew commented, 'Well, I have heard your Nabee Muhammad ﷺ said, 'In marrying, people look at one of four qualities in a lady: wealth, beauty, family and piety.' He ﷺ thereafter advised to marry a pious person as far as possible. Now, of all the candidates that have proposed for your daughter...I see no truly pious person. However, I am aware of a *Taleeb-ul-Ilm* (student of Deen) living in your Masjid who spends his time in the obedience of Allah ﷻ...my advice is marry your daughter to him, Inshã'Allah, there will be great blessings for your daughter.'

This is precisely what the Muslim did and it was noticed his daughter spent her whole life in happiness!'

The moral from this episode is not that we consult with just anybody but we approach a person who is wise and a well-wisher.

ﮞﮞﮞ

Chapter Five

How Should A Muslim Marry?

With notes from the Teachings of

Shaykh Ashraf 'Ali Thãnwi 🌸

Shaykh-ul-Hadeeth Ibrãheem Palanpoori 🌸

& Shaykh Muhammad Saleem Dhorat

Shaykh Maseehullah Khãn 🌸 commented, 'Nowadays it is best to perform nikãh and then make ruksat (allow the couple to live together) quickly. Both are saved from many sins, anxieties and grief...'

What is a honeymoon? Two monkeys drinking honey and looking at the moon for the first week of their marriage at some exotic location...ahh, pure heaven. And thereafter constantly disagreeing, arguing and bickering with each other for the rest of their live...aagh, pure hell!

How to Marry

haykh Muhammad Saleem Dhorat *dāmat barakātuhum* relates, 'Marriage is undoubtedly an institution and occasion of happiness and joy. By nature, at times of jubilation, man is prone to becoming overawed by merriment and loses his intelligence. He/she fails to comprehend what is expected and demanded from them by Allah 🕮 and His Rasool 🕮.

During the time of the Sahābāh 🕮, this phenomena never arose because they had full control over their emotions and intellect...both on occasions of joy and sorrow. Why? Because the thought of forgoing or losing their grip on the 'Rope' of the Deen of Allah 🕮 was unimaginable.

Remember and understand well, the Deen of Islām was revealed unto Qiyāmah and Allah 🕮 was and is fully aware of all the 'developments' to take place in society. Accordingly, the customs in vogue today, 1400 years after revelation, are also being addressed in the Khutbah (Sermon) of Nikāh wherein all three Verses of the Glorious Qur'ān contain reference to Taqwā. And what is this Taqwā? Taqwā is the name of the spiritual veil which saves one from the disobedience of Allah 🕮.

On wedding occasions, we go to great lengths to please everybody; the bride, bridesmaid, bridegroom, their respected parents, relatives, friends and colleagues. Yet in doing so we displease the very Creator who has given us this opportunity and His Rasool ﷺ whose soul is undoubtedly being pained in Madeenah Munnawwarah at our behaviour. All of us, the old and young are guilty of this crime.

The Pressure of Non-Islãmic Customs

Through pressure by relatives, friends and associates, non-Islãmic customs have overpowered and dominated our Muslim homes to such an extent that the thought of pleasing Allah ﷻ and His Rasool ﷺ just does not arise. From the time of *mangni* (engagement) unto the nikãh, departure and waleemah, how often are the overwhelming majority of people involved in the sin of viewing non-mahram? Rasoolullah ﷺ commented,

'The Curse of Allah be upon the person who observes (deliberately without a valid reason a non-mahram) and the person who (allow themselves to be) observed.' (Baihaqee, p264, Vol. 3, Mazãhir Haqq)

Should anybody be even remotely courageous enough to make separate eating and feeding arrangements for men and women, then people become astonished. Generally, when the bridegroom arrives to escort his bride, what happens? He is accompanied by his friends and male relatives; all these young men enter a gathering of young resplendently dressed and adorned non-mahram ladies-in-waiting. Those elders who turn a 'blind-eye' and allow such a vile and evil development should ponder what actions, deeds and thoughts take place on such a heinous occasions. Why do we allow such evil? Because of pressure of such customs which have become entrenched in our society. If none of us are prepared to forgo these evils, how will these customs be broken? It only takes a few brave, sincere and courageous souls to breakaway from this 'mould' and follow the Sunnah of Rasoolullah ﷺ for Allah ﷻ to grant *tawfeeq* to others. Should anybody pressurise, then I always advise my friends and associates to unreservedly say, 'we are following the Sunnah of Rasoolullah ﷺ!'

Remember, at the time of the Nikāh Khutbah a hadeeth is recited, 'Nikāh is my Sunnah.' However, how many evils do we commit in fulfilling this one Sunnah? It appears that at our weddings, apart from the bridegroom's appearance at the Masjid for Nikāh, all other activities are enacted outside the limits of the Sharee'ah.'

The Repercussions of Non-Islāmic Customs

We are witnessing unbelievable transgression of the Sharee'ah at weddings. Huge amounts of money (sometimes funded by interest-bearing loans), time, resources and food is wasted. Such flagrant violation of the Commands of Allah ﷻ and His Rasool ﷺ brings down Divine Punishment. Within a short time of marriage, problems come to the fore and the couple wish to separate. Families who had only come together with such high hopes a few months previously are now at each other's throats; flinging accusations and blaming each other. Moreover, even in business activities and affairs, *barakat* is taken away and families, who were running huge financial empires, soon end up bankrupt and ruined.

Mangni (Engagement)

R asoolullah ﷺ commented:
'When some pious person of noble character sends nikah proposal to your home, then accept his proposal: otherwise, there will be great fitnah & fasãd (anarchy and strife) upon earth.' (Tirmizi)

'No Muslim should propose 'over' the proposal of his brother...until he either marries or withdraws his proposal.' (Muslim, 1414)

What is Mangni? In reality, it is a pledge or promise from one side to another to marry their respective boy and girl with their willing and happy consent. This pledge may be in person, by correspondence or through the agency of some reliable acquaintance. There is no need to accompany it with an engagement party, distribution of sweets, cakes or any other futile custom. Do remember, a promise or pledge is no light matter, consider very carefully before pledging and thereafter honour your promise (unless there is a valid reason). Shaykh Maseehullah Khãn ﷺ commented,

'Please do not take offence, but let me tell you something: The truth is that a Muslim has lost trust and confidence (i'timãd) in his fellow Muslim. Why do I say this? You can see for yourself that, even after the (mangni) agreement is made, it is still necessary to hold a special function (where 400-500 people gather for meals) to re-confirm this agreement!'

What is Permissible for an Engaged Person?

Shaykh Muhammad Saleem Dhorat *dãmat barakãtuhum* commented, 'Meeting each other, before marriage, without nikãh, is impermissible. Touching each other, before marriage, without nikãh is harãm. Every person is aware of this. Seeing each other - non-mahram male (or) female, before marriage, without nikãh, is impermissible. Even after engagement, it is harãm. A male does not become permissible for a female, and a female does not become permissible for a male after engagement alone. They will have to marry each other, i.e. perform proper Nikãh before they become halãl for each other.

Nowadays this is the tragedy of the Ummah. An 'engagement' takes place before the actual engagement. What is engagement? The meaning of engagement is that each party makes a promise to the other saying, 'We will take your daughter,' and 'We will give our daughter.' 'Your daughter will marry our son' and 'Our son will marry your daughter.'

This is engagement. You do not need to invite and feed a large crowd of people for an engagement. The getting together of a few people from both sides, without incurring any expense and indulging in extravagance to make a firm promise of marriage is an engagement. They simply gather to express their intentions saying, 'Yes, we have made the resolution that we will marry our daughter to your son.'

And the other party will say, 'We also affirm that our son will marry your daughter.' This is engagement, which may take place through correspondence, or even over the phone. But nowadays, first a semi-engagement (which in reality is the mangni) takes place after which is the 'official engagement,' where two to three hundred or more people will get together and engage in so many activities, which bring the Displeasure and Anger of Allah ﷻ. We ourselves have made the intention of disobeying and displeasing Allah ﷻ, (but not contented) we want another 200-400 people becoming part of this disobedience as well.

How ungrateful to Allah ﷻ! So between this semi and official engagement there is usually an interval of two to three months and, sometimes even up to a year, during which the engaged couple go out shopping together and spend time elsewhere in solitude, which is all harãm and a means of displeasing Allah ﷻ.

Then, after the 'official engagement' has taken place, again the same sins are repeated. On the day of 'Eed, the boy comes to meet the girl and she goes to meet him. This party has already become in-laws for him, and the other party has already become in-laws for her. The boy sends presents to the girl and she sends presents to him.

Engagement does not make them lawful for each other. As far as the law of Islãm is concerned, they should remain as distant as they were before engagement. By meeting and seeing each other before marriage, we are inviting the Wrath of Allah ﷻ.

To Request Permission from Elders

*S*haykh Ashraf 'Ali Thānwi ❀ narrates, 'The blessings we have observed in marriages where permission was sought from the elders of the household...is not seen in weddings where the couple marry solely on their own. This latter (so-called love) marriage wherein the couple 'decide' everything for themselves is a testimony to their lack of hayā (sense of shame and modesty),

'When you no longer possess hayā; do as you please.'

Islām considers hayā and natural restraint as the supreme treasures for any woman. They are the keys to all goodness and when these no longer remains what hope is there for any virtue?

Remember our Nabee ❀ married his beloved daughter Fātimah ❀ in a manner wherein there were no customs whatsoever...the engagement itself was ever so simple. 'Ali ❀, who was also a cousin, came and sat down quietly, but out of shame was unable to say anything or raise the subject. Our Nabee ❀ spoke:

'I am aware you have arrived to propose marriage to Fātimah ❀...because Jibr'aeel ❀ has already conveyed Allah Ta'ālā's Message that I marry 'Ali to Fātimah (❀).' (Hadeeth)

Nabee ❀ accepted the proposal and engagement. No gathering was arranged or sweetmeats, cake, jewellery or clothing were exchanged.'

Dating Agencies & Blind Dating

haykh Ashraf 'Ali Thãnwi ❀ commented, 'Nowadays the curse and mischief of placing and answering *illicit* adverts by boys and girls in newspapers, magazines, (internet, text and chat lines) has become rampant. Sometimes the boy will boast of his qualifications, profession (and of course good sense of humour). He thereafter lists his desire for a lady with certain qualities...and whomsoever be interested should send a photo and details. Girls too advertise their good points: qualifications, (western birth), beauty, age (and again the G.S.H.) all without any shame or fear. She too outlines her requirements. Thereafter, each other communicate and meet a few times so they may gauge their prospective partner before nikãh...sometimes this produces a match, otherwise one look's elsewhere. What curse and misfortune!' Regarding this total emulation of others our beloved Nabee ❀ predicted:

'Most certainly, you will follow the ways of those who preceded you step by step, inch by inch. If they enter into a lizard's hole, you (will emulate them) and follow them into the lizard's hole.' Somebody asked: 'O Rasoolullah ❀! Do you mean the Yahood and Nasãra?' Nabee ❀ replied: 'Who else?'

(Mishkhãtul Masaabeeh)

Should a genuine need arise to approach a reputable 'Muslim Marriage Bureau,' (authenticated by senior pious Ulamã's) this should be with the consent, knowledge, approval and under the full supervision of mahram elders.

Who is a Walee (Custodian)?

Rasoolullah ﷺ commented:

'*A previously married women has greater right and say over her affairs than her walee; and the father of a virgin (previously unmarried) should also ensure regarding her nikāh that he obtains her consent...*' (Ma'āriful Hadeeth, Vol. 7, p.16)

Shaykh Manzoor Nu'maani ﷺ comments:

'*From this (and other ahadeeth) it is quite obvious that no walee may marry any mature and intelligent lady (whether previously married or not) without her willing consent.*' *(ibid.)*

Shaykh Ashraf 'Ali Thānwi ﷺ commented, 'A person who represents the person marrying is known as a *walee* (custodian). For both the bride and bridegroom, the father enjoys this right, in his absence the grandfather, thereafter real-brother, step paternal brother, paternal & maternal uncle, etc. All of these, must of course, be sane mature Muslims.'

Nowadays, the trend is for one male, from both sides, to be physically present when requesting the girls permission. This is totally wrong and completely against the Sharee' command of *hijāb*. Only mahram male should seek the girl's permission and thereafter ensure they be present when the nikāh is solemnized. What prevents a father, brother or uncle from requesting this consent and how do they tolerate a non-mahram asking their daughter/sister?

Ādāb of Nikāh

1) As far as possible, nikāh should be publicised, announced and performed in public as our beloved Nabee ﷺ advised: *'Perform nikāh with announcement and in the Masjid...'* (Ma'āriful Hadeeth, Vol. 7, p.22)

2) The wisdom behind this 'publicity' is to bring to view the sanctity and legality of this union and ibaadah...in complete contrast to *zina* (adultery), which is harām and always-committed in secret.

3) Another lesson from the above Hadeeth is that it is preferable to perform nikāh in the Masjid ideally after some Salāt; the best occasion being after Jumu'ah Salāh when large numbers of people gather. Herein will be the greatest number of 'Ulamā and Sulahā; whose du'aa the newly married will receive and whose presence will attract the *Rahmat* of Allah ﷻ.

4) Remember, nikah is an *ibaadah* generally performed in a Masjid. Accordingly, even when it is not salāh time...all attending should make intention of *nafl it'ikaaf* and recite the Sunnah du'aa when entering the Masjid. All, especially the bridegroom, should be in the state of *wudhu* (ablution - this is one Ādab of the Masjid) and their clothing, headdress and behaviour must confirm to the *rights* of the Masjid.

5) It is indeed heartbreaking to observe how we Muslims, who are on haqq, behave ever so rowdily and disrespectfully in the Masājids on occasions of nikāh, contrast this with the behaviour of non-Muslims *inside*

their places of worship. At all times we should maintain the sanctity of the Masjid. Rasoolullah ﷺ commented, 'Do not make a commotion like that of markets.' (Aboo Dawood)

6) Many a times it is observed that when people attend the Masājid for nikāh outside of fardh salāh times, they will await in groups leaning against all three side walls and wait for the bridegroom to enter and only then huddle around the *mimber*. Whilst in the Masjid, one should sit in rows and face the qiblah; engage in some form of ibaadat (salāh, recitation of the Glorious Qur'ān, du'aa's, thikr, etc.) and not waste the opportunity in useless and disrespectful behaviour.

7) A pious Ãlim (or Sāleh person, who has received Tāleem from an Ãlim), should perform the nikāh. After recitation of the khutbah should take place *ijāb* (proposal) and *qubul* (acceptance). The bridegroom should ensure he recites the complete sentence: 'I have accepted,' (not merely, 'accepted') clearly, so that the *Khateeb* (performer of nikāh) and the *Walee* may hear.

8) All cultures and people, the world over, have different ways of congratulating the newly married. The Sunnah du'aa is:

بَارَکَ اللهُ لَکَ وَ بَارَکَ عَلَیْکَ وَ جَمَعَ بَیْنَکُمَا فِیْ خَیْرٍ

'May Allah bless you and shower His blessings on you and may He grant you both a pleasant and prosperous life.' (Tirmidhi, Abu Dawood)

Mahr

R asoolullah ﷺ commented:
'*Whomsoever marries a lady, whether for a small or large amount of mahr; with the intention in his heart of not actually paying will be gathered before Allah Ta'ālā on the Day of Qiyāmah as a fornicator!*'

(Ma'āriful Hadeeth, Vol. 7, p.24)

Shaykh Ashraf 'Ali Thānwi ﷺ relates, '*Mahr* is *wājib* (compulsory). Irrespective of whether any mention of *Mahr* is made or not at the time of nikāh, it will be valid; nevertheless, *Mahr* will remain compulsory even if not mentioned.' According to Hanafi Scholars, the minimum quantity of *Mahr* is 10 *dirhams* (i.e. 30.6 grams or 1 troy ounce of Silver). There is no maximum amount, however it is not wise to fix an exorbitant amount.

Mahr-e-Fātimi ﷺ

This is the amount of *Mahr* 'Ali ﷺ gave at the time of his *nikāh* with Fātimah ﷺ. Shaykh Maseehullah Khān ﷺ whilst performing a nikāh in the UK commented, 'This *Mahr-e-Fātimi* is a good sufficient amount full of blessings. The *Mahr* should at least be a reasonable amount to reflect the 'rank' and honour of the bride.' Although differences exists as to the exact amount, according to Shaykh Mufti 'Abdur-Raheem Lajpoori ﷺ, 'The preferred and more cautious view is that *Mahr-e-Fātimi* ﷺ be calculated upon 150 tolas (1750 grams/62 ounces) of silver.' (Fataawa Raheemiya Vol.6, p445)

In January 2008 this equated to approximately £512

The Departure & Arrival of A Muslim Bride

*O*ur Prophet Muhammad ﷺ arranged for Umme Ayman ؋, the noble lady who had breast-fed him and whom he lovingly referred to as 'mother' to escort his daughter Fātimah ؋ to her husband's house after nikāh. No fanfare, no pomp, and no customs: neither did 'Ali ؋ arrive with a 'caravan of friends.' Sheer simplicity from both sides.

It now becomes compulsory upon us to shun the ridiculous rituals and huge expenses on these occasions and adopt the pure, simple and informal Sunnah of Nabee ﷺ. What prevents Muslim parents from personally escorting their daughter to her new home? If it amounts to disgrace or shame why did Nabee ﷺ request his 'mother' to escort the 'Queen of Jannah?' There is no need for a huge entourage of people or cavalcade of limousines to achieve this. One or two vehicles at most are quite adequate to carry the bride and her attendants.

*S*haykh-ul-Hadeeth Ibrāheem Palanpoori ﷺ narrates, 'Both the bride and bridegroom (especially their parent's) should ensure the couple receive sufficient sleep and rest before departure during the wedding day. In this way both will be in a refreshed condition for their first meeting at night.' The bride, about to leave her parents' house for a new life with new people is naturally emotionally strained. Added to this is the well wishes and company of friends; wearing of 'new' (not necessary comfortable) clothes; having to sit in one place embellished for long periods; etc. Her parents should make a special point of removing her away from this 'exposure' and insist she sleeps and rest for a few hours. In addition, they and their daughter should be punctual about Salāh. What greater shame and loss than for a father and mother to see their daughter leave home without having prayed Salāh or be in the state of Sharee' Hijāb?

Brides Arrival

Shaykh Ashraf 'Ali Thānwi ❀ narrates, 'Live amongst your in-law's with dignity from the beginning. Be merciful upon juniors and treat elders with respect. Never delegate any of your responsibilities to other's nor leave things lying around for them to place away. Help your in-law's in their domestic duties...this will create your love in their hearts. Whenever two people are conversing amongst themselves, leave the room and do not assume they are talking about you. Upon arriving at your in -law's, do remember that even if your heart feels uncomfortable with new people and a new place...keep calm and do not pine away your time in tears. Nowadays, many brides go in haste and thereafter wish to leave in haste.

Converse with your new relatives in moderation. Neither be un-lady like, foolish and talk too much, nor withdraw to the extent that people have to plead with you to get a word out. This too is considered a sign of arrogance. Should you find any aspect of living with in-laws displeasing, do not relate this upon return to your parents. Do not make a habit of relating tales of in-laws to your mother...neither should she keep asking you of events at your new home. This backbiting only serves to ignite strife, arguments and disputes...nothing positive is ever achieved. Therefore, until one's father-in-law and mother-in-law are alive, endeavour to serve them and consider this service a source of pride. Also remember, that with great difficulty and sacrifice did they nurture their son and marry him to you. Now in old age, they expect him to serve and comfort them...events should not transpire whereby immediately upon your arrival, you plan and scheme to drive your husband away from his parents. Remember this advice in no way advocates refusing the wife her *wājib* (obligatory right) of separate living quarters if she so wishes; and nowadays in the majority of cases, it is best if couples do separate from parents on good terms.'

An Ideal Wedding

Shaykh Ashraf 'Ali Thānwi ﷺ commented, 'If I had a daughter, then in marrying her, there would be no need for a fanfare from the bridegrooms' side. I would stipulate (in writing), he arrives with only three other attendants and brings his own clothing for the occasion. I would arrange for his stay at a nearby comfortable house (upon rent if necessary). I would clothe my own daughter and not specifically invite anybody to the nikāh. I would take everybody to the local Masjid for Salāh, after which make an announcement requesting *musallees* to stay behind for nikāh. I would either personally, or request some other Ãlim, to perform nikāh and then distribute a small amount of dried dates. Thus, the *fadheelat* (virtues) of having performed nikāh in the Masājid would have been fulfilled.

Upon arrival home, either immediately or quite soon thereafter, I would arrange for my daughter to leave for her husbands' temporary house with a reliable female aide...without any gifts. Next day, I would invite the girl back home and again thereafter arrange for her to return. After a few days, seeing her settled, I would request the couple to depart for their home. As far as gifts are concerned, I would arrange for jewellery and property but no utensils, bed, furnishings, sweetmeats, etc. Neither would I gift anything to any relative (either side on this occasion). Yes, what I would do, as long as I live, is to informally see to their needs, as I feel fit and appropriate. The property I would purchase either in my or their locality, and its rental income would be handed over to the couple on a regular basis with accounts.'

There is much wisdom in this approach, which although may appear lacklustre to 'modern-eyes' nevertheless is devoid of emotionalism and *riya* (showing-off). It is designed for the couples' genuine well being, because the amounts spent nowadays at engagement, weddings and honeymoon, etc. is sufficient to purchase the couples first home.

Shaykh Ashraf 'Ali Thãnwi ﷺ once related an anecdote of great wisdom which is most appropriate for young couples,

'In this era of selfishness and self-importance, people are loathed to listen to the good counselling and advises of others, especially elders. Every person feels he is wise, intelligent, independent and above rebuke from another. I shall illustrate this by means of an example. An allegorical meeting took place between a huge snake and an overworked farmer who commented, 'O boy! Do you have a life worth living...go where ever you want; do whatever you want; eat whatever you want; nobody would dare say anything to you; what a carefree existence!'

The snake replied, 'Undoubtedly, what you have said is true, but I have one problem...one sorrow!' Amazed, the farmer asked, 'What, you and a sorrow?' The snake replied,

'Yes, I have one problem...you see there is nobody to place their hand on my shoulders and affectionately ask, 'Son, how are you?' '

One should remember that **pious** elders give very good advice based on their knowledge, experience, far-sightedness and most importantly because of their genuine well-wishes for the younger person.

Chapter Six

Performing Nikāh

From the teachings

of

Shaykh Manzoor Nu'maani 🏵

Shaykh Mufti Taqee 'Uthmāni

Shaykh Mufti 'Abdur Ra'oof Sakhrawee

*S*haykh Abul Hasan 'Ali Nadwee 🏵 commented, *'There is no aspect of a Muslims life which is bereft of the Sharee'ah. Moreover, acting on each command of the Sharee'ah earns reward and violation thereupon results in sin. What a shame that in the same way we have become totally careless of the Sunnah mode of eating, similarly we are abysmally neglectful of the ibaadah of nikāh wherein we endeavour to appease, accommodate and please everybody except Allah* 🏵 *and His Rasool* 🏵*...to the extent that we regard marriage as an occasion to fulfil every whim and fancy (whether it be permissible or impermissible)...'*

The Nikāh Khutbah

اَلْحَمْدُ لِلَّهِ نَحْمَدُهُ وَ نَسْتَعِيْنُهُ وَ نَسْتَغْفِرُهُ وَ نُؤْمِنُ بِهِ وَ نَتَوَكَّلُ عَلَيْهِ، وَ

نَعُوْذُ بِاللَّهِ مِنْ شُرُوْرِ اَنْفُسِنَا وَ مِنْ سَيِّئَاتِ اَعْمَالِنَا، مَنْ يَّهْدِهِ اللَّهُ فَلَا

مُضِلَّ لَهُ وَ مَنْ يُّضْلِلْهُ فَلَا هَادِىَ لَهُ، وَ اَشْهَدُ اَنْ لَا اِلٰهَ اِلَّا اللَّهُ وَحْدَهُ لَا

شَرِيْكَ لَهُ، وَ اَشْهَدُ اَنَّ مُحَمَّدًا عَبْدُهُ وَ رَسُوْلُهُ، اَرْسَلَهُ بِالْحَقِّ بَشِيْرًا وَ

نَذِيْرًا،

اَمَّا بَعْدُ فَاَعُوْذُ بِاللَّهِ مِنَ الشَّيْطَانِ الرَّجِيْمِ، بِسْمِ اللَّهِ الرَّحْمٰنِ الرَّحِيْمِ:

يَاَيُّهَا النَّاسُ اتَّقُوْا رَبَّكُمُ الَّذِىْ خَلَقَكُمْ مِّنْ نَفْسٍ وَّاحِدَةٍ وَّ خَلَقَ مِنْهَا

زَوْجَهَا وَ بَثَّ مِنْهُمَا رِجَالًا كَثِيْرًا وَّ نِسَآءً ۚ وَ اتَّقُوْا اللَّهَ الَّذِىْ تَسَآئَلُوْنَ

بِهِ وَ الْاَرْحَامَ ۚ اِنَّ اللَّهَ كَانَ عَلَيْكُمْ رَقِيْبًا،

يَاَيُّهَا الَّذِيْنَ اٰمَنُوا اتَّقُوا اللَّهَ حَقَّ تُقَاتِهِ وَ لَاتَمُوْتُنَّ اِلَّا وَ اَنْتُمْ مُّسْلِمُوْنَ،

يَاَيُّهَا الَّذِيْنَ اٰمَنُوا اتَّقُوا اللَّهَ وَ قُوْلُوْا قَوْلًا سَدِيْدًا، يُّصْلِحْ لَكُمْ اَعْمَالَكُمْ

وَ يَغْفِرْ لَكُمْ ذُنُوْبَكُمْ ۚ وَ مَنْ يُّطِعِ اللَّهَ وَ رَسُوْلَهُ فَقَدْ فَازَ فَوْزًا عَظِيْمًا،

قَالَ النَّبِىُّ صَلَّى اللَّهُ عَلَيْهِ وَ سَلَّمَ: النَّكَاحُ مِنْ سُنَّتِىْ، وَ قَالَ: فَمَنْ رَغِبَ عَنْ

سُنَّتِىْ فَلَيْسَ مِنِّىْ،

English Translation

A llah's Thanks & Favour that we praise Him and request His aid. We beseech His forgiveness for our sins, bring Imān and trust upon Him. We seek His protection from the mischief of our nafs (self) and misconduct. Whomsoever Allah (ﷻ) guides: nobody may mislead him: and whom He leads astray: nobody may guide him. I bear witness there is no Creator except Allah (ﷻ), He is Alone, He has no partner and I bear witness Muhammad (ﷺ) is His Servant and Messenger. Allah (ﷻ) sent him with truth; as a harbinger of both good tidings and warning.

A fter Praises and Salāt, we seek Allah's Protection from the accursed Shaytān. With the name of Allah, Most Merciful, Very Merciful.

O People! Fear your Creator, whom created you from one man (i.e. Prophet Adam ﷺ) and from him created his wife (Hawwā ﷺ); and from them both He produced and spread numerous men and women the world over. Fear Allah through Whom you demand (your mutual rights) and (do not cut the relations of) the womb (kinship), for undoubtedly Allah (ﷻ) is Ever Watchful over you! (4: 1)

O Muslims! Fear Allah (ﷻ) as He should be feared, and die not except as Muslims. (3:102)

O Muslims! Fear Allah (ﷻ) and speak the truth so that He may rectify your deeds and forgive your sins. Remember, whomsoever obeys Allah (ﷻ) and His Rasool (ﷺ) has achieved tremendous success. (33:70)

'T o perform Nikāh is my Sunnah,' & 'Whomsoever refuses to act upon my Sunnah is not (from amongst us).'

(P.539, Uswa Rasool ﷺ from Al-Hisnul Hasin)

Lessons from the Nikāh Khutbah

Shaykh Manzoor Nu'maani ﷺ relates:

'Abdullah Ibn Mas'ood ﷺ commented...'This khutbah is so lofty it is worthy for all occasions even besides nikāh. The contents therein are so perfect it appears, quite obviously, that each word is the product of Ilham (Divine Inspiration)...'

On whatever occasion, for a servant of Allah ﷺ to humbly plead and testify to his submission and helplessness in the Divine Court of Allah ﷺ: is all-present in the first part of the khutbah. In addition, the final three Glorious Qur'ānic Āyah's are more than ample for a servants hidāyah (guidance). Whilst this noble khutbah is recited before solemnization of nikāh...it heralds the commencement of marriage.

It is a crying shame that even recitation of this khutbah has become somewhat customary (and nowadays just the one ritual on the wedding day with a 'Deeni' hue): otherwise, it contains everything to remind (and guide) the bridegroom, bride and all others. Should Allah ﷺ grant Tawfeeq to act only upon this khutbah...then it would be sufficient to achieve success in dunya and Ākhirah.'

(Ma'āriful Hadeeth, Vol. 7, p.22)

ഇറ

The Practice of Naseehat at the Time of Nikãh

Shaykh Mufti Taqee Uthmãni *dãmat barakãtuhum* comments, 'During the time of Rasoolullah ﷺ, whilst performing the nikãh khutbah, it was normal to offer some *naseehat* (advise). However, nowadays this practice has become almost obsolete and we remain contented with the somewhat 'ritualistic' recitation of the sermon. Accordingly, it would be prudent to recollect upon the *ruh* (soul and purpose) of the nikãh *khutbah*.

Nikãh is an agreement enacted in our society, wherein two parties propose and accept; for example, the *wakeel* (brides guardian and representative) offers the lady into the bridegroom's nikãh, whereupon he affirms his acceptance. Although this *ijaab* (proposal) and *qabool* (acceptance) may appear similar to monetary transactions, nevertheless, in nikãh it is preceded by a *khutbah* which has been decreed *mustahab* (preferable) by Rasoolullah ﷺ. Although nikah is valid without a khutbah...it is still a very important Sunnah. Why? Because, Allah ﷻ has placed two specific features in the nikãh agreement. The first aspect is the social agreement whilst the second intrinsic feature is one of ibaadah. The great Imãm Aboo Haneefah ﷺ relates,

'In nikãh, the characteristic of mua'amalãt (transaction) is magloob (subdued) whilst the feature of ibaadah is ghãlib (dominant).'

Whilst it is *masnûn* to recite three verses in the khutbah, close study will highlight that these verses contain no specific mention of nikãh, whereas it is mentioned categorically at numerous other places in the Glorious

Qur'ãn. My respected father, Shaykh Mufti Muhammad Shafee' 🕮 used to comment, 'It is a matter of reflection as to why Nabee 🕮 left the other verses and specifically chose these 3 verses?' To understand, it would be appropriate to firstly study the translation of these verses.

First Verse ~ Surah Nisã

يَٰٓأَيُّهَا النَّاسُ اتَّقُوْا رَبَّكُمُ الَّذِىْ خَلَقَكُمْ مِّنْ نَّفْسٍ وَّاحِدَةٍ وَّ خَلَـــقَ مِنْهَا زَوْجَهَا وَ بَثَّ مِنْهُمَا رِجَالًا كَثِيْرًا وَّ نِسَآءً ۚ وَ اتَّقُـــوْا اللهَ الَّذِىْ تَسَآئَلُوْنَ بِهٖ وَ الْاَرْحَامَ ۚ اِنَّ اللهَ كَانَ عَلَيْكُمْ رَقِيْبًا،

'O mankind! Be dutiful to your Lord, Who created you from a single person and from him (Adam 🕮) He created his wife (Hawwã 🕮), and from them both He created many men and women. And fear Allah through Whom you demand (your mutual rights) and (do not cut the relations of) the womb (kinship). Surely Allah is Ever an All-Watcher over you.'   (Glorious Qur'ãn, 4:1)

Second Verse ~ Surah Al-Imrãn

يَٰٓأَيُّهَا الَّذِيْنَ اٰمَنُوا اتَّقُوا اللهَ حَقَّ تُقَاتِهٖ وَ لَاتَمُوْتُنَّ اِلَّا وَ اَنْتُمْ مُّسْلِمُوْنَ،

'O you who believe! Fear Allah as He should be feared (by doing all that He has ordered and by abstaining from all that He has forbidden). (Obey Him, be thankful to Him and, remember Him always) and, die not except in a state of (Islãm) as Muslims.'   (Glorious Qur'ãn, 3:102)

Third Verse ~ Surah Ahzāb

يَـٰٓأَيُّهَا الَّذِينَ ءَامَنُوا اتَّقُوا اللَّهَ وَ قُولُوا قَوْلًا سَدِيدًا، يُصْلِحْ لَـكُـمْ

أَعْمَالَكُمْ وَ يَغْفِرْ لَكُمْ ذُنُوبَكُمْ ۗ وَ مَنْ يُطِعِ اللَّهَ وَ رَسُولَهُ فَقَدْ فَازَ

فَوْزًا عَظِيمًا،

'O you who believe! Keep your duty to Allah and fear him, and speak the truth (always).

He will direct you to (perform) good righteous deeds and will forgive you your sins.

And whomsoever obeys Allah and His Messenger (ﷺ), he has indeed achieved a great achievement (i.e. he will be saved from the Hell-fire and will be admitted to Paradise). (Glorious Qur'ān, 33: 70-1)

Taqwā appears in all three verses

All three Glorious *Āyāt* (Verses) begin with and emphasise *taqwā* and, the reason why on the occasion of nikāh *taqwā* is so emphasised is, because in general, the ceremony of nikāh is considered outside the pale of Islām...with scant, if any, regard given to the commands of the Sharee'ah. Before, during and after nikāh, no thought is ever given to Sharee' commands...this is why the concept of *taqwā* is so highlighted, because if one reflects, it will become apparent that the relationship and institution of marriage cannot produce *true* happiness until the hearts of both contain *taqwā* and the resultant endeavour to fulfil each other's *huqooqs*. And how is *taqwā* acquired? Allah ﷻ Says:

'O you who believe! Be afraid of Allah and join the company of the sãdiqeen (i.e. Awliya)' (Glorious Qur'ãn, 9:119)

Nikãh is so easy ~ We have made it so difficult

Allah ﷻ has made Nikãh so easy in Islãm, that no other matter could be easier. Even recitation of the nikãh khutbah is not compulsory (though it is definitely a Sunnah). Should a man and woman propose and accept in front of Sharee' Muslim witnesses (either two males or one male and two ladies), then nikãh is complete and both are halãl for each other. This is how easy nikãh is: neither is engagement and henna ceremony; stag or hen parties; or any form of invitation/congregation a pre-requisite. Rasoolullah ﷺ commented, 'The nikãh with the greater barakat is the one wherein the least expenditure is expanded.' (Musnad Ahmad)

The wedding wherein is the least formality and effort is the one which contains the most blessings. Although the Sharee'ah is teaching us informality, we ourselves are making this occasion as difficult as possible to the extent that it has become a scourge. Nowadays, until months and thousands are not spent over it, nikãh cannot take place.

Let us look at an incident during the time of Rasoolullah ﷺ. 'Abdu'r-Rahmãn ibn 'Awf ﷺ is a senior Sahãbee who was extremely close to Nabee ﷺ and who was one of the ten Sahãbãh to be given glad tidings of Jannah in this world. Once, when he entered the *Majlis* (blessed gathering) of Nabee ﷺ, the latter noticed signs of marriage; happiness and joy were visible upon his face and clothes. Upon inquiry, Abdu'r-Rahmān ibn 'Awf ﷺ replied, 'O Rasoolullah ﷺ! I have married and because of nikāh I have applied perfume...the stains of which are visible on my clothes.' Nabee ﷺ inquired, 'How was the *Mahr* fulfilled?' He replied, 'gold equivalent to a bag of dates (was presented).' Thereupon, Nabee ﷺ suggested, 'In that case, make Waleemah; even if it be of only one sheep.'   *(Bukhāri)*

We too should adopt this Simplicity & Informality

Now ponder, a senior Sahābee who is distantly related to Nabee ﷺ gets married without even inviting or informing him. Moreover, when Nabee ﷺ inquired, leave aside an iota of complaint or unhappiness, the latter gave du'aa and advised to arrange for an *waleemah*. Such simplicity and informality.

If somebody was to behave in this manner today, just consider how close one's will react and erupt. Contrast this with the behaviour of Nabee ﷺ and the Sahābāh ﷺ; they maintained the simplicity of Nikāh which Allah ﷺ has bestowed to us. I am not saying it is harām to invite your elders and relatives because at the time of the nikāh of Fātimah ﷺ, Nabee ﷺ summoned Aboo Bakr ﷺ, 'Umar ﷺ and other close ones. Accordingly, to invite is permissible, but to rigidly impose so many man-made pre-conditions and customs before nikāh may even take place is not permissible in the Sharee'ah. Today, until a person is able to spend thousands, the pathway to halāl is kept closed. Consequently, people are drifting towards harām as a result of which evil and anarchy is widespread in society.

$\mathcal{QS}$haykh Mufti 'Abdur Ra'oof Sakhrawee *dāmat barakātuhum* relates, 'There are two ways of purifying the many sins that are committed on occasions of nikāh. Firstly, the wise approach suggested by Shaykh Mufti Muhammad Shafee' ﷺ wherein the elders of every family and locality meet to jointly rid our society of the communal sins being enacted at weddings (music, photography, intermingling of the genders, etc.). Secondly, on a personal note to find out what activities will be taking place at particular weddings and to either stay-away or attend as appropriate. It is up to the individual to inquire (almost all wedding cards have a telephone number)...'

The Malpractice of Feeding by the Bride's Family

$\mathcal{QS}$haykh Mufti 'Abdur Ra'oof Sakhrawee *dāmat barakātuhum* continues, 'The practice in vogue of the bride's family feeding others as if it is the Sunnah *waleemah* has been decreed incorrect and impermissible by our Scholars. Although, there is no harm in feeding the very close and immediate family members and associates who have to attend and visit the bride's home (not hall) under the niyyat of 'feeding the guest;' nevertheless there is no leeway for asking the bridegroom's side as to how many (hundreds of) visitors (and coaches) they will be bringing. All these endless expenses and customs which we have adopted are, in reality, a form of self-oppression as a result of which marriage has become extremely difficult. For Muslims, the example of the departure of Fātimah ibn Muhammad ﷺ is a beautiful ideal.' (p57, Vol. 4, Islāhi Lectures)

Shab-ê-Zufãf

(First Night)

&

The Ãdãb of

Muslim Sexual

Behaviour

Shab-ê-Zufãf (First Night)

R asoolullah 🌸 commented:
'*Allah loves a man who caresses his wife. Both of them are awarded thawãb because of this loving attitude and their rizq (earning) is increased.*'

Q🔊 haykh-ul-Hadeeth Ibrãheem Palanpoori 🌸 relates a Hadeeth in his original book 'Tuhfatun Nikãh:'

'*Rasoolullah* 🌸 *commented, 'To make love to your wife too is sadaqãh and one receives reward.' Upon this the Sahãbãh* 🌸 *inquired: 'O Rasoolullah! What, will a person receive thawãb for even fulfilling his carnal desires with his wife?' Rasoolullah* 🌸 *replied, 'If he were to fulfil these desires at some wrong place would he not be a sinner?' The Sahãbãh* 🌸 *replied, 'Of course!' Rasoolullah* 🌸 *commented, 'When he has gone to a halãl place to save himself from harãm, than of a surety he will receive thawãb!'*'

Q🔊 haykh Maseehullah Khãn 🌸 commenting upon the decline in morality, 'Nowadays, in many cases the question of Shab-ê-Zufãf does not arise (when couples are spending time together before nikãh)!' Remember, when the Mu'min is buried and answers successfully the questions posed by Munkir and Nakir (Angels), a caller from the Heavens informs him to sleep and rest in peace in the same manner in which a bride sleeps after receiving her husband on the first night. Such is the significance of Shab-ê-Zufãf and Haya (modesty and chastity).

Etiquette's of Shab-ê-Zufãf

hen the bride arrives at her husband's house...fairly soon, both will meet for the first time. This should be at the husband's own residence or that of a very close sensible relative. Nowadays, people whiz-off to a 5-star 'exotic' remote hotel location for the first night and honeymoon. This is indeed heartbreaking. These places are frequented by impure people with no regard for *tahãrat* (purity). Accordingly, despite the luxurious furnishings, these hotels are dens of physical and spiritual *najaasat* (impurity). It is an open secret that fornicators, prostitutes and drug dealers are frequent clients of these places. In addition, alcohol is served. It is therefore not wise for the bridegroom to take his new bride into such a filthy revolting environment. There have been numerous cases of assault, theft, mugging and rape at even 'well respected' and famous hotels.

The Importance of Esha Salãh & Salãt-e-Shukr

haykh Ashraf 'Ali Thãnwi ﷺ narrates, 'To pray two rakãts nafl Salãh on *Shab-ê-Zufãf* (First Night) does not appear in any hadeeth...however we have heard some of our pious elders recommend the praying of two rakãts Salãt-e-Shukr and thereafter thank Allah ﷻ for having saved one from harãm and granted us halãl...' It is therefore best for the couple to pray these two rak'ãt's together (the husband in front as Imãm and his wife behind as follower) with a combined intention of *shukr, tahajjud, taubah* & *hājat* (i.e. 4 niyyats for one Salāh) *after* the Witr of Esha Salāh which, of course, is compulsory and often neglected by the couple. Thereafter, both should make du'aa for goodness, blessings, mutual love, faithfulness, chastity, marital success and the birth of pious children.

Shaykh In'āmul Hasan ☞ often used to comment upon the awful habit of couples to miss the compulsory Fajr Salāh after their first night. Couples should remember this has a harmful effect on the *akhlaaq* of any offspring conceived. Accordingly, from the first night make a firm resolution to prepare for Fajr Salāh. Always set the alarm whereby both have sufficient time for ghusl.

Parents and relatives should within their means and without resorting to waste or any act contrary to the Sharee'ah, try to 'furnish' the room where the bride and bridegroom will meet. For example, comfortable bedding and furnishing, flowers, perfume, fruit basket, fruit juices, sweetmeats and chocolates, etc.

Some people, especially friends, resort to silly pranks and jokes in order to irritate the newly married on their first night. This is not wise as it may sour the relationship at a delicate stage, nowadays with disastrous consequences. It is therefore important for the couple to have full privacy and not be disturbed in any way. Remember for other's to eavesdrop or for either of the couple to 'report' on the activities of the first night is a grave sin. Nabee ☞ said, 'On the Day of Qiyāmah, that person will be of the lowest rank who makes love to his wife and thereafter reveals details to others.'   (Ma'āriful Hadeeth, p.36, Vol. 7)

When Meeting Your Spouse for the First Night

The normal practice is for the bride to sit resplendently in the bedroom awaiting her husband. Accordingly, elders and friends should ensure the bridegroom does not keep her waiting and proceeds to meet her soon after Esha Salāh. After knocking and requesting permission, the bridegroom should make Salām clearly and audibly. This is a *Sunnah* which should be maintained throughout your married life. The bride should reply to the *salām* and welcome her husband. When *Umm al-Mu'mineen* Umme Salamah ﷺ married Rasoolullah ﷺ, she exclaimed, *Marhaban bi Rasoolillah* ﷺ (Welcome to the Messenger of Allah ﷺ). Thereafter, shake hands and affectionately placing his hand upon her forehead the husband should recite the du'aa:

$$\text{اَللّٰهُمَّ اِنِّىْ اَسْئَلُكَ مِنْ خَيْرِهَا وَ خَيْرِ مَا جَبَلْتَهَا عَلَيْهِ، وَ اَعُوْذُ بِكَ مِـــنْ شَرِّهَا وَ شَرِّ مَا جَبَلْتَهَا عَلَيْهِ}$$

'*O Allah! I seek from You, the good and blessings of this lady, and the goodness, which You have created within her. In addition, I seek Your protection from the evil of this lady, and whatever evil You have created in her.*'

The bride may also recite a similar du'aa:

$$\text{اَللّٰهُمَّ اِنِّىْ اَسْئَلُكَ مِنْ خَيْرِهِ وَ خَيْرِ مَا جَبَلْتَهُ عَلَيْهِ، وَ اَعُوْذُ بِكَ مِنْ شَرِّهِ وَ شَرِّ مَا جَبَلْتَهُ عَلَيْهِ}$$

The benefits of these du'aa's is Allah ﷺ will distance any evil from the spouses and will bless the household with their blessings.

How to start a conversation? Smile and appear happy (even if you are nervous), ask about each other's well-being. Initiate a light discussion on the purpose behind nikāh. Make an agreement with each other to always obey Allah ﷻ and be faithful and loyal to each other. Narrate a short episode of the pious, why? 'Allamāh Ibn Jawzee ﷻ relates, 'The Mercies of Allah ﷻ descends upon those occasions when the virtues of His sāleh (pious) servants are related.'

• The husband should present an appropriate gift (e.g. a necklace) to his new bride at this stage to show his love, commitment and appreciation and offer some light refreshments to further overcome his bride's shyness. One should always remember, the bride before nikāh and this meeting was a complete stranger. Whilst she is now in your presence because of nikāh...her natural restraint (a quite praiseworthy virtue in Muslim ladies) will still prevent her from becoming too intimate or open. She will be shy, nervous and reluctant to undress or get into bed.

• Accordingly, lovemaking, which is the peak of physical expression between lovers, should not be commenced immediately. Rather, resort to winning her over with words of love and light good-humoured talk. All this time, slowly, slowly getting physically closer, caressing and embracing her...prepare for bed. Once in bed, it is a good introduction to discuss the niyyat behind making love: to save oneself from harām, wish for pious children, fulfilment of spouses *haqq*, etc.

• Some men brought up on a diet of TV and 'egged-on' by ignorant and insincere friends think they must make love on the first night to demonstrate their manliness. Never behave so selfishly and cowardly especially if the wife appears too fatigued or reluctant. Both of you have the rest of your married life for this. Pressure at this stage will embed the idea in the bride's mind that you have married her merely to fulfil your carnal desires.

• Also remember, *tab'ee hayã* in Muslim ladies prevents them from making-love immediately, furthermore when she does incline, her initial nervousness and the loss of her virginity will cause physical pain which reduces the chances of her reaching orgasm or sexual pleasure. If the husband behaves rashly at this delicate stage, a revulsion and dislike for him may set in the bride's mind.

• Another point worthy of consideration is that upon marrying a 'new world' appears, especially for the bride. It is therefore prudent for the husband not to over express his emotions, otherwise the wife will consider him her slave expecting him to fulfil her every wish and tantrum. Similarly, if the husband tries to overawe his wife by treating her like a chattel, ordering and 'bossing' around...dislike and hate for him will begin to engulf her heart.

The bride enters her husband's house as 'Queen' and 'Shepherdess.' Whilst physically weaker, she is your 'closest friend' and partner in life: sharing your aspirations, hopes and worries. Like you she is but human, therefore from the beginning treat her with decorum, honour, grace and in the manner you expect others to treat your daughter/sister. Learn to overlook her indiscreetness in matters where the Sharee'ah is not violated.

Making Love

llah ﷻ says in the Glorious Qur'ān:

'Your wives are for you a soil to cultivate. So, come unto your soil from where you will, and advance something for yourselves, and fear Allah and know that you are to meet Him and give good news to the believers.' (2:223)

asoolullah ﷺ commented:

'Allah Ta'ālā states (reciting the above Āyah from the Glorious Qur'ān), therefore come unto your soil from the front in the front part (i.e. the vagina only of one's wife), or come from the back into the front part (vagina). And save yourselves from the back portion (anus) in the way you save yourselves from the pubic region during the period of menstruation.'

(Tirmidhi)

haykh Mufti Muhammad Shafee' ﷺ comments regarding the above Āyah in his epic *Ma'āriful Qur'ān*, that undoubtedly, Allah ﷻ loves those who remain pure. Whilst the wife is in state of purity (free from menses), the couple may make love as long as it is via. the vagina...whether from the front, rear or side...whether lying down or on top.

However, the analogy of the wife is like a fertile field whilst the husband is comparable to the farmer who plants seeds.

In order to reap good fruit, a farmer plants from the top, similarly the husband too should 'plant' from top, i.e. at the time of ejecting *manee* (semen) it is preferable for the husband to be on top and wife below. Avicena (Arabic name: *Ibn Sina*), the great Physician (930-1037 CE) whose medical work *Qanun* was the greatest single influence on medical science; too recommends that the husband be 'on top.' In his opinion, if at the time of ejaculation, the husband is below; *manee* is left in the male organ to putrefy, with danger of venereal infection.

Etiquette's of Making Love

Rasoolullah ﷺ commented:
'*Whenever any of you (commences making love) with his wife, he should recite the following du'aa to Allah Ta'ālā:*

بِسْمِ اللهِ اللَّهُمَّ جَنِّبْنَا الشَّيْطَانَ وَ جَنِّبِ الشَّيْطَانَ مَا رَزَقْتَنَا

'*With the name of Allah! O Allah! Save us from the evil of Shaytān and save whatever children You bestow us.*'   (Tirmidhi, 1092)

Now if a child is destined from this love making; then Shaytān will not be able to harm him in the least, moreover this child will always remain safe from the evil of Shaytān. Shaykh-ul-Hadeeth Ibrāheem Palanpoori ﷺ advices, 'This du'aa should be recited before undressing, however, if one remembers after exposing one's *satr,* recite it by heart only. Both husband and wife should recite this du'aa. Our 'Ulamā have mentioned numerous benefits of this du'aa, one of which is safety of the child conceived from Shaytãn...who will not be able to remove the child from *Imãn*. Allahu Akbar! This is a tremendous bounty.'

*S*haykh Manzoor Nu'maani ﷺ relates, 'Should one not make this type of du'aa to Allah ﷻ at the time of making love; and furthermore, remaining indifferent to Allah ﷻ, if one were to behave like animals in only fulfilling carnal desires...then any offspring from such a union will not remain protected from Shaytãn...This is precisely why, people born nowadays; display such corrupt akhlaaq (character), habits and behaviour.'

Let us now briefly study the various ãdãbs of lovemaking:

Niyyat (Intention)

The great Shaykh Junaid Baghdadi ﷺ stated: 'My requirement and need for sex with my wife is the same as my need for food.'

Muslims should realize that lovemaking is a natural desire and necessity of the human. Accordingly, our Deen has not only discussed this issue openly but in detail. Remember that each action of the Muslim should be to attain the Pleasure of Allah ﷻ. Accordingly, even in making love, we should intend:

- Acquiring of *sãleh* (pious) offspring.
- Protection from *zina* (adultery) of all parts of the body.
- Fulfilment of partners *huqooq* (rights) and of one's self in a halãl manner.

Physical Preparation

Islām lays great emphasis on purity. Accordingly, one should use a miswāk, brush one's teeth, use halāl perfume and ensure no body odours or an unkempt appearance. Whilst this should be a regular part of one's body hygiene...they take on a special significance at the time of lovemaking. The newly married couple should remember a long stress-full day takes a toll on one's body, therefore, before meeting ensure you carefully clean your mouth, shower and preferably be in the state of wudhu. If you fear mouth odour, chew something with a pleasant smell. Remember there is no greater 'put-off' than foul odour. A separate piece of clean cloth should be spread to stop the bed from being soiled and two small towels should be kept nearby to clean the private parts after lovemaking.

Mental Preparation

It is vital for the couple to mentally prepare themselves for lovemaking in advance. This increases enjoyment. Each should express their desire for the other by words, expressions, touch, etc. The wife should adorn herself for her husband (by using all permissible means), similarly, it is commendable for a husband also to adorn himself for his wife. This is collaborated by a statement of Ibn Abbas ﷺ, 'I love to adorn myself for my wife as much as I like (her) to beautify (herself) for me.' Nowadays, people dress very 'scruffily' at home: whilst outside with non-mahram they adorn themselves to the full. The Sharee'ah has granted a Muslim lady much leeway and *thawāb* in 'dressing-up' for her husband.

Timing

It is worth remembering, that according to homeopathic doctors on a number of occasions every month, usually just after *haidh*...a special craving and restlessness for lovemaking arises in most women. Husbands should try to recognize these moments and endeavour to fulfil her desires. This will increase mutual love, pleasure and respect. For a husband to allow such opportunities to pass without fulfilling his wife's desires without a real reason, is contrary to manliness.

Foreplay

A Muslim lady is the 'Queen' of her home and the *mahbub* (beloved). Consequently, she is to be treated and is to behave with nobility at all occasions. In making love the husband should always 'seduce' his wife by foreplay, there is greater enjoyment and pleasure; especially for the wife. This too is a Sunnah of our beloved Nabee ﷺ... 'When the husband and wife hold each others' hands with love and affection; Allah Ta'ālā forgives their sins.' Massaging, kissing, fondling (kissing and sucking of breasts ~ as long as there is no possibility of milk entering the mouth), alluring talk, caressing, necking, stroking, rubbing of oil and talc on the body, etc., all arouse passion, craving and 'enthusiasm' for sex. Love itself teaches one the art of love. The couple should therefore spend some considerable time indulging in these activities. The couple, in making love should physically 'talk' (with their bodies). It is oral sex (licking and sucking of genitals) which is strictly forbidden and physically destructive.

Positions

The Sharee'ah allows husband and wife to view and benefit from each others' body in every way except, of course, anal and sexual intercourse during the days of *haidh* and *nifaas* (monthly and post natal bleeding), all of which are totally harãm. Whilst the wife's vagina maybe approached from any direction, do note the following: recite *Bismillah* and the Sunnah du'aa at commencement of lovemaking and try not to face the *qiblah*. As far as specific positions for making love is concerned, two are mentioned:

- Wife below and husband on top. This has already been discussed at the beginning of this chapter and is very effective when the lady is trying to conceive.

- Entry into vagina from rear. Upon the query of a Sahãbi ⬡, this position too was approved.

Orgasm, After Play & After Care

When the time arrives for orgasm, it is best not to speak, and should the husband fear early ejaculation he should divert his attention away: though do remember it is harãm and comparable to *zina* for either husband or wife to 'fantasize' about some other person. One 'essential' of lovemaking is for both to make sure they do not separate until each achieves orgasm. Generally, the husband reaches 'climax' first, however he should not selfishly withdraw, rather continue (as long as necessary) with his motion or after play so that his wife too achieves full orgasm and 'relief.' Otherwise, there is great danger of both physical harm to the wife and discontentment setting into her heart.

It appears in a hadeeth, 'When any of you makes love to his wife, then he should do so with relish, vigour and enthusiasm. And when the husband reaches his desire (orgasm and wishes to ejaculate) then he should not hasten until his wife's desire (orgasm) is achieved.' (p36, Ādāb-ul-Jimā')
At the time of ejaculating semen, both should recite (silently within the heart):

اَللّٰهُمَّ لَاتَجْعَلْ لِلشَّيْطَانِ فِيْمَا رِزَقْتَنِىْ نَصِيْبًا

'O Allah! Do not allow Shaytān any share of what You grant us.' (p65, Radiant Prayers)

After lovemaking, both should wipe their genital organs with different pieces of clean cloth and then endeavour to urinate and wash these parts and thereafter make wudhu or ghusl before either making love again or sleeping. Should one not make wudhu, then at least make *tayyamum* so that purity to some extent is achieved. Do remember that until the body is warm (due to the rigours of lovemaking)...to expose it to cold air or cold water is harmful. Nevertheless, newly-married brides and those who suffer from a burning sensation in passing urine or vaginal discharge are advised by experienced Muslim Doctors to pass urine and make *istinja* (wash) just before and quite soon after lovemaking. To make love a second or more times until a 'true desire' arises in one; although permissible in the Sharee'ah, is nevertheless according to our Akābir harmful to health. The sign of 'true desire' is a heartfelt craving from within without having to physically arouse one's organs. Remember, in making love a second or more time; one must again indulge in foreplay and prepare the wife.

Aphrodisiacs

(Foods Renown for Potency)

The quality and type of food one eats play a very important role upon sexual capacity, because it is nourishment which develops blood and thereafter semen. Therefore, one should always eat such nutritious, healthy and invigorating foods, which maintain and develop the physique, mental health and sexual potency:

Dates both fresh and dried are beneficial. This is why they have been traditionally distributed at time of *nikāh*. Sucking dates distances thirst. Many *halwa* preparations contain dates; homeopathic doctors consider it especially beneficial to potency and *date ma'jun* is a famous homeopathic medicine. Fresh (or even dried) dates are the best form of nourishment during childbirth, for Allah ﷻ reveals regarding the birth of Prophet 'Eesa ﷺ in the Glorious Qur'ān:

'And the pains of childbirth drove her (Maryam ﷺ) to the trunk of a date-palm... 'And shake the trunk of date-palm towards you, it will let fall fresh ripe-dates upon you.' (19:23-25)

Honey. Ā'ishah ﷺ relates that Nabee ﷺ was very fond of honey because Allah ﷻ reveals in the Glorious Qur'ān:

'...There comes forth from their (bees) bellies, a drink (honey) of varying colour wherein is healing for men...' (16:69)

The homeopathic doctors suggests that unlike other foods, honey does not lose the potency of its vitamins even over a period of time. It is assimilated into the blood stream within minutes, generates great energy without disturbing the bodies system, and is a cure for many illnesses.

*M*ilk according to Ibne Abbas 🙵 was the favourite drink of our Nabee 🙵. The homeopathic doctors suggests milk develops sexual potency, dispels dryness and because it is so easily digested provides energy to body organs. Milk and honey, two bounties of Allah 🙵 are the essence of many flowers and meats. If all medical experts of the world were to try to produce a better product for sexual potency, they would not be able to do so. It is the Mercy of Allah 🙵 that we are blessed with two such bounties.

*G*arlic although advised by our Nabee 🙵 not to be eaten raw before entry into the Masjid, according to weaker *hadeeth* contains healing properties. The homeopathic doctors suggests garlic is very beneficial and creates sexual potency in weak temperaments; increases semen and is known as one of the ambrosia's of life.

*H*alāl perfumes have an unique relationship and effect upon the human heart and soul, producing exhilaration and cheerfulness. This is why flowers are so widely employed at weddings with both bride and bridegroom garlanded as their sweet smells instigate sexual potency. Our Nabee 🙵 never refused *itr* when offered and often applied *musk* to his *mubarak* beard. Couples should employ *itr* before lovemaking.

Other aphrodisiacs reported by homeopathic doctors are:

Hareera ~ a dish of wheat, meat, clarified (low fat) butter and spices. This dish was suggested to Nabee 🕮 by Jibr'aeel as having the potent power of 40 men.

Beetroot ~ Recommended to 'Ali 🕮 by Nabee 🕮. It is also good for the eyesight.

Saffron ~ as part of other medicines increases sexual potency and improves the heart, brain and eyesight.

Eggs ~ Recommended by Nabee 🕮.

Other foods recommended by Dr. Ãftãb Ahmad Shãh in his excellent Urdu book *Ãdãb of Mubbãsharat*:

Pulses & Grains ~ *Wheat, Chana, Peas, Beans, Rice, Sesame Seeds.*

Vegetables ~ *Onions, Garlic, Okra, Pumpkin, Gourds, Turnips, Carrots, Potato, Ginger, Coconut.*

Fruits ~ *Ripe Mango, Grapes, Pomegranate, Bananas, Figs, Apple, Pineapples, Sweet Melons, Guavas.*

Nuts ~ *Cashews, Peanuts, Walnuts, Dried Dates, Raisins, Olives, Sultanas,*

Animals ~ *The meat and brains of all halãl birds, baby Chicken, Pigeon, Duck, Fish, Red Meat (lamb), Fish.*

Dairy Products ~ *Cow's Milk, Yoghurt, Low-fat Butter and Cheese.*

Spices ~ *Black Pepper, Elachi, Cloves (lawang), Nutmeg.*

Foods that are Harmful to Potency ~ *All types of Sour Fruits, Pickles, Chutneys, Amli, Vinegar, Red Chillies, Hot Spices, Tea & Coffee, Saunf, Fresh Coriander Seeds.*

haykh Ashraf 'Ali Thãnwi 🕮 narrates:

1) The best time to make love is at least three (3) hours after having eaten. To make love immediately after having eaten a heavy meal, or when completely famished or tired is detrimental to health.

2) To drink cold water immediately after lovemaking is harmful.

3) In lovemaking, physical strain is placed on the body. Should one practice on these advises of our *Akãbir* and after at least washing one's hands and mouth (and preferably after ghusl) try and eat some invigorating food then, Inshã'Allah, no physical harm or weakness will result.

4) Some good foods to eat after lovemaking include milk, honey, egg, halwã (dates, carrots, egg, sweetmeat), dried dates, or a mixture of these in milk, chicken, *ghaur* (jaggary or raw sugar).

5) Mother of the Believers, Umme Salamãh 🕮 narrates that whenever the eyes of any of the pure wives of Nabee 🕮 ached, he would not make love to them. From this it is obvious that when one's wife is ill or in pain, it is a demand of one's manliness not to make love.

6) If a person suffers on account of frequent lovemaking, he should stay away from cold/heat and try to sleep more. He should also enrich his diet by eating foods that increase blood, e.g., drink milk, eat carrot *halwã* and half boiled eggs.

Ghusl Janābat

(The Compulsory Bath after Lovemaking)

Ghusl is the Islāmic way of completely washing one's body to obtain purity from *hadathe akbar* (greater impurity). Remember any of the following acts causes a person to be in the state of *janābat* (hadathe akbar or greater impurity):

1) Sexual Intercourse. Entry of the penis head (gland) into the vagina (or anus, Allah Forbid), whereby top of the penis is not visible: and irrespective of whether *manee* (semen) is ejaculated.

2) Discharge of *manee* accompanied by sexual lust: whether in the state of sleep (wet dream) or wakefulness: irrespective of whether it is caused by touching or fantasizing about a person.

3) *Haidh* (menses) & *Nifaas* (blood flow after childbirth).

In all these cases, purification from the state of *janābat* is obtained by means of *ghusl*.

Rules for the state of Janābat

Whilst in this state of *janābat* the following things are prohibited:

1) Salāt, touching or even reciting the Glorious Qur'ān.

2) To enter a Masjid or to make *tawaaf* of the Holy Ka'bah.

3) Cutting or breaking nails or any hair of the body.

The Farãidh (Compulsory Elements) of Ghusl

The Islãmic *ghusl* has three compulsory elements (*farãidh*), which must be carried out to achieve purity:

1) Deep gargling of the entire mouth with water (except in the state of saum: when one merely rinses the mouth).

2) Taking water into the nostrils up to the soft bone of the nose.

3) Washing the entire body, from head to toe, whereby not a single hair remains dry.

The Sunnah Method of Ghusl

Carrying out the three *farãidh* of ghusl will, of course, achieve purity. However, following the *sunnah* method will also transform this act into an *ibaadah* and means of obtaining thawãb.

1) Make *niyyat* (intention) for *ghusl-e-janãbat* in any language in the heart, e.g. *'I intend to make ghusl to achieve purity from janãbat.'*

2) As far as possible, make sure you do not face or have your back towards the *qiblah*.

3) Wash both hands up to the wrist preferably under the tap.

4) Wash the private parts, surrounding areas and whatever parts of the body where there be impurity thoroughly.

5) Perform a full wudhu, however, should ghusl be made in a place where water pools; then delay washing of the feet until the end.

6) Now pour water over one's head three times. Thereafter, pour water over the right and left shoulders three times; in such a way, that water reaches the entire body.

7) Wash the feet if they were not washed earlier.

8) Remember, whilst pouring water ensure you rub well over the entire body so not a single hair remains dry. Pay special attention to concealed areas: such as the navel; behind knees; and back of the ankles.

9) Rings (finger, ear, nose, etc.) should be removed during *ghusl* to enable water to reach the parts covered by them.

Shaykh Ashraf 'Ali Thānwi ﷺ advices, 'If after having a ghusl, one remembers that a particular area was left dry, then it is not necessary to repeat the entire ghusl. Instead, only the dry area should be washed. However, it is not sufficient to just pass a wet hand over this area: water must flow over it. If one forgot to rinse the mouth or wet the nostrils, then they should be washed. In brief, whichever portion has been left dry should be washed. It is not necessary to repeat the entire ghusl.'

Wisdom of Ghusl Janābat

Shaykh Ashraf 'Ali Thānwi ﷺ narrated, 'For *ghusl* to be Wājib after emergence of semen from the body, is a distinguished and salient feature of Islām. It is indeed a Mercy of Allah ﷻ and full of wisdom because *manee* is the product of the whole body. Allah ﷻ mentions in the Glorious Qur'ān:

'And indeed We created man (Adam ﷺ) out of sullallath (an extract of clay-water and earth). Thereafter We made him (the offspring of Adam ﷺ) as a nutfah (mixed drops of the male and female sexual discharge and lodged it) in a safe lodging (womb of the mother).' (23:12-13)

Hence, semen is the 'core product,' which although emerging out of the private area nevertheless originates from the whole body. Its discharge considerably weakens the body, but by using water this weakness no longer remains. Remember, when semen is discharged, all the pore's of one's body open with sweat. Together with this sweat, impurities of the body also emerge and stick to the pores. Now, should the body remain unwashed, the grave danger exists of contracting illnesses. This is one reason why the Sharee'ah has imposed *ghusl-e-janābat*. Another reason is that when humans emerge from sexual intercourse, their hearts experience spiritual contraction, narrowness and a form of sorrow, apathy, weakness, negligence and depression. However when both types of impurities are removed by washing, bathing, donning clean clothes and scent...this narrowness disappears and vitality, happiness and vibrancy appears; strengthening and refreshing the soul and body. Aboo Zarr Ghiffāri ﷺ, the famous Sahābi commented,

'After ghusl-e-janābat, it appeared as if a mountain had been lifted off my shoulder's...and this reality is noticeable to any person possessing fahme saleem (correct heart and temperament).'

Homeopathic doctors have stated that *ghusl-e-janābat* overcomes the weakness in the body's digestive system (following love making) and even some western medical experts encourage bathing with warm water after lovemaking, so as to wash away impurities and save one self from venereal infection. Another point to note is that unduly remaining in the state of *janābat* creates a distance between man and the Angels. This separation disappears with *ghusl*. Many of the senior Sahābāh ؓ have reported that when one sleeps away in the state of *janābat*...one's soul is deprived of the opportunity to visit the upper heavens and prostrate before the *Arsh* (Throne of Allah ﷻ). This is precisely why our beloved Nabee ﷺ commented,

'*When the janubee (the one in the state of janābat) sleeps, he should make wudhu (ablution).*' (p323, Islāmic Weddings)

Obviously, pleasure and joy are derived in love making and this diverts one's attention away from the Remembrance of Allah ﷻ. Ghusl-e-Janābat serves as a recompense for this negligence.'

What is Madhi & Does it Necessitate Ghusl?

In the early stages of sexual excitement a sticky translucent fluid is discharged from the reproductive organs known as *madhi* (in both men and women). It differs from semen in the sense that its emergence does not provide any intrinsic pleasure nor does it herald the end of desires. Discharge of *madhi* in itself does not make *ghusl* compulsory though it is impure, hence breaks *wudhu* and necessitates washing of the genitals and soiled garments. (p55, Noorul Eedhā')

An Episode

haykh Ashraf 'Ali Thānwi ☙ narrated, 'Once in Makkah, an educated person passed away and was buried. After some years, another person also died and his relatives wished that he too be buried in this scholar's grave. This is normal practice in Makkah. Accordingly, the scholar's grave was dug-up...and to everybody's surprise and bewilderment, there present instead of the remains of the scholar; was lying an extremely beautiful young European lady!

Dumbfounded, the people began to ponder and fathom a reason. Coincidentally, amongst those present was an Ãlim who had just arrived from France. Upon witnessing the dead girls' face, he shouted out:

> *'Why...I recognize her! She was a student of mine in France. She is the daughter of a Christian priest and became a Muslim secretly. She used to come to me for Deeni Tãleem and to learn the Glorious Qur'ãn. Sadly, she became ill, only recently died, and was buried in France. At this, I was so sad, I left to come here for Hajj.'*

The locals concluded, 'Well, we are aware of the reason for her transfer here (to the blessed city of Makkah)...that she was a pious Muslim. However, this begs the awful question, 'Where is the body of the scholar and why?'' Some concluded, 'Allah Forbid, but it is possible his body may have been exchanged with the lady's back in France!'

Subsequently, the locals requested the Ãlim to make inquiries upon his return to Europe and gave him some documents to vouchsafe his story. Upon his return to France, the Ãlim headed straight for the home of the Christian priest and related the amazing story of his daughters secret conversion to Islãm and 'transfer' from a grave in *darul kufr* (non-muslim country) to the holy city of Makkah.

The accompanying documentary proof convinced the Christian priest to go together with the Ãlim, a magistrate and some locals to the graveyard and see. They exhumed the grave and upon opening the coffin found the body of the scholar who had been buried in Makkah so many thousands of miles away! Immediately, the Muslim teacher notified the Ulamã back in Makkah who became very worried, 'Whilst we are aware the lady's arrival in Makkah means her acceptance by Allah ﷻ...what then was the reason for this scholars 'transfer' from Makkah to *darul kufr* and what was the cause for his turning away from the Deen of Islãm?'

All concluded, 'A man's true condition is only known to his wife, we should inquire from her.' Accordingly, a small delegation arrived at the scholar's house and queried his wife, 'Were there any anti-Islãmic qualities in your husband?'

Wife: 'None! quite the contrary, he was punctual in salãh, saum, zakãt, hajj and recitation of the Glorious Qur'ãn!'

Locals: 'Think hard madam! His body has been found in

France, and in his place here in Makkah is a Muslim revert, surely there must have been something!'

Wife: '...Well, there was one habit of his which always worried me. After making love he had this habit... prior to getting up to make *ghusl-e-janābat* of saying, 'One very nice thing about the Christian religion is that they do not have to bathe after lovemaking."

Locals: 'Yes, this is precisely why Allah ﷻ ejected his body from Makkah towards *darul kufr* whose 'style' he so admired.'

Externally, this educated person appeared to be a pious Muslim. However, events and investigations 'unearthed' his true colour of giving preference to a kuffar method over one of the noble teachings of Islām (ghusl-e-janābat). This *istehsāne kufr* (preference of kufr) too is kufr. Sometimes, Allah ﷻ causes such events to unfold thereby enabling people to witness the result of misbehaviour and mockery of Deen.' May Allah ﷻ save all of us from such a calamity.

Ashraf's Advice Upon the

DEATH

of a Muslim

A Comprehensive & Essential Manual of

'What to do & What Not to do'

Ashraf's Amānat©

PO Box 12, Dewsbury, W. Yorkshire, UK, WF12 9YX

Order On-line from www.amanahstudio.org

Chapter Seven

The Sunnah Waleemah

(Post Marital Meal)

*R*asoolullah ﷺ *commented:*

'Whenever anybody is invited to a Waleemah, then they should accept and attend.'

'To eat of that Waleemah is reprehensible wherein only the affluent are invited and not the needy or destitute. Also, whomsoever (without a valid Sharee' reason ~ which includes places where non-mahram intermingle) declines an invitation, then he has acted contrary to the Command of Allah and His Rasool ﷺ.'

(Ma'āriful Hadeeth, p34, Vol. 7)

haykh Manzoor Nu'maani 🕮 narrates, 'To be blessed with a bride of one's choice is undoubtedly a tremendous Nemat of Allah 🕮. One right of this bounty is to express the shukr (gratefulness) of Allah 🕮 and display one's heartfelt joy. (The Sunnah) Waleemah is this demonstration...wherein the husband and his family beautifully proclaim their happiness and gratitude to Allah 🕮 for this union...' (Ma'āriful Hadeeth, p34, Vol. 7)

haykh Ashraf 'Ali Thānwi 🕮 narrated, 'Obviously, this (Waleemah) is an act of respect and nobility towards one's new bride and her family...wherein the wealth spent and people gathered serves to demonstrate the husbands appreciation and acknowledgement for his wife. This is why Rasoolullah 🕮 stressed and acted upon this Waleemah...'

Waleemah's of Nabee 🕮

When Nabee 🕮 married Saffiyah 🕮 on the return journey from Khaybar, he 🕮 requested his Companions 🕮 to bring whatever food was available for Waleemah...dates, butter, cheese, etc. Complete informality, no pomp or pretence whatsoever.

ishah 🕮 relates that at her Waleemah neither was a camel or sheep slaughtered. A bowl of milk arrived from the house of Sa'd bin Ubaadah 🕮 and this was the Waleemah! As Muslims nowadays abhor such austerity...we should carefully study this Sunnah. Anas 🕮 narrates, 'The waleemah Nabee 🕮 gave after marrying Zaynab binte Jahsh 🕮 was larger than for any of the other wives.'

On this happy occasion, Nabee ﷺ arranged for the slaughter of a sheep (to feed the guests), whilst Umme Sulaym ؓ (the mother of Anas ؓ) sent *hareera* (soup). Nabee ﷺ had instructed Anas ؓ to invite many by name, as well as all others he happened to meet. In this way, a large number of men totalling some 300 gathered at the residence of Nabee ﷺ...who whilst reciting a du'aa instructed people to eat in batches of 10 at a time from near to them. After all had eaten to their fill, Nabee ﷺ requested the food be removed. Anas ؓ comments, 'At the time of removal, I was unable to distinguish, whether more food was present when I had served the meal...or now upon its completion!' Although Nabee ﷺ did generously invite a large number of people, do also remember the conditions and arrangements for this Waleemah. No halls were hired, obviously no music or photography, no gheebat, no intermingling, no time wasting after the food had been eaten.

Shaykh Ashraf 'Ali Thānwi ﷺ narrated, 'At my Waleemah, I never invited anyone. We arranged for food to be cooked at our residence and thereafter distributed it to the homes of our neighbourhood. One lady objected and returned the food saying, 'What kind of Waleemah is this?' We replied, 'If she does not wish to accept, then its up to her.' She must have assumed we would plead and appease her...but what need is there for this? We had sent food from home, yet she also wanted us to flatter and pamper her! Next day, she arrived at our home and requested, 'Let me have yesterday's food please.'

I replied, 'That was all eaten up last night.' Hearing this reply so saddened her, she mumbled, 'What misfortune, I have deprived myself of such blessed food.' This is the way the *Ahl-e-Ilm* should respond towards worldly people, with an air of indifference...'

Some points to remember regarding Waleemah:

1) Although it is *Sunnah* for the bridegroom's family to make *Waleemah,* the unnecessary expenses incurred by the bride's family in holding a feast has no basis in the *Sharee'ah.*

2) It is totally un-Islāmic for those, who do not possess the means, to incur debt in order to have grand Waleemah's.

3) Great care must be taken as regards to *salāh* on occasion of Waleemah by all - the couple and all the participants.

4) It is a fallacy to think that one's respect will be lost if one does not hold an extravagant meal and invite many. What is our respect compared to that of Nabee ﷺ?

5) Present day practices of intermingling of sexes, music/ photography are sins totally against the *Sharee'ah.*

6) It is not permissible to 'take along' any extra people to those who have been invited, this applies to children also.

7) Whilst one should not unnecessarily cast suspicions on the income of a brother Muslim; nevertheless where there are grounds for justified doubt as to the nature of a persons revenue; then his invitation should be shunned.

8) Should one arrive at a *Waleemah* and find sin taking place, then leave immediately with *hikmat* and grace.

Chapter Eight

Advice for the Muslim Couple

*T*here are four qualities which are wonderful if every man is able to acquire them; but if certain pertinent persons of the Ummah possess them, then it will enhance the beauty of these features.

Justice, fairness and equality are brilliant attributes for anybody, but Wallah it would be superb if the rulers (and those with authority) have it!

Generosity is wonderful if the wealthy have it, but Wallah it would be outstanding if the poor man shares from the little that Allah ﷻ has given him!

Modesty and bashfulness is wonderful if men have it, but Wallah it is unique if women possess it!

Repentance is wonderful if the hunched aged person does it, but Wallah it is exceptional if the youngster enacts it!'

Key Points for the Newly Wed

*S*haykh Muhammad Saleem Dhorat *dãmat barakãtuhum* advises,

1) Every action is dependent upon intention. When marrying, both partners should rectify their niyyat (intention) to ensure three objectives:

* Following the Sunnah of Nabee Muhammad ﷺ.

* Safeguarding oneself from sins.

* Parenting pious children

2) When marrying, each becomes the other's lifetime companion. Each should understand and appreciate that Allah ﷻ has enjoined both together whereby their destiny in life now becomes one. Whatever the circumstances: happiness or sorrow; health or sickness; wealth or poverty; comfort or hardship; trials or ease; all events are to be confronted together as a couple with mutual affection and respect. No matter how wealthy, affluent, materially prosperous and 'better-off' another couple may appear, one's circumstances are to be happily accepted with *qanã'at* (contentment upon the choice of Allah ﷻ). The wife should happily accept her husband, his home and income as her lot and should always feel that her husband is her true beloved, best friend and well-wisher in all family decisions. The husband too should accept his wife as his partner-for-life and not cast a glance towards another.

3) Nowadays, the husband reads and is well-informed of his rights and demands them. Similarly, the wife reads of her rights and expects them. However, both should concentrate on being aware of each other's rights and then strive to fulfil them...this is true love and the prescription for a prosperous marriage

4) During the first year of marriage, the couple must try and spend as much time as possible together. This is especially true for the first two months as it provides an opportunity to understand the temperament of each other and establishes a firm foundation and goes a long way towards securing a prosperous marriage.

5) The couple (especially the husband) must make a point to arrive home early after *'Isha Salāh* and scrupulously avoid the habit of socialising with friends late into the evening. Wherever possible, business, employment and other activities should be concluded beforehand or curtailed and time set aside for spending together.

6) True and everlasting prosperity is only possible for Muslims when they follow the Sunnah of Nabee ﷺ in all affairs. It is the only panacea for being blessed with pious children.

7) In the initial stages of marriage, the love between the couple is a physical bond, wherein emotional changes take place all the time. Despite great passion and physical love for each other, affection between the couple is not yet well-established or on a rational basis...such intellectual love comes after many years

together. It is therefore extremely important for the husband not to succumb to emotional weaknesses at the onset and let the marriage waver towards an irreligious direction. Both the husband and wife should make a pledge to each other to steadfastly follow the Deen, especially in the performance of Salāh and in avoiding all sins.

8) Marriage is like the weather...forever changing. Sometimes it is cloudy and raining, life appears gloomy, then the sun appears and rays of happiness break through bringing joy. At times, one experiences rain, wind and sunshine all in one day. Such is life, and like the seasons, we go through different experiences. The secret is to remain devoted and steadfast to one's Deen and spouse.

9) The husband should be sympathetic to the fact that his wife has left her parents, brothers and sisters to start a new life with him. Her sacrifice and her feelings should be respected and joy should be felt by both partners at the expansion of their families. Just as the wife should treat her husband's parents as her own, he should also extend affection, courtesy and respect to his new in-laws.

10) As soon as one experiences a problem, no matter how trivial, which remains unresolved for more than one to a maximum of three days, then consult a person who is both knowledgeable and your sincere well-wisher.

Zaujain (Married Couple)

llah ﷻ says in the Glorious Qur'ān:

'They (women) are libãs (cover or screen) for you and you (men) are the same for them.' (2:187)

haykh Ashraf 'Ali Thãnwi ﵒ commented, 'This Āyah highlights the 'uniqueness' of the bond between husband and wife. Upon their *nikãh*, both acquire responsibilities and rights for each other, which they should strive to fulfil to the best of their abilities in order to achieve peace and success. It is the *Rahmat* (Mercy) of Allah ﷻ that He establishes such a relationship between the couple which is unequalled anywhere in the universe...the reason for this strong bond is precisely to fulfil the rights of each other...for both although different in body become one in life.

Just as life is unbearable without clothes, similarly, minus *nikãh* both men and women are unable to achieve tranquillity. This does not refer to only carnal desires, for whilst the wife is in need of her husbands' assistance; in terms of service and comfort, the husband is also in need of his wife.

Ponder, during illness, nobody but the wife will provide greater service. One old man of 80 years decided to remarry after the death of his first wife. All his children, daughters-in-law and grandchildren discouraged him saying, 'We are all present here to serve you, why then do you need to remarry in old age?' The old man replied,

'Nobody is able to serve and comfort as one's wife...at the appropriate time I shall show you.' Thereafter he remarried but within a short time, he fell ill. Suffering from acute diarrhoea, he would pass loose and nauseating stool some thirty-five (35) times a day upon his bed. All his children and daughters-in-law soon took leave from this stench. Only his wife sitting at the bedside remained, faithfully washing him, his bedding and clothes on each occasion! Upon recovery, the old man addressed his children, 'I married for just such (devotion)...observe, nobody besides she stood by me.' Therefore, like clothes, men are in need of wives, whilst ladies also need their husband...both are each other's aides and helpers, however, the husband occupies the rank of *hākeem* (ruler).'

Three Sharee' Huqooqs

Shaykh-ul-Hadeeth Ibrāheem Palanpoori ☘ comments, 'Accordingly, when the husband performs *Nikāh* and brings his wife home, immediately the Sharee'ah imposes three external duties upon him. These are the cost and responsibility of;

1) Feeding. 2) Clothing. 3) Housing.

Regarding the first two duties, the husband is responsible totally for feeding and clothing his wife within his means. Whatever he eats or wears, he should ensure the same (quality) for his wife. There is no need for the wife to go out to work. She enters her husbands' house as 'Queen,' and whoever heard of a queen going out to work? Both the husband and wife should appreciate each other's *maqām* (rank) commanded by Allah ﷻ: for a Muslim Lady was never created to 'earn a living.' Moreover, in fulfilling these obligations, the husband should take into consideration his wife's tastes and wishes. As long as they be within limits of the Sharee'ah, he should try to fulfil these, within his means, with love, sacrifice and happiness.

Before discussing the often-vexed right of separate living quarters, women should realize that a good Muslim wife does not resort to placing her husband in a situation where he is forced to choose between her and his parents even when her rights are at stake.

Housing ~ Separate Living after Nikāh

Shaykh Ashraf 'Ali Thānwi ﷺ advises, 'Nowadays it is prudent for young couples to live separately from their parents immediately upon marrying. There is benefit for all parties in this arrangement. I had observed a family in Meerath (India)...they were always in-fighting and quarrelling. One gentleman from this household, who was an acquaintance wrote to me complaining of these constant disputes. I advised him to rent a separate house; immediately he acted upon this suggestion and began to live alone with his wife. From that day peace and tranquillity prevailed!

My advice is for parents and children to arrange separate households immediately upon marriage, this is the panacea for good relationship between daughter-in-law and mother-in-law. Why? Because nowadays women are liberal, and (wish) to live separately. They are more willing to put up with the modest income of their husband, even if it means poverty, than enjoy luxuries living with in-laws. This is precisely the cause of many domestic quarrels.'

A Common Question ~ What if Parents Object?

'It is the wife's wãjib (compulsory) right, if she so wishes, to live separately with her husband. However, it appears in the Glorious Qur'ãn, that besides Shirk (idol worship) one should uphold all commands of one's parents and this is fardh (compulsory). Would you kindly advise, if parents do not desire their married son to live alone, whilst the wife wishes to live separately, whether in the one or separate building, what should be done? Do we follow the fardh or wãjib?'

Reply of Shaykh Ashraf 'Ali Thãnwi 🕮

'Assalamualaikum Warahmatullahi Wabarakatuhu, Obedience to parents does not apply in 'Tarke wãjib' (abandonment of compulsory duties)...and this right of the wife (to separate living quarters) is wãjib (compulsory). Therefore, should parents insist on ignoring this right, then one does not comply, for it appears in Hadeeth, 'There is no obedience for creation in disobedience to the Creator.'

Remember to provide separate living quarters for the wife when she demands is wãjib...and to omit a wãjib is sinful. Therefore, should parents insist (upon their married son) committing this sin, their demand will be ignored.'

haykh Ahmad Sãdiq Desai *dãmat barakãtuhum* comments, 'Separate living quarters do not necessarily mean a separate house. If the house is big enough, (the wife's) quarters should be demarcated with the (sole) keys in her possession. Privacy in her home is her (undeniable) right and, in fact, necessary. Many a time, the mother-in-law intrudes in her daughter-in-law's privacy. She considers such unlawful intrusion justified and her right simply because the girl happens to be the wife of her son. But the Sharee'ah does not give the mother-in-law any such right...The wife has the Sharee' right of debarring her mother-in-law from entering her room. Whilst good wives treat their mother-in-law with utmost respect, the latter should not take advantage of their daughter-in-law. They should respect them and seek permission before entering the room (or residence) of their daughter-in-law.

Some mothers-in-law consider it their right to even open the cupboards and wardrobes of their daughters-in-law to examine the contents. This is a despicable invasion of privacy, a show of scant respect and unlawful in terms of the Sharee'ah. Living separately does not mean that the man should sever his ties with his parents.'

haykh Ashraf 'Ali Thãnwi ◉ advises, 'My late respected father, immediately upon marrying us, separated our living quarters. This is the norm in our locality, that upon marrying, parents would arrange for a separate house. (My father) paid for all expenses which embarrassed and prompted me to seek employment. Through the Grace of Allah ◉, I received a high salary.

Before (as a bachelor), I had questioned the real need for a high income...and thought a fair amount would be sufficient. Within a short time of living separately, we realized that even this modest income would be used up.

My wife often requested me to arrange for the construction of a new house...whereupon I would convince her of the temporary nature of this dunyā. When we arrived for hajj in Makkah, my wife complained to (my Shaykh) Hajji Imdaadullah ﷺ of my reluctance to construct a house. Hajji Imdaadullah ﷺ advised me, 'Your wife is requesting you to build a house, why delay, it is a good idea for there is greater peace and comfort in one's own house.' Upon this I thought, 'She has come up with a very good way of having a house built.' I replied, 'Yes, I shall arrange it.' Thereafter, upon our return from hajj, we had a house built and informed my Shaykh ﷺ, who replied, 'Congratulations! May your house be blessed.' Shortly after moving in, I realized that indeed without one's own residence, true comfort is not possible. Yes, should somebody lack the means and is unable to build (or buy) a house, then it is different.'

Both parties should realize, living separately will strengthen not weaken the relationship between mother and daughter-in-law, there will be greater love, respect and much less friction.

Nowadays, living separately is an almost inevitable development; parents especially should realise this reality, suppress their emotions and allow their children to separate with their blessings.

Moral Rights

llah ﷻ mentions in the Glorious Qur'ān:

'Men are the rulers over women because of the excellence which Allah has granted to some of them over others and because of that which they spend of their wealth (to maintain women).' (4:34)

haykh-ul-Hadeeth Ibrāheem Palanpoori ﷫ comments: 'Undoubtedly, Allah ﷻ has blessed men with many such qualities generally lacking in women; courage, valour, honour, benevolence. Similarly many other faculties are present in men at a stage of perfection; leadership, physical strength, judgement, wisdom.' This is why men enjoy a loftier rank and command over women; thus, it is his responsibility to oversee the wife's morals and character. Without doubt, the husband is duty bound to provide more than merely the material and physical needs of his wife and family. He is obliged to maintain a constant 'eye' on his wife and family's spiritual and educational needs and training. In this aspect, an overwhelming majority of husbands fail in their duty and this is the major cause for the ills rocking our society. 'Umar ﵁ stated, 'The leader of a nation is its servant!' Thus leadership, at any level of society, will impose tremendous responsibilities and sacrifice. For a husband, this means a greater need to observe the religious welfare of his wife and family so that their *Ākhirah* is secured. Leadership does not entail the barking of dictatorial orders.

Husband-Wife Relationship

abee 🕯 commented:

'The Mu'min with the most perfect Imān is one who has the best character and who is the kindest to his wife.' *(Tirmidhi 1162)*

haykh Ashraf 'Ali Thānwi 🕯 advises, 'Remember well, success in both worldly and Deeni affairs is only possible when one person leads whilst the other is subservient and follows. Nowadays, people raise fancy slogans of unity and equality and pass many a resolution...however; they fail to observe its root cause.

The core of unity and equality is to recognise and accept one as leader whilst all others are subservient to him. Any organization (at whatever level of society), which fails to uphold this belief, is unable to achieve unity. Therefore, when this central precept of success is understood, women should remove from their hearts the false notion of equality...because this in itself is the cause of *fasad* (strife).

We now face two possible outcomes: either women rule and men become subservient; or men lead whilst women follow. Women should themselves, with an unbiased mind decide whether they or men are more able to command? Any lady with *fitrateh saleemah* (correct temperament) would not be able to refute the fact that physically and mentally men are more able and therefore capable of supporting and protecting women. On the contrary, women are unable to support or protect men. Therefore (women should rid themselves of this false and alien notion of equality) and act in accordance to the Qur'ānic Verse, *'Men are the rulers over women...'*

Husband and wife do not just have the ruler and ruled relationship; but one more of lovers. It is necessary to uphold the rights of both. When the need arises...it is necessary to enforce as ruler; however, this should be within the limits of the Sharee'ah. Our Akābir and Ulamā have practically demonstrated the ideal.

Shaykh Abrārul Haqq ۞ advises, 'The whole world is aware that a husband is *hākeem* (ruler) whilst his wife is *tābe'* (subordinate); however, there is another angle to this relationship. The husband is *muhib* (lover) whilst the wife is *mahbûb* (beloved)...now conclude, who is subordinate, the *muhib* or *mahbûb*?

Was it Layla or Majnun who was tābe'? (These were two famous lovers...Majnun was totally dedicated to his beloved Layla). Obviously, from this viewpoint the husband (muhib) is *tābe'* to his wife (mahbûb). Therefore, on the one hand, he is a *hākeem,* whilst on the other, she is *hākeem...*but hold on, how is this possible?

Well, our Sharee'ah has designated limits (*hudoods*) and responsibilities. In brief, the *hākeem* should not allow any infringements of (Sharee') laws, otherwise he will be termed a puppet governor...his wife's slave! When the wife demands or insists upon anything contrary to the Sharee'ah, then here a *hākeemānah* (authoritative) stance will be taken; however, when she requests any permissible (halāl) item such as food, clothing, meeting relatives and (appropriate) friends, etc., here full cognition will have to be taken of her wishes as a *mahbûb*. Will life not become a pleasure under these circumstances? Yes, true Jannah; but do remember the *hākimānah* approach is not for all occasions, as some people are too strict and authoritative *all* the time. Our Akābir and Ulamā have practically demonstrated the ideal.

Shaykh Ashraf 'Ali Thānwi ﷺ once arrived at the Masjid to perform the Sunnah of Fajr Salāh. Our Akābir advise the Ulamā to pray these two rakāts in the Masjid thereby avoiding the idea amongst the masses that these Sunnahs are not important. Shaykh Ashraf 'Ali Thānwi ﷺ had performed the first rakāt...when news arrived that his wife ﷺ had fallen from the balcony. Immediately, he broke his Salāh and rushed to attend to her. Only after comforting her, did he return to re-perform Salāh. What, such a great Ālim and breaking Salāh in the Masjid? Yes, this is what the Sharee'ah commands...break your Salāh if somebody is in mortal danger; be oblivious to the comments and opinions of others and ensure you fulfil the *huqooq* of creation. Another incident to illustrate this ideal and equilibrium.

Shaykh Ashraf 'Ali Thānwi ﷺ once arrived home from the *Academy* at midday and sat down for lunch with his wife...when she mentioned, 'Your elder brother's servants have said and done so-and-so...'

Immediately, he summoned these servants and ordered them to stand outside with himself at the centre of the doorway. His wife was requested to stand inside the room. Thereafter, he asked the servant, 'Munshi! My wife claims you have committed and said so-and-so, what is the reality?' Both servants denied the charge, whereupon, Shaykh Ashraf 'Ali Thānwi ﷺ asked his wife, 'Bring your witnesses to this accusation.' Unable to tender any proof, he reproached his wife, 'What! You make *fazeehat* (defame) somebody upon the smallest pretext? I now give *naseehat* (advice), in future unless you have Sharee' proof, never ever accuse anybody!'

Shaykh Abrārul Haqq ﷺ concludes, 'Allah ﷻ is advising the couple... 'Whilst we are granting each of you a *rafeeq-e-hayāt* (companion in life), do not become so drowned in this *nemat* that you become forgetful of our Command's; remember the *huqooqs* of your parents, elders, brothers and sisters, etc.' There have been many instances of young people leaving our locality (in India), ostensibly to acquire knowledge...yet they have lost themselves totally and failed to return home. The second Verse in the sermon states:

'O Muslims! Fear Allah ﷻ as He should be feared, and die not except in a state of Islām (as Muslims).' (3:102)

Understand that you are being blessed with many *nemats*...however, do not become so emerged in these bounties, that you end up losing or allowing weakness in the greatest *nemat* al-Islām...

'And die not except in a state of Islām (as Muslims).'

With the Command of Allah ﷻ, you receive this new *nemat* and with it another set of parents...one more bounty! Therefore, never behave so rashly, whereby these gifts are snatched away. Obviously, these nemats will only be fully appreciated when one has *taqwā* (fear of Allah ﷻ), and how do we acquire and maintain taqwā?

'O you who believe! Fear Allah, and join the company of the Sādiqeen (i.e. the Awliya).' (9:119)

Every skill and excellence is achieved by associating with experts of that profession. How many people have become chefs by merely reading books on cookery? How many people have become drivers by reading transport manuals? Obviously, only by receiving tuition from a chef or driver does one acquire their skills. Similarly, by associating with people of *taqwā* (the Awliya) will one receive this *nemat*. Another point worthy of note and borne by experience and current events is related in the third Āyah:

'O Muslims! Fear Allah Ta'ālā and speak the truth so that He may rectify your deeds and forgive your sins...'

Nowadays, sometimes the girl is at her parents and needs to be recalled. Both parties should avoid suspicions or a dictatorial stance and request she departs. Neither those on the boy's or girl's side should become dogmatic; 'we want her by this date.' Think well, *husn-ê-zann,* and each should try their utmost to resolve any differences... 'What date do you have in mind?' 'Why, you may come today.' Notice the effect of *husn-ê-zann,* it works wonders and ensures your speech is mild and noble... *'And speak the truth...'*

We must also ponder upon how to maintain this bond. Remember, the husbands similitude is that of a driver...who takes into consideration his co-passengers; those road users in front, rear and sides as well as road regulations; traffic lights and signs. Similarly, the husband has to uphold *huqooqs* of various people. Shaykh Ashraf 'Ali Thãnwi 🏵 has written a book, *Rights in Islãm,* wherein are related rights of the wife, parents, brothers and sisters, etc. Familiarize yourself with these so that you may ensure correct fulfilment and commit no injustice or shortcomings. Events should not transpire, whereby in pleasing one party you harm or hurt another.

Understand, the girl in marrying has *qaul-õ-qarãr* (bonded herself in covenant to her husband). She places rocks upon her heart in leaving behind her parents and family in coming to us. We too have *qaul-õ-qarãr* (bonded ourselves) by reciting the *Kaleemah*...that we shall enslave ourselves to the Sunnah of Muhammad 🏵 in every avenue of human existence: *Aqaaid, Ibãdãt, Muãmalãt, Muãsharat* and *Akhlãq.*

Now reflect to what extent do we fulfil our *qaul-õ-qarãr*? Yet, we expect total obedience from those who are under our jurisdiction. Reflect! She is weaker, yet upholds her *qaul-õ-qarãr*, whilst we commit many shortcomings in our obligations. We demand 100% compliance from our spouse and children whilst we fail to fulfil even 50%. This is the degeneration within us.'

Recipe for a Happy Marriage

Shaykh Mufti Muhammad Shafee' 🌸 used to comment, 'The husband/wife relationship cannot become truly prosperous until *taqwã* and the Fear of Allah 🌸 becomes ingrained into the hearts of both.' The bond between the husband and wife is so intimate that no other human relationship is as close. Both are each other's bosom friend and confidante...it is impossible to even envisage a closer bond or similitude. When both are alone and should either decide to violate, harm or forfeit the others huqooq; then nobody is able to intervene. There are many rights in this world; which if violated, redress of some form is possible either through law enforcement agencies or the judiciary. However, many of the *huqooq* of nikāh are such that no police officer or judge is able to enforce them. At most, they may apportion maintenance to the wife; but if the husband comes home and broods away; replies with sarcasm and vulgarity; and enacts matters whereby the wife's heart is pained...which police officer or court is able to charge or reform him?

The only possible remedy for such problems and conflicts is the Fear of Allah 🌸. Both need to appreciate that the other's existence Allah 🌸 has enjoined with me and if I fail to fulfil their haqq (right), I shall be held liable. Until this reality does not become entrenched in the heart, both husband and wife are unable to truly honour the other's huqooq.

haykh Mufti Taqee Uthmāni *dāmat barakātuhum* narrates, 'Sometimes, in order to train us, my Shaykh Dr. 'Abdul-Hayy 'Ārifee ✿ used to comment,

'We have been married fifty-five (55) years, however, Alhamdulillah, I have never talked harshly (to my wife).'

Moreover, even his respected wife often commented,

'He never ever ordered me to do anything...for example, 'fetch me some water...or do this.' I used to undertake all the tasks for him with enthusiasm and regarded it as my good fortune and honour...nevertheless, throughout our life together he never once ordered me to do anything.'

(p148, Statements of the Akābir)

People think that walking on water, or flying in the air are miracles whereas in reality this is a true miracle (and a feat worthy of mention). Such steadfastness is higher in rank than a thousand miracles. Over such a long period of time, undoubtedly there must have been differences of views and disagreements...yet he never spoke to her with bitterness! Such chivalrous behaviour is also the Sunnah of Nabee ✿.

Once a person who had stayed as a student for many years with the great Junaid Baghdadi ✿ commented, 'Shaykh! I have not seen you performing a miracle.' Shaykh Junaid ✿ replied, 'O ignorant one! Have you ever observed me doing anything contrary to the Sharee'ah or Sunnah?'

How Every Muslim Should Behave

*S*haykh Ashraf 'Ali Thãnwi ﷺ had formulated a list of advices based upon the Glorious Qur'ãn and Hadeeth of how every Muslim should behave:

1) Acquire the necessary level of Deeni Knowledge; either by studying authentic books or by asking an Ãlim.

2) Refrain from all sins. If a sin is committed; immediately repent.

3) Do not harbour another person's right; do not inconvenience by hand or speech nor speak bad of another.

4) Do not hanker after materialism or fame; nor crave after exquisite food dishes or clothes.

5) Should somebody reproach for a fault; do not make excuses; immediately accept your error and apologise.

6) Do not travel without a genuine need, for during journeys many events come to the fore; many good deeds are missed and; matters are not completed on time.

7) Do not laugh or talk excessively; and with non-mahram people do not become informal.

8) Never ever lie, dispute or argue with anybody.

9) Always bear the Sharee'ah in mind.

10) Do not become lax or lazy in ibaadah.

11) Spend greater time aloof and in seclusion.

12) When the need arises to meet others; be of service to them without expecting any return.

13) Remain detached from the wealthy and irreligious people.

14) Do not seek the faults of or think bad of others; rather fix your gaze on your own shortcomings and endeavour to rectify them.

15) Endeavour to pray Salāh punctually and correctly; with the utmost concentration.

16) At all times remember Allah ﷻ; whether by the heart or tongue. Do not remain negligent.

17) Should you derive pleasure in remembering Allah ﷻ; thank Allah ﷻ.

18) Speak with mildness.

19) Enact all activities and tasks to a schedule and on time.

20) Whatever harm, sorrow or grief arrives, consider it to be from Allah ﷻ and do not become disheartened; rather convince yourself that you will be rewarded.

21) Do not think about worldly affairs all the time; fix the thought of only Allah ﷻ.

22) As far as possible be of benefit to others; whether worldly or Deeni.

23) As far as food and drink are concerned, do not be so stringent that you become weak or ill; nor eat so excessively that you become (obese) and laziness appears in your ibaadah.

24) Do not have any hope on anyone besides Allah ﷻ nor conjecture that so-and-so will be of benefit to me.

25) Remain perplexed in seeking the Pleasure of Allah ﷻ.

26) Whatever the bounty; little or large; be grateful to Allah ﷻ and do not become despondent upon poverty.

27) Whomsoever is under your jurisdiction, tolerate their shortcomings.

28) If you become aware of the faults of another, keep it hidden. However, if they are endeavouring to harm somebody, then make them aware of this possibility.

29) Be of service to the guest, travellers, poor, scholars and pious. Select the company of the pious and at all times fear Allah ﷻ.

30) Always bear in mind your death. Every day, allocate a few moments wherein you take account your actions and behaviour of the day. For good deeds, be grateful; and repent for any sins.

31) Never attend any gathering which is against the Sharee'ah.

32) Constantly make du'aa to Allah ﷻ for correct guidance.

33) Behave with shame, modesty and patience. Never become arrogant or proud of piety. (p554, vol. 7, Bahishtee Zewar)

Shaykh Hakeem Muhammad Akhtar *dãmat barakãtuhum* narrates, 'There are four tasteless sins very prevalent amongst Muslims today which deprive one from becoming the Friend of Allah ﷻ;

* For men, allowing trousers or any upper garment to drape or overlap the ankles.

* A beard less than one fist length all around the face.

* Unrestricted gazing at non-mahram.

* Fantasising about non-mahram.'

The latter two sins also deprive one from truly appreciating and enjoying one's spouse and marital bliss.

Chapter Nine

Common Sexual Problems & Wholesome Cures

Rasoolullah ﷺ commented, *'In regard to two bounties, most people remain in loss (i.e. deprived of their benefits). One is health and the other is peace of mind.'*

$\mathcal{S}$haykh Hakeem Muhammad Akhtar dãmat barakãtuhum narrates, *'When your gaze falls upon a non-muslim person then do not pacify your nafs by ogling at them as if they are war booty (maal-e-ghaneemat)...but address your self, 'they too are the grandchildren of Adam* عَلَيْهِ السَّلَام.*''*

Kindly Reviewed by

Dr. 'Abdur Rahmãn Rajpura

MBBS, LRCP (London), MRCS (England)

Lovemaking - How Often?

Shaykh Ashraf 'Ali Thãnwi 🕮 narrates, 'To keep every matter at its equilibrium and within moderation is true achievement. In my opinion, the preservation of one's health is extremely necessary and important. In placing undue stress and strain, some have succumbed to illnesses; some have been mentally incapacitated whilst other's have brought an early death upon themselves. Life and good health should be well-protected; for once they depart there is no return. What is the value of pleasures at the expense of good health? A few seconds of ecstasy and then eternal pain!

Therefore, pay great attention in preserving good health...for there are repercussions in fulfilling even every lawful carnal desire...excessive indulgence of which destroys vitality and enthusiasm. Our pious elders have forbidden this. Moderation (in love making) ensures peace, satisfaction, tranquillity, real enjoyment and progress in life. Affection between the couple increases and true fulfilment of the wife's desires results in her considering her husband to be a real man and not impotent.'

(p243, Islãmic Weddings)

The Sharee'ah has not stipulated any specific limits for lovemaking as the temperament and physique of people varies considerably. Whilst in a hadeeth one is encouraged to make love and bathe on the night of Friday (p22, Ãdãb-ul-Jimã'), those with a greater appetite may make love twice or more a week. However, to make a habit of making love every night or more than once a night *may* prove harmful to health. This is especially true nowadays with the comparatively weaker physique of people combined with a lack or dearth of 'natural' (unmodified) foodstuff.

Lovemaking too often has been attributed to an early ending of youth because ejaculation of semen once, drains a considerable supply, which must be replenished; thus quickly depriving other vital body organs from nourishment. Hence, repeated depletion of energy too quickly results in illnesses...one of which is premature ejaculation. This disease drastically reduces the pleasure and enjoyment of lovemaking and the ability to satisfy the wife's natural appetite; leading to friction and marital problems. In addition, semen continues to weaken with a resultant harmful effect on any offspring born.

Another harm of over indulgence is to become a 'burden' upon the wife. Generally, women are 'sexually satisfied' with 'quality' love making (wherein she achieves full orgasm) at moderate intervals.

Shaykh Maseehullah Khān ※ advises young men, 'When you (selfishly 'come' too early) and cannot wait to fulfil the rightful desire, craving, appetite and orgasm of your wife (as is commanded by the Sharee'ah), what moral grounds do you then have in objecting to her *wishing* to have her desires satisfied otherwise?' This comment is meant to jolt husbands into getting their act together and should not be misconstrued by others as a licence for self-masturbation or adultery.

Psychological & Spiritual Factors

*P*rophet Muhammad ﷺ commented,

> *'Indeed, there is a piece of flesh in the body: when it is in order, the entire body remains in order and when it corrupts, the entire body becomes corrupted. Understand well! It is the heart.'* (Bukhāree & Muslim)

The soul, heart and brain of a person ~ vital organs which enjoy the rank of kingship ~ also govern and dictate the correct functioning of the entire body. Just as the body has been blessed with physical features: eyes, ears, hands, legs, reproductive organs, tongue, etc., so is it endowed with spiritual organs: the soul and nafs (self). Just as external features differ in every person, so do these spiritual organs which are categorised into four faculties:

1) Faculty of 'Ilm (Knowledge)

2) Faculty of Shahwat (Desires)

3) Faculty of 'Adl (Justice)

4) Faculty of 'Gadhab (Anger)

Externally, a person is said to be handsome when all his body features are well proportioned and active. Similarly, nay more importantly, a person will be described as cultured, well-mannered, intelligent, responsible and dignified if all of his spiritual faculties are also well proportioned and operating at the level of moderation. Moreover, their correct functioning will ensure that the external bodily organs correctly operate at the level of moderation stipulated by the Sharee'ah. Some modern psychologists now acknowledge this theory of Islām.

*A*llah ﷻ mentions in the Glorious Qur'ān:

'Our servants are those who are neither extravagant nor stingy, but they remain in a condition in between.'

When one's faculty of desire operates at this equilibrium, it is termed *parsāee* (chastity). Should it increase beyond moderation, it will be termed greed and lustful. Chastity is the state pleasing to Allah ﷻ, for this state heralds the virtuous qualities of compassion, generosity, shame, patience, contentment, desire to aid others, lack of avarice and the fear of Allah ﷻ. However, any extreme in this faculty will result in greed, avarice, flattery, sycophancy, shamelessness, jealousy, extravagance, insincerity, narrow mindedness and impotence.

One should now appreciate that this faculty of desire (of which virility is a branch) differs in every person, male and female. It is affected by both physical and psychological factors. Physically, one's diet, health, exercise and the environment play a part. Nevertheless, it is psychological factors, an entity within one's control, which play the dominant role. Obviously, a husband with a healthy power of virility will be able to fully satisfy his wife's sexual desire. A husband of weak virility due to an incorrect mental outlook, diet or lack of exercise leaves his wife unsatisfied. Nevertheless, people suffering from erectile dysfunction (ED ~ problems in getting or maintaining an erection) caused by physical illnesses will need to seek the services of a qualified doctor as there are proven drugs available to help such people overcome impotency.

Faculty of Thought (Quwwat-e-Khiyaleeyah)

$\mathcal{O\!S}$haykh Maseehullah Khãn 🏵 commented, 'Humans have a natural ability to think, ponder and reflect...this is known as *quwwat-e-khiyãleeyah* (the faculty of thought). If this ability is used correctly (as envisaged by the Sharee'ah), its effects will be beneficial and correct. If employed wrongly (or negatively), its effects will be harmful. People with a positive outlook are able to use this faculty to overcome many minor illnesses and ailments and carry on with their normal routine.'

Unfortunately, indifference to Deen, the upsurge for instant gratification and constant entertainment, lack of patience and constant exposure to photography and nudity from an early age (especially through the medium of TV) has resulted in minds becoming befogged with images of lewdness and ungratefulness. Combine this with a reduction in the inclination to stay connected with the pious; the result is alien cultures and outsiders now influence our chain of thoughts. The real values and teachings of Islãm which had been passed down from bosom to bosom over generations ~ spanning over 1400 years ~ have almost disappeared.

Understand well, all sexual misbehaviour has a harmful and damaging effect on one's virility. Muslim couple's who spend hours in front of the TV viewing non-mahram people and their amorous antics should not be surprised when they appear ordinary and boring to each other and as a consequence their sex-life declines. The choice is 'either the TV or Beevi (wife/spouse)!'

Lack of Self-Esteem

True manliness has vanished from the Ummah. Why? Muslims have drifted far away from the Sunnah and despite any lip service to the contrary, their hearts give greater precedence to the values and culture of others. Alien methods and norms which may externally appear to be a medium of 'progress' for others are not the basis of real success for Muslims. If we rebel, as we are doing, Allah ﷻ will overcome our hearts with fear, lack of confidence and loss of self-esteem.

Self praise, conceit and *takkabur* (arrogance) are of course harãm qualities, but self-esteem is a necessary facet for a sound character and true progress. Many Muslim parents make the mistake of alienating their children from Islãmic values (they feel everything to do with Deen is the responsibility of the Madrasah), now when these very children adopt the norms of other cultures and rebel; parents compound the issue by heavy criticism, ridicule, abuse and harshness. As a result Muslim youth feel abandoned, unloved, inferior and disorientated.

Living in an environment which encourages lewdness, Muslims lacking in Islãmic identity, character, self-confidence and true purpose in life, quickly fall prey to an inferiority complex and pine away their life in day-dreams and fantasy. As a consequence, they grope blindly everywhere to seek recognition, attention and gratification. Vices such as drugs, alcohol, masturbation, adultery and homosexuality which have reeked havoc in society appear acceptable.

Sexual Problems ~ Real or Imaginary?

A further point to understand is that a sexual problem for one person might not seem or actually be a problem to another. Every person is different and their perceptions vary, accordingly each of the couple should be willing and forthright in discussing any problems and their solutions with each other. When the need does arise to seek expert advice, one should appreciate that problems in this field are not new and there are halāl, tried and trusted cures available. Therefore, be very wary of seeking miracle cures offered by quacks nowadays over the Internet.

Common sexual problems for men include:

- Premature ejaculation or 'coming' too quickly
- Low libido ~ a decreased or low sexual desire
- Erectile Dysfunction or ED (problems in getting or maintaining an erection)
- Not being able to have an orgasm
- An increased sexual drive

Common sexual problems for women include:

- Not being able to have an orgasm
- Low sexual arousal
- Pain during intercourse
- Burning sensation in vagina and when passing urine
- Thrush, vaginal discharge and *istihādhā*
- Vaginismus (vaginal muscles tighten)
- Decrease or increase in sexual desire
- Pre Menstrual Tension (PMT) & Menopause

Amorous Glances

(A Common & Major Sexual Problem in Men & Women)

llah ﷻ mentions in the Glorious Qur'ān:

'Inform the Muslim males to lower their gazes (from looking at forbidden things) and protect their private parts (from harām). That is purer for them. Indeed Allah is All-Aware of what they do.' (24:30)

'Allah is aware of the fraud of the eyes and what the bosoms conceal.' (40:19)

abee Muhammad ﷺ commented:

'The gaze is a poisonous arrow from the arrows of Shaytān. Whomsoever, out of Fear for Allah refrains there from, then Allah will bless him (her) with such Nur of Imān that he (she) will perceive it's pleasure in his (her) heart.'

Although wrongful gazing is a grave sin, nevertheless the majority of Muslims, both men and women, young and old, are all involved in this evil. Our nafs has duped us into considering it to be an insignificant act, hence we do it all the time and do not even contemplate that we are sinning or realise the considerable spiritual and physical harm to ourselves. Shaykh Sa'ādee ﷺ once visited a Saint living in a mountain cave and suggested he sometimes visits the cities to enliven his heart. The Saint replied, 'Handsome people live there and, where there is mud around even an elephant is in danger of slipping.'

Shaykh Muhammad Wastee ⬡ advises,

'Whenever Allah ⬡ wishes to disgrace somebody (because of their intransigence), then He inclines and casts them towards the wicked and evil...'

Shaykh Sufyan Thãwree ⬡ advises,

'There is one Shaytãn with a girl and two Shaytãn with a young boy...this is why I am forever fearful of my nafs...' (p19, Tahzeeb-ul-Akhlaaq)

Once Shaykh Junaid al-Baghdãdi ⬡ was walking with a group of students when one of them, after staring at a passing handsome Christian boy commented, 'Will Allah ⬡ casts such people into Hell Fire?' Shaykh Junaid ⬡ commented, 'It appears you have stared at him wrongfully...you will soon experience the consequences of your misbehaviour.' Within a short time, the student who was a Hãfiz forgot the entire Qur'ãn. Although surreptitious gazing and sinning may provide temporary pleasure, nevertheless they are always followed by painful repercussions and spiritual darkness. Amorous gazing damages a person's ability to be aroused. What we hear, what we see, what we take into our stomachs, all affect us. Shaykh Ibn Qayyum Jawzee ⬡ comments, 'Four things are the poison of the heart:

1) Unrestrained glances (every new one is a delight).

2) Unnecessary talk.

3) Bad company.

4) Overeating.'

Treatment for Wrongful Gazing

haykh Ashraf 'Ali Thānwi ☙ narrates, 'The only treatment for wrongful gazing is to strive against ones self with courage, determination and vigour (*mujāhadah*). Even in mundane worldly affairs nothing is achieved without effort; observe how we swallow bitter medicine (at regular intervals over a period of time) to cure a physical ailment because the intention or desire is to be cured. Similar is (or should be) the approach for spiritual diseases.

1) When casting a gaze at a woman (or man), consider what would happen if their and your *mahrām* and seniors (parents, husband, wife, son, etc.) came to know of this misdeed? Now ponder, 'Allah ☙ is forever watching, should I therefore not be ashamed?'

2) Ask yourself, 'should a non-mahrām look at my wife, sister or mother in this manner, how would I feel?' Obviously, a person with any honour would not be able to tolerate such misbehaviour and would take physical steps (including assault) to stop such wickedness.

3) Whenever one desires to view a non-mahrām, instantly ponder that Allah ☙ will ask me on the Day of Qiyāmah, 'Did We bestow the nemat of eyesight for this purpose?' Thereafter, reflect upon the punishment in-store for sinning.

4) Whenever one succumbs and views a non-mahrām wrongfully, then immediately make ablution and pray two rakāts Salāt Taubah and thereafter repent. If one

repeatedly adopts this technique, then Inshã'Allah within a short while one will not be only cured from this vile habit but will also experience spiritual tranquillity.

(p17, Tahzeeb Akhlaaq)

*O*nce an old-aged person, who had suffered from this disease for a very long time finally wrote to Shaykh Ashraf 'Ali Thãnwi ﷺ who suggested the above advices. However, the problem remained, he continued to goggle at young ladies. Nevertheless, he did not stop writing to his Shaykh and informing him of his condition. Finally, Shaykh Ashraf 'Ali Thãnwi ﷺ suggested, 'make a banner and write upon it, 'I suffer from the habit of ogling at young women, please make du'aa for me,' and hang it around your neck whenever you leave home.' Being a sincere person, he made the banner and hung it around his neck...but was too embarrassed to step outside. Firstly, his wife castigated him, 'Oho! Been fooling everybody all these years with your image of piety, beard, turban, kurta and rosary...right, go on, get out the house and let everybody know what an amorous old person you are!' He pleaded with her to let him stay and promised never to do it again. He wrote to Shaykh Ashraf 'Ali Thãnwi ﷺ of what had happened and how he was now 'cured' of this vile habit.

This incident highlights the need for a spiritual guide, for no matter how knowledgeable, dedicated and self-determined one may be, without a qualified guide one will not be able to achieve spiritual good health and reformation.

Common Sexual Problems for Men

llamah Ibn Jawzee 👒 used to supplicate, 'O Allah! Strengthen my reproductive organ whereby my wife's Deen and dunya becomes pleasurable.' *(Ādāb of Jimā)*

Premature Ejaculation (PE)

Probably the most common sexual problem (or dysfunction) for a husband is premature ejaculation (PE) of semen when making love. It is estimated that almost 75% of men suffer from this problem at some time, especially the young, sexually inexperienced and middle-aged men. Experts define PE as the husband climaxing or coming too early ~ within two minutes of penetration into his wife's vagina when it should be greater than this. A better definition is the state where the wife is left persistently sexually unsatisfied. Although very rarely there may be physical causes for this problem, which only a competent and experienced doctor is able to treat, in the majority of cases the reasons are psychological and therefore within one's will-power.

Primary Premature Ejaculation (PE)

Primary PE which usually affects young men is caused by undue anxiety, ignorance and sexual misdemeanour (failure to keep one's thoughts and gaze pure; watching pornographic filth; masturbation, etc.). Many young men wrongly worry that their penis is too short...why? The pornographic and sex-aid industry (to increase their sales and profits) have, through media advertising entrenched the view amongst lay people that to conquer, overpower and truly satisfy a female it is necessary to have a very broad and long penis. Although the physique of each person differs, the organs of the body generally grow in natural proportion until late adolescence...and this development is beyond one's control.

According to experienced medical doctors a penis 6+ finger -width (120 mm) in length (when erect) and 2 to 3 finger-width in breadth is normal. Nevertheless, people with smaller penises should not fall prey to *wahm* (suspicion) that they are impotent, lacking in manliness or unfit to marry. Medically speaking, the length of a penis is irrelevant...just like the size of the wife's vagina is irrelevant. The man who worries about the size of his penis, should be more worried about the size of his brain.

Remember, your wife's sensitive genital tissues (clitoris) are located internally around the circumference of the vagina. It is therefore not the length or width of the penis but more importantly the love, affection, foreplay, sensitivity, enthusiasm, technique, consideration, care and after-play shown by a husband when making love which determines and fulfils the sexual appetite and orgasm of his wife. Whilst there is no place in Islām to foolishly boast of one's sexual prowess to others, nevertheless there is also no need to feel inhibited with one's wife or suffer emotionally from an inferiority complex generally because of harām images and material viewed elsewhere.

Secondary PE ~ which affects middle-aged+ men may arise when a man takes too much notice of the natural loss with age in the quality, frequency and duration of his erections. Even modern research shows that the much publicised male 'menopause' may be all in the mind and men can be as sexually active in their 60s as they were in their 20s. Sexual desires do not stop in old age, this is why the Sharee'ah has stipulated *purdah* for even elderly men.

Treating Premature Ejaculation (PE)

Before undressing and approaching one's wife recite the following Qur'ānic verse three times (but remember it is forbidden to recite when in the state of *janābat* ~ greater impurity):

$$ اِنَّ خَيْرَ مَنِ اسْتَأْجَرْتَ الْقَوِىُّ الْاَمِيْنُ $$

'...Verily, the best of men for you to hire is the strong, the trustworthy.' (28:26)

1) Courage & Mental Preparation

A person suffering from PE should not bring thoughts of sexual pleasure or beauty into his heart before lovemaking as such thinking may hasten early discharge. Rather remain calm, composed and confident of satisfying your wife. Rid your mind from any thought of failure. If you think negatively and lose courage beforehand, you will definitely ejaculate too quickly. However, if you rigidly hold on to the thought that you will succeed, then most often you will be successful; it is a case of 'mind over matter.' If necessary 'fantasize and role play' with your wife...but to think of any other woman or man is harām.

2) Prolonged Foreplay

It is estimated that 12% of women never experience an orgasm and 75% have difficulty achieving one by sexual intercourse alone, why? Because, it is not penetration of the penis alone which allows a lady to experience climax; she needs prior mental/emotional preparation and seduction, prolonged foreplay and stimulation of her clitoris.

3) Breathing Upwards

During intercourse, the husband should try and breath upwards and hold his breath, whilst the wife should breath deeply and arch her back to maximise clitoral stimulation.

4) Stop, Squeeze, Dry & Start Again

When experiencing a climax and the urge to eject, the husband should breath upwards, withdraw the penis, squeeze its base and wipe with a handkerchief. Thereafter, breathing upwards and releasing air slowly start again.

5) Never Become Despondent

Even if you ejaculate early, do not become despondent and separate...continue with your rhythm, fondling and caressing, as most often this too instigates her orgasm.

6) The Need For Reform

The overwhelming majority of men who suffer from this problem are those who have failed to reform their character. It is not about physical strength. Therefore, a genuine effort needs to be made to follow the Sunnah in all aspects of life; secondly, a strenuous and genuine effort must be made to reform and rid oneself of the bad qualities which makes a person feeble, timid and a spiritual weakling.

Low libido ~ a decreased or low sexual desire

There are many reasons, both physical and psychological why a person may have a low libido. It is essential to try and diagnose the cause, so that effective treatment is prescribed:

Depression

Depression is the all embracing by-word used by psychologists to describe many character disorders...the chief amongst which, though never accepted, is constant ungratefulness and rebellion to Allah ﷻ. If a person has a positive approach to life, is optimistic and prepared to be patient and forbearing when matters go against his temperament and wishes, many if not all events and occurrences in life will be taken in their stride and accepted for what they are ~ as trials for a Muslim.

Positive thoughts are the body's best healing tool and driving force. Remember, the brain too is an organ of the body and derives its nutrients from the same source as other organs. Accordingly, constant brooding, worry, grief, negative thoughts, lack of spiritual tranquillity and the constant and monotonous craving for superficial excitement, adventure and variety causes the brain to sap vital potassium and sodium from the blood stream with consequent fatigue of the mind, body and ultimately the soul. As a result, one's mood's swing wildly...consisting of peaks but mostly troughs.

Lack of sexual appetite is reported in almost 75% of all depressant cases, therefore the cause of this must be traced and it is not enough to turn towards only a medical doctor, one will need to make *ruju* (incline) also towards a spiritual doctor (the Mashã-ikh) and spend time in the company of the pious (whether in person or by correspondence). Even the most weak-hearted, naïve and feeble-minded person will benefit from a short while spent in the company of the Mashã-ikh. Shaykh Maseehullah Khãn ﷺ narrated:

> *'A short while spent in the companionship of the Awliya-e-kiram is nobler, superior and more beneficial than a century of unostentatious obedience...'* (p29, Sharee'ah & Self-Purification)

Just what is the connection between a person's marital life, the Deen and the company of the pious when numerous non-believers seem to be doing okay? Well, animals also appear to be doing okay but true sweetness in all aspects of human existence will only be experienced when our bond with Allah ﷻ has been rectified. The proof for this claim? When both husband and wife follow the Sunnah of Rasoolullah ﷺ in all affairs...such mental, physical and spiritual exhilaration, tranquillity and satisfaction is experienced which leaves no place for depression. In the overwhelming majority of cases, depression is of one's own making and the result of rebellion, sins, lukewarm allegiance to the Sharee'ah, inadequate upbringing and befriending the company of wicked people. Accordingly, the remedy for this is to adopt *taqwã* in the manner prescribed by the Glorious Qur'ãn and Sunnah:

> *'O you who believe! Be afraid of Allah and join the company of the sãdiqeen (i.e. Awliya)'* (9:119)

Treating Depression

Although the following method of treating depression will appear anathema to non-believers, for a Muslim it is the best way:

1) Repent & Abstain from Sins.

All sins are harmful and cause the heart to become darkened, agitated and ultimately depressed. Such a person becomes distanced from Allah ﷻ. Taubah (repentance) is to feel remorse in one's heart when remembering a sin and to turn towards Allah ﷻ to seek forgiveness. Rasoolullah ﷺ commented:

> *'Every human is a sinner. However, amongst sinners, the best are they who, after sinning or erring, sincerely repent and turn towards Allah Ta'ālā.'* (Ma'āriful Hadeeth)

Whenever a sin is committed, immediately perform two rakat's Salāh, thereafter make taubah with the heart, shedding tears and promising never to commit any sin again. The Rahmat (Mercy) and Forgiveness of Allah ﷻ is limitless. Nevertheless, if the sin committed involves *huqooqul ibaad* (rights of others), then these will have to be honoured or forgiveness (from the person) sought. Moreover, other duties such as *qadhā* (missed) salāh, saum, zakāt, hajj, etc. will also need to be discharged. When any servant fulfils all these conditions, then it appears in hadeeth:

> *'A person who repents is like one who has never committed a sin.'* (p206, Chapter of Forgiveness, Mishkhāt)

2) Adopt a Positive & Optimistic Outlook

Research shows that of the patients who visit the out-patient department at hospital, almost three-quarters of them have no physical cause for their complain, in another words, much of it is in the mind. We should therefore try and adopt a positive and optimistic outlook in all aspects of life: at home and work; avoiding all unnecessary stress.

'Whenever Nabee ﷺ had the option of selecting one of two matters, then he always selected the easier of the two...as long as no sin was involved...' (p350, Mazāhir Haqq)

Today, having failed to inculcate contentment we hanker after the 'latest' in all aspects of material life. Consequently we become frustrated and forever remain dissatisfied and ungrateful to Allah ﷻ. Sister Karima Burns relates:

'...The best method of avoiding negative attitudes and emotions whereby control is established over our bodies is simply to practice the wisdoms that we have been given throughout the Glorious Qur'ān and hadeeth. We should say, Alhamdulillah (All Praise to Allah) for what we have; Inshā'Allah (Allah Willing) for what we intend; and, Subhana'Allah (Glory be to Allah) when we see something exciting or amazing. We should remember to say, Astaghfiru'Allah (Seek forgiveness from Allah) when we lose our tempers or become weak, and most importantly, Allahu Akbar (Allah is the Greatest) when we are faced with the challenges of life. These five phrases, said regularly, are like taking a multi-vitamin for holistic health!'

(Courtesy Riyādul Jannah)

3) Sunnah Du'aa To Eliminate Depression

haykh Hakeem Muhammad Akhtar *dãmat barakãtuhum* relates, 'Rasoolullah ﷺ commented:

*'Whomsoever recites 7 **times** morning and evening the following du'aa, Allah Ta'ãlã will suffice for him by removing his grief of this world and the Ãkhirah:*

$$\text{حَسْبِىَ اللهُ لَا اِلٰهَ اِلاَّ هُوَ عَلَيْهِ تَوَكَّلْتُ}$$

$$\text{وَ هُوَ رَبُّ الْعَرْشِ الْعَظِيْمِ}$$

'Allah suffices me. There is none worthy of worship but He alone. On Him is my trust, He is the Lord of the Supreme Throne.'   (p53, Roohulmaa'ni)

Ill Health

t is extremely necessary to be aware whether any loss of libido is due to a decrease in *quwwate bah* (virility) or *quwwate mardee* (impotence). The latter (*na-mardee* or lack of manhood) is when a person is totally unable to perform sexual intercourse; irrespective of whether this is a defect from birth or due to other causes. A low libido (weakness in virility) is when a person is unable to sexually satisfy his wife. In such cases, either semen is discharged during foreplay or immediately upon entry of the penis into the vagina. Nowadays, the latter is quite common. It is imperative for the person suffering to consult a competent and qualified physician to diagnose the cause and not labour under the notion that eating aphrodisiacs or self-prescribing remedies such as the much publicised wonder-drug sildenafil citrate will overcome the problem.

NHS Prescribed Drugs for Erectile Dysfunction

In the UK, the Government's Department of Health, allows doctors under the provisions of the NHS (General Medical Services) to prescribe for certain patients drugs which have been proven to cure erectile dysfunction (ED). Patients who suffer from the following illnesses which may lead to low libido or impotence as well as those receiving treatment for ED before September 1998 are eligible as are those who suffer from severe distress and have been referred by a specialist:

* Diabetes
* Renal Failure ~ transparent and dialysis
* Spinal Cord Injury
* Radical Pelvic Surgery
* Prostrate Cancer
* Poliomyelitis

* Multiple Sclerosis
* Men who have had a prostactectomy
* Spina bifida
* Parkinson's disease
* Severe pelvic injury

According to homeopathic doctors, illnesses which affect a person's virility are:

* Mental Suspicion
* Liver problems
* Heart problems
* Weak mind
* Constipation
* Kidney problems

* Excessive Sorrow or Fear
* Influenza
* High blood pressure
* Oedema
* Absence of semen
* Weak genital organs

* Masturbation/Sodomy
* Prolonged Abstention
* Diabetes
* Injury
* Side-effects of medicine
* Obesity & Stomach problems

Stomach Problems ~ Rasoolullah ﷺ commented,

'The stomach is the fountain of the body. If it is maintained in a healthy state, one remains healthy. If it is despoiled, the health deteriorates.'

(Shu'bul Imān, Baihaqee)

The stomach plays the dominant role in digesting food consumed; accordingly any illnesses such as constant pain, dyspepsia (disturbed digestion or indigestion), gastritis, ulcers, etc., whereby food eaten is not fully converted to blood and subsequently semen, may lead to a weakness in virility. Accordingly, it is important to adopt all those 'common sense' measures (many of which are also Sunnah) advocated for centuries by physicians:

1) Eat only when truly hungry, not merely to pacify a routine timetable. Take cognition of the fact that different types of foods digest differently.

2) It is better to eat only one type of food on one occasion...to regularly consume various dishes in one sitting is not wise. The proof of this claim? Study the life of poor peasants who only get to eat one type of dish at meal times. Generally, they suffer from less illnesses.

3) 'Fast junk foods' are named quite aptly; going down the throat and leaving without nourishing as faeces very quickly. They are a chief cause of heart and blood problems, many other diseases and obesity.

4) Eat only wholesome foods and they too after thorough chewing. Try and stop eating when there is place left yet for one or two morsels. Avoid drinking water during meals but

drink a minimum of 6 to 12 glasses throughout the day. After the mid-day lunch, try to have a short nap (with the niyyat of following the Sunnah *qaylullah*), even if it means dozing for only half- a-hour on an easy chair.

5) The evening meal should be eaten at least two to three hours before sleeping and should be followed by a short stroll to aid digestion (a brisk 20 minute walk is ideal).

6) During meal times, the whole family should make a point of following the Sunnah: talking only light-heartedly and keeping matters of anger, grief, unhappiness and the TV and radio well away.

7) One should neither make love on a full nor an empty stomach. Lovemaking between the husband and wife is an *ibaadah* that requires the body to draw upon and burn a plentiful supply of energy. Avoid very spicy, hot, salty, bitter dishes. A sensible balanced diet and food rich in carbohydrates and proteins (especially pasta, bread/ chapatti, rice, fish, white meat and fruit) will guarantee you have the 'fuel' required to 'perform' in the bedroom.

Diet & Exercise

Diet and exercise have a profound effect on a person's sexual performance. Many people think kicking a ball or swinging a bat keeps them fit. One need's to exercise (and build up the stamina and aerobic capacity) for at least 30-minutes five (5) times a week to attain fitness. In general, sex puts the same amount of pressure on the heart as a brisk 20-minute walk, with an orgasm putting the same strain on the heart as walking up a flight of stairs.

Problems in getting or maintaining an erection

Erection of the penis occurs when blood vessels dilate to allow an increase in blood flow. Muscles around these vessels then contract to stop the blood flowing backwards thereby maintaining the erection. Modern research shows that approximately 10% of men, not necessarily old, though the quality and frequency of erections does decrease with age, have a recurrent problem with their erections. Why?

The most common reasons are fear/anxiety, extreme fatigue, over-consumption of alcohol, tobacco and recreational drugs. Basically, factors within one's control and which have no place in the life of a Muslim.

Erectile Dysfunction may also arise because of diseases affecting the blood flow (such as diabetes), high blood pressure (when caused by certain medicines), pelvic surgery and a low level of testosterone ~ the male hormone.

Loss of erection caused by physical reasons may be treated by: using a dynamic vacuum pump which traps blood into the penis to maintain an erection; by using a 'cock ring' (for a maximum of twenty minutes to avoid tissue damage); by self-injecting medicine (prescribed by a doctor) into the penis; by using a pellet inserted into the tip of the penis using an applicator; spraying the penis with a developer spray which dilates the blood vessels; by taking certain drugs which although not actually causing erections nevertheless increase the response of the penis to sexual stimulation. Obviously, such medical solutions require the services of a qualified and competent doctor.

Not Being Able to Have an Orgasm

Strictly speaking, ejaculation and orgasm are two separate experiences during lovemaking, notwithstanding the fact that they are synonymous and usually occur and are more pleasurable when together.

Nevertheless, it is possible for a man to ejaculate and not have an orgasm...which are reflexes in the pelvic floor muscles contracting between 5 to 15 times at rapid intervals...a sort of psychological tension relief.

Exercising of the PC (Pubococcygeus) Muscles

To improve one's orgasm, carry out regular exercise of the PC muscles. To locate these muscles (for test purposes only) try holding your urine momentarily whilst passing water. The sensation felt is the tightening of the PC muscles which: support the contents of the pelvis, prevent urine incontinence, improve blood circulation to the private area thereby aiding erection, control over-ejaculation and ultimately increase sexual orgasm and pleasure.

These PC muscles may be easily enhanced and toned by carrying out the 'Kegal Exercise,' which involves contracting these muscles for two seconds, 15 times, twice a day at the beginning to a gradual increase up to 40-50 times, twice a day, over a two month period. It is important to only contract the PC muscles and not be deceived by tightening the stomach and thighs. Many people have reported an improvement and confidence over both ejaculation and orgasm and this simple exercise may be carried out whilst sitting or lying.

An Increased Sexual Drive

Allāh ﷻ mentions in the Glorious Qur'ān:

'Tell the believing men to lower their gaze (from looking at forbidden items), and protect their private parts (from harām). This is purer for them. Indeed, Allah is All-Aware of what they do.' (24:30)

In a hadeeth, Rasoolullah ﷺ narrated:

'Zina (fornication) of one's hands is to touch a non-mahram...zina of one's eyes is to look at a non-mahram...zina of one's tongue is to speak with a non -mahram...' (Muslim, p10, Ahqam Purdah)

'It would be better for an iron rod to be pierced into your head than for you to touch a female who is harām to you!' (ibid.)

Second Nikah ~ In this era of promiscuity, when images of nudity are all around us, people who are not inspired by the Fear of Allah ﷻ are liable to gratify themselves by committing *zina* and other harām acts. This is why the Sharee'ah has stipulated *nikāh,* for it provides a pure, lawful and mutually beneficial outlet for a couple's desires. Nowadays, many men who imagine they have an increased sex drive are those who fail to keep their gaze under control. It is only a superficial 'increase' brought about by misbehaviour and the viewing of lewdness, whether in media format, on the streets or at the workplace. Nevertheless, it is the undisputed right granted to a Muslim man to marry up to four wives (if he is able to treat all of them with the lofty justice stipulated by the Sharee'ah).

*Sh*aykh Ashraf 'Ali Thānwi ❀ comments, 'Taqwā is such a benevolent and beautiful concept that each human should adopt it as a standard. Some people have greater carnal desires than others...and for such people, one wife may not be enough. Moreover, if such people are not allowed to perform a second, third or fourth *nikāh*, then the result is discarding of *taqwā* and submergence into adultery...an evil which removes any and all thoughts of purity and chastity from the heart and replaces it with poison.' (p.221, Islāmic Weddings)

'Nevertheless, in this day and age, without an over-pressing need, one should never ever perform another nikāh (whilst the first wife is present). Moreover, the 'pressing need' should be the view and judgement of wise counselling not the whim of one's desire.

To marry a second wife after middle-age...usually the time when the first wife has become 'settled' and 'carefree' (because the children are now grown-up) is in effect to place the latter in turmoil. The second wife will bring her 'colour,' which will definitely influence the husband to some extent...the result will be that all three will become submerged in agony...especially if the husband is not an Ãlim (scholar) and one who possesses impeccable forbearance. Without Deeni 'Uloom, a person will not be able to comprehend the limits of justice and without true patience, he will not be able to enforce these limits. As a consequence, he will definitely be guilty of *zulm* (tyranny). This is why many husbands who take more than one wife are submerged in the sin of oppression and injustice.

Second Nikāh is Akin to Placing a Foot on Pul Sirāt

In performing a second nikāh, many matters come to the fore, but such circumstances are like the road to Paradise wherein one has to pass over the *Pul Sirāt* (the extremely hair-thin and razor-sharp bridge over Hell). Whomsoever is unable to fulfil the rights of both wives (which implies the over-whelming majority of husbands) will end up falling into Hell. Therefore, do not even consider such a proposition.

The qualities that are required to overcome such a hurdle are not cheap: perfect intelligence; spiritual *nur* (effulgence); perfect reformation of one's *nafs* (self ~ by means of spiritual exercises under the supervision of a Shaykh). Generally, because such attributes are almost non -existent (in the Ummah today), to become embroiled in the 'dream' of marrying more than one wife is in effect a recipe for disaster. You will embitter and ruin your worldly existence and destroy your Ākhirah.'   (p229, ibid.)

How to Control Excessive Desires?

Shaykh Dr. Habeebullah Mukhtaar ﷺ advises, 'Doctors of medicine give the following suggestions on how to restrain lustful desires and sexual urges:

- Have cold baths in summer and pour cold water on the penis in other seasons.

- Engage in physical exercises and permissible sports (some doctors recommend special exercises to curb lustful desires).

- Abstain from spices and all types of food that excite sex.

- Cut down on tea, coffee and invigorating beverages. Reduce intake of meat and eggs to a minimum.

- Refrain from pursuing things that incite sexual passions and desires. Abstain from listening to romantic tales or reading pornographic novels and magazines, hearing music and indecent songs or viewing such films.

- Spend your time carefully and correctly so that lustful ideas do not play havoc.

- Select the company of good pious friends and companions who may guard us from erring. Stay far away from evil company.

- Attend gatherings where Allah ﷻ is eulogized. Be punctual in performing the Fardh Salāh and make a habit to offer naf'l Salāh and recite the Glorious Qur'ān on a regular basis. (Courtesy of Riyādul Jannah)

Shaykh Ashraf 'Ali Thānwi ﷫ comments, 'Should your view fall upon a lady, then immediately turn your gaze away...and should thoughts about her remain in your heart then make love to your own wife. By doing so, *wasāwis* (thoughts of temptation) will disappear. This is the method taught by Rasoolullah ﷺ. Remember, the person prone to thinking about other ladies, even if all the women of the world were to be presented to him except one...then such a lustful person will still desire the latter in the expectation of deriving some different pleasure from her...therefore inculcate *qanā'at* (contentment).'

(p245, Islāmic Weddings)

haykh Maseehullah Khãn ﷺ related,

'Once a lady (in purdah) visited Shaykh Junaid Baghdãdi ﷺ to request a mas'alah (ruling). She was seated behind a screen from where she inquired, 'Shaykh! My husband wishes to marry another woman, is it permissible for him?' Shaykh Junaid Baghdãdi ﷺ replied, 'The Sharee'ah allows a man to marry four wives if he is able to treat all of them justly.'

The lady continued, 'If the Sharee'ah had given me permission I would have removed my veil and asked you, 'with a wife such as me in his marriage, is it permissible for him to raise his gaze towards another and remarry?' (In this statement, the lady was indicating towards her outstanding beauty).

Instantly upon hearing this reply, Shaykh Junaid Baghdãdi ﷺ cried-out and fainted. The lady fearing what had happened arose and discreetly left.

One of the attendants rushed to the Shaykh's aid and as he regained consciousness inquired, 'Shaykh, what happened?' Shaykh Junaid ﷺ replied, 'Did you not hear what she said? When she made the comment, 'with a wife such as me in his marriage, is it permissible for him to raise his gaze towards another?' I immediately remembered the statement of Allah ﷻ, 'O My servant! With a Creator such as Me, is it appropriate for you to raise your gaze towards another?"

Oral & Sex during Menstruation

llah 🕮 says in the Glorious Qur'ān:

'They ask you about menstruation. Say, 'It is an Adha (an impurity and harmful act for a husband to have sexual intercourse with his wife whilst she is undergoing menses), therefore keep away from women during menstruation; and do not have intimacy with them until they are cleansed...' (2:222)

ayd bin Aslam 🕮 (a Tābee') relates:

'Once a person asked Nabee 🕮, 'During the days of my wife's monthly periods, what leeway is their for me regarding intimate relationships?' He 🕮 replied, 'Cover a tahnaband (cloth between her navel to knees), thereafter you may derive pleasure from her upper torso (e.g. kissing).' (Mishkhāt)

haykh Mufti 'Āshiq Ellahi 🕮 narrates, 'During the days of menstruation, it is *harām* for a husband to make love to his wife or touch or view any part of her body between the navel and knees. However, besides this, the husband may derive pleasure from all the other parts of her body (head, breasts, lower legs, and back).' If during haidh, a person makes the grave mistake of making love then it is *wājib* (compulsory) to repent abundantly and it is better to also make a donation to charity; 'The person who (commits the error) of making love to his wife during haidh, then Nabee 🕮 has instructed the donating of one or half a dinar in charity as recompense.' (Ibn Mājah, p281, Islāmic Weddings)

There is ample evidence to show that during *haidh* and *nifaas* it is physically harmful for both the wife and husband to engage in lovemaking. There have been recorded cases of women suffering lethal blood loss and haemorrhages having made love too soon after giving birth. Moreover, homeopathic doctors claim there exists the grave danger of insanity (to the husband ~ remember *haidh* blood is extremely impure), venereal inflammation and damage to uterus should couples make love during days of impurity.

Oral Sex ~ A case of monkey see; monkey do!

Shaykh Mufti 'Abdur-Raheem Lajpoori comments, 'Undoubtedly the external areas of the genital organs (of those Muslims who wash with water) are pure; however, it does not follow that every clean item be placed in the mouth (to be licked, kissed or chewed). The nostrils are also pure, but could any (right-minded person) tolerate licking and tasting the nasal passages or secretion and could it ever be permissible? The external opening around the anus is not impure but clean, but is it permissible to lick it? No, never, similarly, it is *makruh* (impermissible) and sinful to lick, kiss (or suck) the genital areas of a person; such is the behaviour of dogs and animals...! Ponder, the mouth and tongue which recites the Kaleemah, Glorious Qur'ān and Durood; is it appropriate and acceptable to the (heart and conscience of any sane person) to employ it in such bestial acts...?' Many sexually transmitted diseases spread through oral sex.

(Fatāwā Raheemeeyah Vol. 6, p270: p47, Ādāb-ul-Jimā' Mubāsharat)

Common Sexual
Problems for Ladies

Failure to Experience Orgasm

An orgasm has been described as 'an explosive discharge of neuro-muscular tension,' which in plain English means complete sexual relief for the wife in the form of a 'reflex' throughout her spine, pelvic floor muscles and ultimately her body. After a full orgasm, one instinctively drifts into 'sleep' for a brief moment.

It is estimated that 10% of women never experience an orgasm and 75 % have difficulty reaching one during sexual intercourse. Why? Usually, it is attributed to a lack of foreplay, lack of stimulation of the clitoris/G-spot and early ejaculation by the husband. The G-spot is reported to be a pea-sized zone 25-50 mm inside the vagina, towards the top wall. When this area is stimulated and aroused by the husband, either by stroking with his finger or penis, it increases in size and provides pleasure and sensation to the wife. If sufficiently simulated, it prepares her for the eventual orgasm. There are physical reasons why a lady may have difficulty; generally these are either vascular, neurological or hormone deficient disorders. It may also be due to the effects of medicine, surgery or psychology; obviously the field of qualified doctors whose expertise must be sought.

Early Ejaculation & Insufficient Foreplay

The most common cause of lack of orgasm is too early ejaculation by the husband and insufficient foreplay. So what does a Muslim wife do when it obviously is not her fault and she remains sexually unsatisfied so often? Firstly, she shall have to politely though frankly let her husband know of the problem. Some ignorant men think that sex is all about going like the 'clappers' and 'coming' whenever he feels like it. Let him know that by ejaculating too early, you feel sexually unsatisfied, in physical pain and experience mental turmoil and agitation.

Secondly, she should indulge in intense foreplay encouraging him to 'finger' and stroke her clitoris whereby she becomes fully aroused and only then let him enter his penis into the vagina. Thereafter, knowing your husbands urge to ejaculate too early, try to control him during lovemaking. When she feels he is about to come too early, talk and get him to take deep breaths and withdraw his penis. Gently pinch the junction of the penis/testicles and wipe the penis. Thereafter, allowing him to regain his breath, start again encouraging him all the time. Repeat this process as many times as necessary, no matter how long *you* have to persist. It is the wife who will have to take the leading role and not let him become despondent. Often, by curbing and addressing the problem as it arises, the wife by 'preserving his self-belief' can work wonders. If the problem persists, seek medical counselling as this problem is not incurable. For this perseverance, faithfulness, loyalty and chastity a Muslim wife receives huge *thawãb*.

Exercising of the PC (Pubococcygeus) Muscles

In women, the PC (Pubococcygeus) Muscles are those that encircle and support the vagina. Ladies who have toned and strengthened their PC Muscles by means of regular exercise claim they are more able and find it easier to reach a climax than before. These PC muscles may be easily enhanced and toned by carrying out the 'Kegal Exercise' as described for men and improvements should be noticeable within 6 weeks.

Lack of Lubrication

Another common reason for failing to experience an 'orgasm' is lack of lubrication (due to either the onset of menopause or inadequate foreplay or dryness) of the vagina which reduces the chances of enjoying sex. Lack of lubrication may be overcome by using a water-based cream.

Vaginal Infections

The vagina is a very sensitive organ and is easily irritated by lack of hygiene, usage of strong soaps (natural unperfumed soap is best), vaginal deodorants, talcs, shower gels, perfumes and inappropriate (nylon), uncomfortable, dirty underwear, tight-fitting trousers and even an infection on the husband's penis. Every Muslim lady should have a personal hygiene routine whereby she showers regularly (even during and especially immediately after her monthly period). It is part of purity to change underwear daily, shave the pubic area regularly (once a week) and wear such underwear (like cotton) and light-fitting trousers that allow the private organs to breath 'naturally.'

Muslim Ladies & Washing After Call of Nature

When answering the call of nature, generally Muslim ladies cleaning their private parts with tissue paper and water have the habit to stroke 'upwards' from the rectum past the vagina and up to the urethra. Although it is necessary to clean and wash these areas to achieve purity, nevertheless by stroking upwards, the natural bacteria present in the rectum (stool) may enter the vagina and cause infection. It would be more appropriate to alter the washing technique and stroke 'downwards' away from the vagina thereby reducing the chances and possibilities of vaginal infection.

Thrush

'Thrush' is probably the most common vaginal infection and a chief cause of painful sex. It is recognisable by its thick white 'cottage-cheese' like appearance, however it is easily treatable (by antifungal pessaries and often preventable by urinating and washing the private areas soon before and after making love ~ in the manner described above). This is one more benefit of ghusl-e-janãbat ~ it rids the body from both spiritual and physical impurities.

When treating 'thrush' one should avoid making love until the infection clears. Should any infection persist, create a burning sensation when passing urine or cause pain during lovemaking then medical treatment should be obtained immediately from your GP (Doctor). The husband should also apply an ointment (recommended by the Doctor) to his penis to avoid the possibility of re-infection.

Increase in Sexual Desire

Nowadays, constant exposure to pornographic 'material' has led to a deterioration and in many cases to the destruction of *tab'ee haya* (natural modesty and chastity) present in Muslim ladies. Sexual desires aroused in a promiscuous and unhealthy manner reek havoc to the body and soul. What may *appear* as an increased sex drive is in fact a sign of moral destruction. Therefore, a Muslim lady (and men also) should inculcate *taqwã*, discipline herself to keep her gaze, mind and thoughts as pure as possible. Nevertheless, ladies, like men have differing sexual appetites. This is but natural and nothing to be ashamed about as long as one satisfies such 'natural' desires in a halãl manner. If a Muslim wife has a greater sexual appetite then it is the responsibility of her husband to satisfy and fulfil it spending as much time and energy as necessary.

Decrease in Sexual Desire & Vaginismus

Illnesses such as diabetes, high blood pressure and neurological disorders (such as multiple sclerosis), menopause and surgery (removal of ovaries, etc.) as well as the increasing use of drugs, alcohol and smoking may lead to a decrease in sexual desires. It is therefore important for a Muslim lady suffering from this problem to let her husband know of her predicament for recent research suggests that up to 40% of women may suffer from sexual dysfunction. Why and how? Apart from illnesses this may be due to a reaction to certain contraceptives and many a times due to depression. Throughout pregnancy and sometimes during breast-feeding, sexual desires lessen as the body and mind undergo physical, hormonal and emotional changes. Muslim husbands need to appreciate these added responsibilities and a wife should let her husband understand her feelings rather than bottle them up. Medical reasons aside, a lack of sexual desire may be the consequence of when young girls are left in the custody of, or as is very common nowadays, allowed to come into contact with unscrupulous people and they are either emotionally distressed, sexually molested or abused. Such childhood 'experiences' often leave the girl traumatised, wary and frightened of sex.

Although non-Muslims also attribute a strict upbringing as being a possible cause of low sexual desires and vaginismus (an involuntary tightening of the vaginal muscles, which can make penetration difficult, painful and often impossible); a Muslim wife who feels disinclined towards sex with her husband should remember that it is an act of *ibaadah*. It appears in a hadeeth, 'Allah loves a man who caresses his wife. Both of them are awarded thawāb because of this loving attitude and their rizq is increased.' Such a positive outlook with appropriate counselling and medical treatment will *inshā'Allah* solve the problem.

Istihādhā (Abnormal Vaginal Bleeding)

Any abnormal bleeding from the vagina which occurs for either less than 3 days; or when accompanying haidh more than 10 days; and when accompanying nifaas is greater than 40 days is known as *istihādhā* and breaks *wudhu* only. Salāh and saum remain compulsory during *istihādhā* and it is permissible to make love.

Pre Menstrual Tension (PMT)

A llah ﷻ says in the Glorious Qur'ān:

'Whomsoever practises righteous deeds, be they male or female, while he/she has Imān, then assuredly, We shall grant him/her a wholesome (i.e. peaceful and honourable) life. And We shall certainly reward them (the pious ones) in return for their righteous deeds.' (16:97)

I t is estimated that almost 90% of women (and wives claim just as many husbands also) experience pre-menstrual tension (PMT) in the few days before the start of their monthly periods. Why? It is assumed in women these symptoms are the result of hormonal changes in the body as it gears up for *haidh*. The most common symptoms are:

Psychological	Physical	Spiritual
Irritability	Tiredness	Lack of Patience
Anxiety	Bloated Feeling	Restlessness
Depression	Greasy Skin/Hair/Acne	Anger
Mental fatigue	Stomach Cramps	Frustration
Mood swings	Constipation	Aggressive
Tension	Discomfort in breasts, lower back & abdomen	Argumentative

How To Cope with PMT?

PMT usually disappears within a day or two of the period starting. Accordingly, unless severe discomfort or pain is experienced there is no need to worry or take any medicine.

It is wiser to concentrate on the factors within one's control whereby the symptoms are overcome or minimised:

1) Avoid physical, intellectual and emotional over-exertion during the 'heavy days;' the few days before and after the start of your periods when the body is experiencing the greatest strain. Surprisingly, many women appear to undertake extra-strenuous domestic tasks during this time and self-aggravate the symptoms and problems.

2) Inform your husband of your impending period and symptoms whereby he understands. If possible delay burdensome and stressful tasks until later.

3) Bathe and change clothing daily. Try to stay in the state of *wudhu* ~ great tranquillity is noticeable.

4) Maintain a healthy diet; foods high in protein, carbohydrates, vitamin B and magnesium are helpful; especially bananas, whole grains, meat and fish.

5) Try and make a habit of reading a 'monumental Deeni book' in the few days before and during your period whereby your thoughts and emotions are focused, captivated and enlightened.

6) Maintain your physical and spiritual exercise program; recite Tasbeeh-e-Fātimah ﷺ whenever you feel 'down' and after every fardh Salāh; also read the du'aa:

لَا اِلٰهَ اِلَّا اللهُ الْعَظِيْمُ الْحَلِيْمُ، لَا اِلٰهَ اِلَّا اللهُ رَبُّ الْعَرْشِ الْعَظِيْمِ، لَا اِلٰهَ اِلَّا اللهُ رَبُّ السَّمٰوٰتِ وَ رَبُّ الْأَرْضِ وَ رَبُّ الْعَرْشِ الْكَرِيْمِ

La hawla walaquwwata is the medicine of 99 illnesses the least intensive of which is grief and sorrow. (p300, Virtues Du'aa)

Menopause

N*abee* 🕮 *commented, 'He amongst you who arises in the morning with Imãn, health and sufficient food for that day, should consider himself as being in possession of the whole world.'* (Tirmizee)

Every lady who experiences menstruation will have to go through the stage of menopause; usually sometime between the mid 40's to mid 50's. Menopause literally means the 'end of menstruation' and the ability to conceive children. It is a natural phenomena, part of the ageing process involving physical and emotional changes to oneself. This is not a time to panic, worry or become depressed. Be grateful to Allah 🕮 for having brought you to this phase in life with dignity and your Imãn, honour, intellect, health and wealth intact; when so many others have either died, become terminally ill or suffered so much hardship.

The Bounty & Blessings of Old-Age

S*haykh* Muhammad Shafee' 🕮 narrates, 'Rasoolullah 🕮 commented,

'Until a child attains buloogh (maturity), his good deeds are accrued in the accounts of his parents and whatever bad deeds he enacts are neither written in his or his parents' records. When he reaches maturity, his (written) accounts are established and the two angels who are to stay with him are instructed to safeguard and guide him unto full strength.

When, in the state of Islām, he attains forty-years of age, then Allah saves him from three types of illnesses: insanity; leprosy and leukoderma (vitiligo or white patches on the skin). When he reaches fifty years, Allah lightens his reckoning. When he reaches sixty years, Allah grants him tawfeeq to incline towards Him. When he reaches seventy years, all those in the Heavens begin to love him and, when he reaches eighty years, Allah records his good deeds and forgives his sins. When he reaches ninety years of age then Allah forgives all his past and future sins and grants him the right to intercede on behalf of members of his family and accepts his intercession. His title (henceforth) is Ameen'ullah and Aseer'ullah fil ardh (i.e. Allah's Prisoner on earth because at this age generally a person's strength weakens and the sense of pleasure diminishes...his days pass like those of a prisoner). When he reaches the zenith of life then all the good deeds which he used to perform in good health and strength are written in his records. And should any sin be committed then they are not recorded.' (Musnad Ahmad, Ma'āriful Qur'ān, p242, Vol. 6)

Menopause usually occurs at a time when most women also experience changes in responsibilities at home; when the children have grown-up and are in the process of leaving the mother's nest; and when the middle-aged couple are generally less inclined towards sex. As the circumstances, personality and outlook of each woman differs, so does their apparent ability to cope with menopause.

For some, there is absolutely no noticeable difference in their lifestyle...just the gradual stopping of monthly periods. Others may notice irregular periods over two years before final stoppage. Most women however will notice minor physical and emotional changes.

Nowadays, some women fall prey to hallucinations. Instead of changing one's diet, outlook, exercise and seeking medical treatment from a doctor and being concerned with spiritual reformation, many ladies head for the nearest practitioner of *taweez* (talisman) and seek his paid services under the illusion they have succumbed to or are the victims of witchcraft or the jinni. Understand well, according to pious and senior scholars with knowledge of this field, in almost 99.9% of cases there are no supernatural causes connected to menopause. The causes are either physical, i.e. medical or psychological and therefore, Inshã'Allah, curable. Of the remaining 0.1%, the majority of victims themselves acted with impropriety providing an opportunity for others to harm them. Should one resort to practising the daily Sunnah du'aa's then, Inshã'Allah one will find relief and cure from all worries.

What are the Symptoms of Menopause?

- Dryness and infection of the vagina and pain during intercourse.
- Loss of libido and mood swings. Emotionalism.
- Incontinence ~ the need to frequently pass urine and sometimes inability to control urine.
- Dry hair/skin, generalised itching and hot flushes (a

sudden sensation of uncomfortable heat).

- Constant tiredness, headaches, aches, pains, insomnia (irregular sleep) and night sweat. Weight gain.

How to Cope with Menopause?

The best way of treating menopause is to positively regard it as part and parcel of life and to change your outlook and lifestyle. With advice from your doctor, alter your diet and exercise program.

- Eat plenty of fruit, vegetables, cereals, pulses, wholemeal bread and chapatti.
- Ensure sensible portions of semi-skimmed milk and low-fat dairy products (the body needs 1500 mg of calcium per day).
- Avoid fatty foods (red meat and ghee) and select white meat, fish and; cook in olive oil. Drink plenty of water.

Physical Exercise

The best form of exercise is to go for walks (suitably dressed in hijāb/comfortable footwear) with your husband for 30 minutes a day. Invest in a good exercise bicycle (for 'rainy' days) and draw up a training schedule which you are able to maintain daily. Try and remain physically active instead of sitting and brooding. Even when there are others at home to undertake domestic tasks; learn and adjust to become helpful and supportive without becoming over-assertive. Take an interest in gardening. For the sake of pleasing your husband, be concerned and maintain your figure, appearance, beauty and attractiveness. Do not become plump or overweight. Strictly control what you eat.

Spiritual Exercise

Ensure you are punctual with *tahārat* (physical purity), salāh, saum, zakāt and perform hajj if it is compulsory upon you. Daily recite a portion of the Glorious Qur'ān and the Tasbeeh-e-Fātimah ﷺ after every Fardh Salāh. Make the Hereafter your main concern because Allah ﷻ fills the heart of such a person with contentment and independence. With the willing consent and knowledge of your husband, if possible, establish a spiritual link with a pious, qualified and authentic Shaykh and strictly follow his teachings. Try and spend your free time in studying authentic Islāmic books/deeni lectures and in wholesome activities. Save yourself from all sins; especially the TV, gheebat (backbiting) and the company of the wicked. Adopt Sharee' purdah. Do not pine away the final years of your life initiating customs; moaning, winging and being unreasonable towards juniors (especially daughter-in-laws). Treat all children/grandchildren equally. Be cordial and on good terms with relatives and neighbours. Allow trivial differences to pass and let bygones be bygones.

What is Hormone Replacement Therapy (HRT)?

Hormone replacement therapy (HRT) is the medical way of treating many of the symptoms of menopause by replacing some of the hormones the body no longer produces with oestrogen and progestogen. It is only possible under the supervision of a medical doctor as there is substantial risk of side-effects: cancer of the womb and especially of the breasts; headaches and mood changes. HRT should only be taken for as long as it is absolutely necessary.

Chapter Ten

Advice for the Muslim Wife & Mother

Based upon the Teachings of
Shaykh Ashraf 'Ali Thānwi ৠ

Rasoolullah ৠ commented,
'To view (your own) beautiful wife and greenery
is a means of strengthening one's vision.' *(Kanzul 'Ummal)*

Shaykh Sa'dee ৠ states in Bustān, 'A pious,
faithful and beautiful Muslim lady will make even an
impoverished husband into a king!'

Rank of the Husband

haykh Ashraf 'Ali Thānwi ☙ advises, 'Allah ☙ has blessed a high rank and many rights of the husband. His happiness and pleasure (in lawful avenues) is a great *ibaadah* (worship), whilst his (justified) displeasure is a grave sin. Nabee ☙ commented,

1) *'Whichever lady performs the five Fardh Salāh; fasts the month of Ramadhān; protects her chastity and honour; and obeys her husband, may enter Jannah by whichever portal she desires.'* (Mishkhāt)

2) *'A women who dies whilst her husband is pleased with her will enter Jannah.'* (Tirmidhi)

3) *'If I had to order anyone to make Sajdah for another person, I would have commanded the wife to make Sajdah for her husband...'* (Mishkhāt)

4) *'When a husband calls his wife for his need, then of a surety she should tend to him...even if she is engaged in cooking (at the stove).'* (p 50, Islāmic Weddings)

5) *'Whenever any wife vexes her husband in this world; those Hûrs (Heavenly Maidens) who are to become his wives come Qiyāmah speak out, 'May Allah destroy you, do not vex him! He is your guest for only a few days, he will be coming to us soon.'* (ibid.)

6) *'There are three types of persons whose Salāh is not accepted nor does any of their good deeds rise (towards heaven)...(Amongst these three, one is), 'A women whose husband is angry with her.'*

Naseehat for Wives

How to live with one's Husband

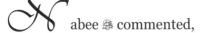abee 🌸 commented,

> *'The best of women is she who makes her husband feel happy when he glances at her; she obeys him when he instructs her and she does not oppose him in regard to herself and her wealth by doing what he dislikes.'*

(Baihaqee)

Shaykh Ashraf 'Ali Thānwi 🌸 advises, 'Understand well, the relationship between husband and wife is a life-long affair. If both their hearts remain united...then there is no greater *nemat* (bounty). But Heaven forbid, should discord settle between both, then there is no greater misery. Therefore, as far as possible, try to capture and win his heart by acting upon his facial expressions, to the extent that should he command one to stand with arms folded the whole night or call daytime as night time, you would be willing to accept his tantrum.

Never say or commit any act contrary to his temperament. Many wives blurt out just anything; jibes, insults, etc., without thinking...thus planting seeds of abhorrence or dislike in their husband's heart. Thereafter they go around crying and complaining of his indifference...remember well, once the damage has been done, any attempt to reconcile will never cover the 'scars' in his heart. When again any disagreement arises...the 'old wound' will reappear in his mind, 'she said or did so and so...' Therefore, from the beginning, endeavour to live with your husband on good loving sensible terms...in this is both the Pleasure of Allah ﷻ and His Rasool ﷺ and; your dunyā and Ãkhirah are secured. Intelligent wives do not need to be lectured to...they themselves are able to discern between what is appropriate or not. Nevertheless, a few advises are mentioned; when these are fully understood, they will, Inshā'Allah make clear more delicate issues.

Recognizing the Husband's Temperament

Always act or speak after recognizing your husband's temperament (his disposition, character and moods). Should you find him in a pleasant humorous mood...engage him in light-hearted talk and jokes. Should he be sombre, then treat him accordingly. React in accordance to his personality (and note, each person differs...it is up to you to fathom and win your husband).

Remember well, the husband-wife relationship is not one of only love, play and humour...it is also necessary to couple love with respect for one's husband. To try to think of him as one's equal is a grave mistake. Never ever ask him to physically serve you (it is, of course, quite another aspect for him to act in accordance with the Sunnah of Nabee ﷺ and help you). Even if he should lovingly come and massage your head and feet...politely, ask him not to take the trouble...Why? Because would you prefer your father to physically serve you? Do remember a husbands' rank is higher than one's father. (Of course, if he insists out of love and concern, there is nothing wrong, for he is your lover, but do not be so audacious as to ask him to physically serve you). In brief, at all times maintain his respect and rank.

To ask for more than his means

Do not ask for anything more than your husbands means. Whatever he provides...(no matter how modest)...gladly accept as your lot. Should you desire some clothes or jewellery; consider carefully whether your husband will be able to afford it (before asking). If he is unable to provide, do not pine away, jibe or present a gloomy face. Always ponder, 'If I ask at an inopportune moment he will think, 'She just does not understand...asking at totally wrong occasions!" Even if your husband is wealthy, as far as possible do not request...of course when he himself asks, there is no harm in informing. Remember, by asking a person lowers his esteem...'

Gratitude for items your Husband brings

Whenever your husband brings anything...irrespective of whether it is to your liking or not, always express happiness with his choice. Never ever find fault...you will break his heart and he will forever be reluctant to bring something for you. Should you wisely accept with joy even the little he brings, his heart will gladden and he will be more inclined to bring items of greater value.

Never ever express your ingratitude when in anger... 'Just what have I seen in this house except unhappiness and difficulties all the time!' Such statements totally remove your respect from his heart. It appears in Hadeeth, that our beloved Nabee ﷺ commented:

> 'O assembly of women! Give charity, for indeed, I
> have seen you to be the majority of the inmates of the
> Fire (Hell).' Someone asked; 'O Rasoolullah ﷺ why?'
> Nabee ﷺ replied, 'You curse in abundance and you
> are ungrateful to your husband.'

Even if you have to undergo poverty and want, never complain; always remain joyful and contented. Observing this patience of yours: not only will your husband feel happy and indebted to you; his heart will be in your hand!

Similarly, whenever your husband returns from a journey (and to a lesser extent also from work), always ask into his health...how was the journey, his stay, etc. Massage him, cuddle him, kiss him, and prepare his meals for him: i.e. see to his comfort. Do not mention money, bills or ask of what he has brought for you. He will, of a surety, present what he had so lovingly brought for you in due time.

Domestic Chores

You should endeavour to keep all your husbands' possessions and household items as a trust and in order. The house should be kept neat and tidy. All bedding and laundry should be regularly cleaned and replaced in their pre-arranged places. To act only when he comments is no big achievement. Success is to organize all domestic chores upon one's initiative without him having to prompt you. By relieving the husband from domestic worries, his heart and mind will become contented and forever indebted to you.

Silence is Golden & the Key to Marital Bliss

Nowadays, many husbands make the error of erupting and losing control over trivialities; wives thereafter compound the issue by answering back. They refuse to keep quiet; this is one of the main reasons for marital conflict. Some husbands become irritable upon return from work in the evening, for whatever reason, whether rightly or wrongly, and an intelligent wife should learn to read the 'storm signals' and react accordingly. If he appears perplexed, stop whatever you are doing and welcome him home. Smile, sit and sympathise with him. Help him unwind.

A venerable scholar narrated, 'A lady once came to a Shaykh and requested a *taweez* (talisman) whereby her husband, who was always quarrelling would live with her in peace. The Shaykh ordered a bottle of water be given to her with the instructions that she keeps a mouthful of this water in her mouth whenever she be with her husband. Under no circumstances is she to swallow or throw the water out in his presence.

Accordingly, whenever the husband came home from work, she would place this water in her mouth. The husband would exchange greetings, sit down to eat and thereafter rest. None of the usual arguments or dispute. Surprised and delighted, after a short time she informed the Shaykh of this 'miraculous' cure and requested to know what he had recited upon the water. The Shaykh informed her, 'I have recited nothing! When you arrived and complained of your husbands' excesses, I immediately realized your problem:

for every one word your husband ever spoke you replied with ten! Thus by asking you to keep water in your mouth, your habit of excessive talking was curbed...and this is why your husband no longer disputes with you.' Many women despoil their marriages by talking too much, rudely answering back and speaking at the wrong time and without thinking. Our beloved Nabee 🌸 said, 'He who maintains silence has attained salvation.'

Inappropriate talk - a classic example

Shaykh Ashraf 'Ali Thānwi 🌸 advises, 'Reducing speech does not mean reduction in such talk which is necessary. However, it means shunning useless and inappropriate speech, even if such talk happens to be lawful.

Once a young lady was about to marry. Her mother (aware of her daughter's habit of speaking nonsense) advised at the time of leaving, 'When you go to your in-laws, for heavens sake keep quiet, do not say anything!' Accordingly when she arrived at her in-laws, she sat there motionless. Surprised and puzzled, her mother-in-law asked, 'Dear, why do you not speak?' The new bride replied, 'My mother told me not to speak at the in-laws!' 'If so then your mother is a fool, of course you should speak!' replied her mother-in -law. 'Should I really speak?' 'Do speak dear...this is your new home.' 'Well, I would like to ask...if your son dies and I become a widow, will you keep me sitting here or will you remarry me?' The flabbergasted mother-in-law replied, 'Your mother was quite correct, you should just not speak at all!'

How to win your Husband

$\mathcal{Q}\mathcal{S}$ haykh Ashraf 'Ali Thānwi 🌿 related, 'Remember well, Allah 🌿 has created men as dominating. (Women) cannot overcome him by pressure or force. To confront him by displaying anger is the height of folly. Although one may not discern any harms, only when the damage has been done will a wife notice and suffer the effects of her harshness. Yet, the easiest way to win or control him is to appease and obey him (in all halāl ways).' A wife should not remain satisfied upon only fulfilling the huqooqs of her husband. She should capture his heart by endeavouring to keep him as happy as possible.

What to do when one's Husband is Angry

Whenever your husband becomes displeased or angry with you, for whatever reason, irrespective of who is at fault, never sulk, display anger, let loose a mouthful or withdraw. Adopt humility and apologize, even when he is clearly at fault...in this noble way the situation will be 'defused' and ended. Never resort to lies or excuses to cover up one's shortcomings or faults; for he will lose faith in you. Thereafter, even when you do speak the truth, he will mentally question your motive.

Should your husband become angry and start shouting: keep quiet, do not say a word or do anything, just sit down and listen. By adopting this beautiful patient response, just observe how shameful he becomes once his anger cools and how much more he will respect and love you! By adopting silence when he is angry, his courage to ever again display anger will, Inshā'Allah break.

Huqooq's of one's Husband

For a Muslim wife, these are the huqooq's (rights') of her husband:

1) Always remember he is your Crown. At all times please and obey him as long as no sin is involved.

2) Without his permission do not perform *nafl* salāh or *nafl* saum (fasts).

3) Do not request or seek expenses beyond his means.

4) Do not allow anybody into your home without his permission nor leave home without his permission.

5) Do not give of his wealth and belongings without his permission.

6) Should he beckon you to make love, then do not refuse unless there is a Sharee' reason; *haidh, nifaas,* (ill health), etc.

7) Do not consider your husband inferior because of his poverty or appearance.

8) Should you observe any wrong Sharee' habits in your husband, advise him with respect (and always make du'aa for him).

9) Never call him by his name nor abuse or speak above him. Do not complain of your husband to others.

10) Do not dispute or wrangle with his relatives. Regard your husband's parents' as your elders and treat them especially with respect.

Family Ties & Squabbles

*R*asoolullah ﷺ commented,

'O people! You should be aware of your relatives to the extent that you are able to perform silah-ê-rahmee (loving kind relationships) with them. (For example, your parents, grandparents, uncles, aunts, cousins, should all be known by name). Because by means of silah-ê-rahmee, love is created and maintained between relations; barakat and expansion appears in wealth; and one's age is increased.'

(Tirmidhi, quoted in *Uswa Rasool Akram* ﷺ, p 410)

A Muslim wife should, as far as possible aid, serve and treat her father and mother-in-law like her own parents. Nevertheless, this is no license for husbands to assume and consider it a 'good fortune' for their wife to act as some personal servant and slave to his mother. This is one of the excesses and *zulm* some wives suffer. It is not at all compulsory for wives to serve their mother-in-laws. Should the husband desire this blessing, let *him* serve or provide a paid servant. Should the husband wish his wife to be of service to his other relatives without any real reason of helplessness...then it is not at all necessary for the wife, for example, to cook food or prepare clothes for others, etc. However, should there be a genuine need, it is best she carries out these acts (to the best of her ability and resources) so as to please her husband.

Aboo Hurairah ﷺ relates, 'A person once came to Nabee ﷺ and asked, 'O Rasoolullah ﷺ, I have a few relatives who respond with me in a very distressing manner. Whilst I treat them with kindness and goodness, they reciprocate with ignorance and aloofness towards me!' Rasoolullah ﷺ commented:

> *'If reality is as you have stated, then you are putting hot ashes into their mouths (i.e. your kindness becomes harãm for them and is transformed into their stomach as Fire). Allah Ta'ãlã will always help you over them as long as you stay steadfast on this approach (of silah-ê-rahmee) with them.'*

(Muslim, quoted in ibid., p 410)

Rasoolullah ﷺ commented,
'Allah Ta'ãlã says, 'My Name is Allah; My Name is Rahman; I have attributed My Name to Rah'm (Mercy). Whomsoever enjoins (love and mercy amongst relatives) I shall endear him, and whomsoever will perform qatah rahmee (break relationships) I too shall break him!'

(Tirmidhi quoted in ibid.)

Shaykh Ashraf 'Ali Thãnwi ﷺ narrates, 'Live with all your in-laws with respect and friendliness from the beginning. Remember that squabbling amongst women although not (often violent) is nevertheless characterized by disunity over a longer period. Men possess agitation in their temperament: they thereby turn hostile and violent quickly when angered. Women by comparison, are restrained and more modest; they therefore are more likely to express their anger (no less in intensity) by...seething time consuming *keenah* (malice), screaming and jealousy.

Whenever women argue, they have the tendency to regurgitate 'old wounds and scores,' which only serves to inflame petty issues into all-out hostility. This is why the anger of women is the cause of a thousand sins...men become agitated and erupt easily and thereafter cool down, not so women, their anger is the slow bubbling type. In addition, most women suffer from *gheebat* (backbiting)...they readily indulge in this sin and remain in anticipation of hearing *gheebat* from others...especially from neighbours and visitors. Understand well, this *gheebat,* a major sin; inflames disunity, hatred and infighting. Upon the slightest pretext, women have the habit of brooding...there is probably no home wherein women are not involved in this: mother fighting against daughter; daughter-in-law against mother-in-law; and (it appears) as if sister-in-laws were created precisely for this purpose (to squabble)!

The overwhelming arguments within families are due to suspicions. It never occurs to our ladies to 'clear the air.' This is the praiseworthy method...to ask one's acquaintance if one is aware of some real suspicion, 'My heart harbours such and such a thought or complaint, is it true?' Remember, to act or pass judgement on hearsay is both ignorance and totally against the Sharee'ah. There are always two sides to any story or argument and intelligent people always inquire.

Allah ﷻ mentions in the Glorious Qur'ān:

'O you who believe! If a fāsiq (liar - evil person) comes to you with news, verify it, lest you should harm people in ignorance, and afterwards you become regretful for what you have done.'

'O you who believe! Avoid much suspicion; indeed some suspicions are sins. Moreover do not spy nor backbite one another. Would one of you like to eat the flesh of his dead brother? You would hate it (therefore hate gheebat).' (49:6 & 12)

Rasoolullah ﷺ commented,
'Beware of suspicions, for suspicion is the worst of false tales; and do not look for the faults of other's; do not spy upon one another; do not overbid one another nor be jealous of one another; do not hate one another and do not desert (stop talking to) one another. O Allah's worshippers (Muslims)! Be brothers!'   (Bukhāri, Vol. 8, No. 92)

Ladies (especially) should learn to let 'matters' rest, many a marriage and home would then be saved from heartbreaking disputes and divorce. Remember, our elders often commented, 'Glassware placed next to each other always rattles!' It is just natural to have differences and sometimes disputes within homes and families. But, nowadays, what we are witnessing is the incomprehensible habit of lengthening the most trivial dispute into all-out fraternal warfare and divorce!

Therefore, men should never follow the 'tales' of women blindly. In addition, it is compulsory for women never to keep instigating such conversations, which flare up their men's anger. Whenever one hears a complaint (from anybody), always ponder, 'Maybe this person is relating one 'truth' mixed with ten lies.'

Power or Control over the Weak

$\mathcal{S}$haykh Ashraf 'Ali Thānwi ﷺ narrates, 'Many a times, women, through unforeseen circumstances (such as death of a relative or divorce) have to foster other members of the family. This may entail the upbringing of, say a brother-in-law's orphaned children (or a weak and frail mother-in-law). As husbands are usually out working, it devolves upon lady of the household to supervise and see to their everyday needs at home. Some women take their hatred and dislike for the husband's relatives out on these orphaned children at their mercy. They constantly abuse, scold, deprive and disgrace these defenceless weak people and not contented; relate incorrect and false reports and lies of them upon her husbands' return home. Therefore, men should make proper inquiries and act intelligently. Nowadays some Muslims have become so selfish, ungrateful and uncaring; they will not hesitate to ape other cultures and even dump aged parents into 'old people's homes' and mental asylums...under some fictitious pretext of depression. Ladies, if they so wish, are able to stop this evil development within our community by insisting weak relative's stay at home under their supervision and care. Despite our drift from Deen, Muslim ladies are still synonymous for being caring, affectionate and always willing to sacrifice their comfort and rest for the sake of other relatives and little one's.

How a Muslim Wife should live at home

Many couples, after the initial 'honeymoon' period of their marriage make the mistake of taking each other for granted. Couples fail to see the numerous good features and qualities in their spouse and living in era where lack of purdah and TV is the norm fail to appreciate the beauty of each other. The wife who initially appeared as a 'gorgeous queen' and the answer to the husbands dream now appears ordinary. Shaykh Ashraf 'Ali Thānwi ❁ advised, 'The Sharee'ah commands that a wife adorns herself for her husband and she receives thawāb for this. Nowadays the majority of women live at home like tramps (scruffy), yet when the time arrives to depart elsewhere, they adorn themselves from head to foot. This is indeed surprising and shameful...*'Earns the husband; whilst enjoys the fruit others; what justice is this?'* Similarly, wives will seldom talk sweetly with their husbands, but with others, enticing soft tones and body language are employed, Moreover, should any lady be honest and courageous enough to beautify herself for her husband, other's mock and ridicule her... 'What! Has she no shame? Look how she dolls up for her husband!'

'There was a pious Muslim lady who every night after Esha Salāh would beautifully dress up for her husband...the finest clothes, jewellery, hairdo, make-up, etc., and thereafter approach her husband and ask him lovingly, 'Do you wish to make love?' Whenever he desired her, she would happily go to sleep with him. When he wished to rest, she would seek his permission to worship Allah ﷻ. After receiving her husbands permission, she would remove her finery, wear clean simple clothes and spend the whole night in *ibaadah*. Observe how this noble pious lady adopted both beauty and simplicity in one night...anybody observing her in her finery would question, 'How can she be pious in this adorned state?' But who was aware of her *niyyat* (intention)...she did not beautify herself for her *nafs* (self) rather because the Sharee'ah commands a wife to beautify herself for her husband and for which she receives *thawāb*. The pious adopt or forgo beauty with the Command of Allah ﷻ and not for the sake of their *nafs*.'

When a Husband is having an affair

Shaykh Ashraf 'Ali Thãnwi < narrates, 'Muslim wives should not accuse (their husbands) on the slightest pretext or suspicions, 'You are very mild towards so-and-so or you keep visiting so-and-so's residence, why do you go there for? etc.' Should the husband be totally innocent, such accusations will deeply hurt him and, Heaven forbid, if these suspicions are true and his habits are corrupt, remember by angrily nagging, threatening or abusing him...you will only worsen the situation and end up driving him further away from you. Ponder, will your harshness cause him to give up this illicit relationship? To turn him away from such a disastrous evil, you will need to react wisely and with patience. When in private, calmly and softly remind him of the harms: Inshã'Allah, the day he is blessed with Tawfeeq to repent, he will appreciate your kind, loving and caring support and become your slave. Allah ﷻ Forbid, but should he fail to heed your sincere advice, adopt *sabr,* maintain du'aa and turn towards Allah ﷻ. Never try to disgrace him by nagging, displaying anger or mentioning his evil to others...this will only make him more obstinate and incline him further towards the other woman. If you insist on angrily confronting and disgracing him...you will inevitably end up losing whatever hold and influence you had over him. He will stop talking and there will remain nothing for you but tears.' People often get entangled in affairs because of dissatisfaction with their spouse's failure to meet an important emotional need; many a times it is due to a lack of understanding and ability to communicate.

Shaykh Ahmad Sadeeq Desai *hafizahullah* advises, 'The husband involved with another women is emotionally disturbed. (A harsh attitude by his wife) will convince him that the other women possess qualities of love and charm, which his wife lacks. Her fighting attitude, which wives usually display when they hear of their husbands' extra-marital affairs, will make her appear as a hag and a witch to him. Her harsh confrontation with him will eliminate any guilt feelings, which he had hitherto cherished in his heart. He will now (falsely) feel that the other woman is offering him love and happiness, which he cannot obtain from his wife. An intelligent wife, who desires to salvage her husband and keep intact her marriage, will not allow the situation to deteriorate to this level.'

The Wife's Smile & Gaiety

R asoolullah ﷺ commented,

'Do not despise even the smallest of virtue, even though meeting with one's brother in a state of happiness is also a virtue.'

Amongst the bounties of Allah ﷻ, one great favour is the blessings of a happy and smiling face. There is no greater nemat for a household than to see the 'Queen and hostess' of the residence forever joyful and affectionate towards her husband, children and mahram relatives/visitors. This one blessing is enough to enliven the heart of the gloomiest person.

It is part of human psychology for a person to be affected by the moods of those around him. The heart is enlivened when it observes another human smiling, laughing and happy. Notice how a gloomy and stubborn child (even an adult) walking into a room full of playful children immediately changes colour. Therefore, the wife should always be aware of her role and responsibility and remain optimistic and smiling. Women are able to do this for a large part of the working day when sitting behind the reception and sales desk for others, even when having to deal with the most obstinate, rude and uncultured person; accordingly, this is ample testimony to their ability and power of influence. Doctors have for long described gaiety and happiness as one of the alchemies for good health and it also assists in food digestion.

Reciting the Glorious Qur'ān

uslim homes nowadays are devoid of happiness and blessings. Why? Firstly, failure by the overwhelming majority of Muslims to pray Fajr Salāh. Secondly, open indulgence in sins. Thirdly, reluctance to recite the Glorious Qur'ān. In bygone times, anybody passing a Muslim locality after Fajr time would be only too aware of the sound of Qur'ānic recitation. In fact, mothers would refuse to serve breakfast until children had read a portion of the Glorious Qur'ān because the zakāt of 'ilm is *amal* (practice). Despite lavish furnishings, our homes have become graveyards. Allah ﷻ has taken away *barakat* from those Muslim homes wherein the Glorious Qur'ān is not recited. The income of the head of the household, which was sufficient to meet the needs of his family, parents, other needy ones and causes is no longer able to cover his own expenses. Even with everybody 'going-out' to work, there is always 'never enough.' *Barakat* means, the amount that the head of the household earns, is more than sufficient to see to the needs of everyone he is responsible for. The small salary of the late Shaykh Mufti Shafee' ﷺ would see to the needs of his immediate family, his widowed mother and the family of his widowed sister.

Another grave mistake in our household is the habit of throwing away quite edible left-overs which could easily have been re-served or at the very least left for birds to eat. Remember well, once rizq is lifted away from a household, it never returns.

Chapter Eleven

Advice For the Muslim Husband

haykh Maseehullah Khān ﷺ narrated, 'The great Scholar 'Abdullah ibn Mubārak ﷺ (741-804 CE) was once standing outside the Jāme Masjid in Baghdad observing the multitude of people leaving after Jumu'ah Salāh. Smiling, he commented; 'They are all People of Jannah...however there are only one or two insān (gentlemen) amongst them!'

True manliness implies the chivalrous manner in which one conducts oneself whereby neither physically, orally, mentally, emotionally or financially another is harmed or inconvenienced. A stage further in being of comfort is to tolerate the inconvenience and indiscreetness of others. This is why Shaykh Ashraf 'Ali Thānwi ﷺ used to say, 'If you wish to become a Mufti, a Gauth or Abdal go elsewhere. Yes, if you wish to become an insān come to me...and understand well, to become an insān is difficult.'

Advice for Husbands

Allah ﷻ Says in the Glorious Qur'ãn:
'And live with them (women) in a beautiful manner. If then you are displeased with them, (then know) perhaps you dislike something wherein Allah has created abundant goodness in it.' (4:19)

'Indeed, there is for you in the Rasool of Allah, a beautiful model (character, way, style) - for him who has hope (in meeting) Allah and the Last Day.'

Rasoolullah ﷺ commented,
'The Mu'min with the most perfect Imãn is one who has the best character and who is the kindest to his wife.'

'The Mu'min (husband) should not harbour enmity for his wife. If he dislikes something in her, then surely, he will be pleased with another quality in her.' (Muslim)

'Whoever has been given four things, indeed, he has been given the best of the world and the Ãkhirah: a grateful heart; a tongue engaged in thikr, a body patient in adversity and a wife who does not betray him, neither with regard to herself nor his wealth.'

(Miskhãt)

'O people! Fear Allah with regards to your wives. You have taken them in your marriage upon aman (pledge) to Allah...and through the very Kaleemah and Command of this same Allah have they become halãl for you...' (Bukhãri, p. 79, Vol. 6. Ma'ãriful Hadeeth)

Huqooq's of Wives

Q*S*haykh Ashraf 'Ali Thãnwi ☸ narrates the following huqooqs of wives:

1) *Husne Khulq,* that is to live with her with love, respect, nobility, kindness, happiness and a good character.

2) To bear patiently (in moderation) her errors, indiscreetness and shortcomings...after all she is but human and dedicated to you.

3) To be modest towards her...that is not to be over suspicious nor be too lax.

4) To adopt moderation in spending upon her...neither adopt *bukhl* (stinginess) nor allow wastage. Also, grant her additional pocket expenses whereby she may purchase personal items.

5) To learn and impart to her all the *farã'idh* (compulsory and necessary) *ahqãms* (rulings) of the Sharee'ah, for example, *aqãeed* (beliefs), Salãh, *haidh* (periods), etc. Just as important is to emphasize and save her from all sins and *bidah* (baseless customs).

6) To make love to her.

7) Not to perform *'azal* (eject semen outside the vagina) without her permission when making love.

8) Not to physically, verbally, emotionally or sexually abuse her or take unfair advantage of her love, dedication and faithfulness.

9) To allow her to meet her *mahram* relatives (father,

mother, brothers, sisters, uncles, aunts) at reasonable intervals and to make sure she is not exposed to non-*mahram*.

10) Not to express intimate details (e.g., how you make love to her) to others.

11) Never to humiliate, abandon or force her out of the house.

12) When there is more than one wife, to treat them all equally.

13) Never ever to divorce her except in the case of severe necessity.

Shaykh Ashraf 'Ali Thānwi ☙ comments, 'Brothers! When Allah ☙ has ordained these rights for women, then who may change them? Understand well, if a man fails to fulfil these *huqooqs* he will be guilty of not upholding *huqooqul ibaad* (rights of creation).

Men should ponder how beautifully Allah ☙ has interceded on behalf of women in the Glorious Qur'ān. Whilst there may be various reasons for being displeased with one's wife, the main reason usually is bad character and this becomes a source of grief for her husband. Nevertheless, Allah ☙ has promised, that even this bad character will become a means of attaining goodness - He is *Hakeem* (All Wise) and able to do anything. For example, she may bear you children who will become the means of your salvation come Qiyāmah...Just ponder how clearly the *huqooqs* of women are emphasized in the Glorious Qur'ān.'

Husne Sûlook (Chivalry)

haykh Ashraf 'Ali Thãnwi ☙ advises husbands, 'Whatever ease and comfort Allah ☙ has granted and which you enjoy; you should choose the same for your wife. This is the teaching of our Sharee'ah, wherever possible provide her with comfort and refrain from burdening her. Grant generous expenses, keep her happy, and tolerate her indiscreetness and shortcomings. Muslim husbands should behave towards their wives in the noble manner shown by our beloved Nabee ☙. Remember, merely providing food and clothing is not her only rights. It is one of her huqooqs that she be kept happy. It appears in a hadeeth:

'Treat women with kindness, for verily their similitude is like prisoners by you...'

(Quoted in *Huqooqe Muaasharat,* p.108)

Indeed that person who is like a prisoner and under your control in every way, to commit any excess upon her is contrary to manliness and chivalry. Keeping her happy means refraining from every such (uncalled for) act that would grieve her. Everybody is aware of the need to provide adequate maintenance and its limits; however, there are no limits (except boundaries of the Sharee'ah) in pleasing her...Remember, our *Fuqaha* (Jurists) have stated that it is permissible to even 'lie' if the sole intention is to please your wife. Ponder, Allah ☙ is here waiving one of His *huqooqs* in order that you may please your wife!

Hijāb is, of course, compulsory upon all Muslim women. Rasoolullah ﷺ stated:

'It is not permissible for a lady to venture outside the home except out of dire necessity.'

(Ahqām-e-Purdah)

However, this should be coupled with the provision of means within the home to keep her happy. Events should not transpire, whereby the husband leaves for Salāh (and other Deeni duties) locking his wife inside with nobody allowed to meet, talk or associate with her.

The Need for Companionship

Do appreciate, whenever a man feels lonely, he does not hesitate to meet his friends and acquaintances...well, to whom are women supposed to turn? Therefore, the husband should make a point of spending reasonable amounts of time with his wife...and should this not be possible, he should allow her good female friends to meet her. Whenever she does complain, even about trivialities; do remember she generally has nobody except you to talk to. Associate her complaints and whims as an indirect informal expression of her love, faith, commitment, dedication and reliance upon you. Many husbands, even those ostensibly 'pious,' punctual in Salāh (and attending lectures, meeting great Ulamā's and going out in Tableegh etc.); but ignorant of the need to keep their wives happy. The very great scholars whom they claim to follow strenuously upheld the Sunnah of keeping their wives happy. This too is an important and binding part of Deen.

haykh Ashraf 'Ali Thānwi ۞ continues, 'This is why, although not passing a *Fatwā*, I sincerely advise that home management and expenditure should remain in the control of either the husband or wife and not be delegated to (other kinfolk, even parents). Otherwise, it is burdensome and unfair for the wife.

Remember, it is not at all wasteful to spend on halāl items, if one is by the means, merely for making one's wife happy. Similarly to buy (delicacies for her, e.g. chocolates, flowers, jewellery, etc.) too is Sadaqāh.

Another important reason for pleasing Muslim women is that they remain in *hijāb*...she should therefore never feel... 'If I were not in *hijāb* like others, I too would be able to do such-and-such, etc.' Therefore, serve her (happily with all your energy and resources) to the extent that she concludes... 'If I were not in *hijāb*, my husband would never serve me in this manner.' In brief, the husband's behaviour should convey a message of ease, comfort and happiness for the lady who remains in *hijāb*...and thereby not incline her towards abandonment of *hijāb*.'

Airs & Whims of Wives - The Example of Ã'ishah ۞

haykh Ashraf 'Ali Thānwi ۞ commented, 'On the occasion of *ifk*' (slander); when the *munāfiqûn* (hypocrites) had made *buhtān* (false accusations) upon Ã'ishah ۞, our Prophet Muhammad ۞ arrived and asked her, 'O Ã'ishah! If you are innocent Allah Ta'ālā will vouchsafe your innocence...and if in reality you have made a mistake then make Taubah and Istighfār to Allah Ta'ālā.'

Ã'ishah ⚘ replied respectfully to Nabee ﷺ:

'If I were to acknowledge, even though Allah is fully aware that I am innocent, will anybody doubt the truth of this slander? Further, if I deny, what, will people ever believe? My condition at present is identical to that of Prophet Yousuf's عليه السلام *father (Yaqoob* عليه السلام*) who (at time of his sons' abduction) uttered, 'My (only) course is beautiful patience.'*

She returned to her bed and started crying. Immediately, signs of the descent of *Wahi* (Divine Revelation) were observable upon the Face of Nabee ﷺ. After a short while he ﷺ spoke, 'O Ã'ishah, listen to the good news, Allah Ta'ālā has announced your innocence!' Thereafter Nabee ﷺ recited the then revealed Ãyah:

'Indeed, those who brought forth the slander (against Ã'ishah ⚘) are a group amongst you. Consider it not a bad thing for you. Nay, it is good for you. Unto every man amongst them will be paid that which he had earned of the sin, and as for him amongst them who had the greater share therein, his will be a greater torment. Why then, did not the believers, men and women, when you heard it (the slander), think good of their own people and say: 'This (charge) is an obvious lie?' (24:11-12)

Hearing these Verses, all Muslims became overjoyed...and Aboo Bakr ⚘ advised Ã'ishah ⚘, 'Go to Nabee ﷺ and thank him.' Her mother also suggested, 'O Ã'ishah! Arise and make salām to Nabee ﷺ.'

Ã'ishah ✿ replied:

> *'By Allah! I shall not get up and go to him...I shall praise none besides Allah ﷻ because You had already concluded me as being impure. It is Allah ﷻ Who has vouchsafed my chastity. Wallah! I shall not get up nor will I thank anybody except Allah ﷻ...for He has revealed my chastity.'*

Ponder, externally this was a severe remark made in front of Nabee ﷺ however, he ﷺ took not the least offence because the 'airs' was from a beloved. Husbands should appreciate these tantrums and whims of wives are because of their love and friendship for you. This is why the Sharee'ah overlooks such apparent disrespect made without (any foul intention). If this was not the case, Nabee ﷺ would have reprimanded Ã'ishah ✿ because in applying the *ahqãms* of the Sharee'ah, he ﷺ was impartial. This maybe gauged from an incident when a Sahãbeeya by the name of Fãtimah ✿ had erred and committed theft. Nabee ﷺ acted in accordance with the Sharee'ah and ordered corporal punishment. People began to plead leniency on her behalf: and decided to send Usãmah bin Zayd ✿, who had been a protégée of Nabee ﷺ. Naively, he proceeded to go and plead, whereupon Nabee ﷺ became angry and spoke:

> *'What! Pleading where hudoods (legal laws and limits) are concerned has destroyed Ummah's before you! Even if it had been Fãtimah, the daughter of Muhammad ﷺ, I would have ordered (the same punishment).'*

Examples of other Mothers of the Believers ﷺ

haykh Ashraf 'Ali Thãnwi ﷺ commented, 'Sometimes, in the household's of our beloved Nabee ﷺ, the Mothers of the Believers ﷺ would become cross (over some domestic issue); whereupon Nabee ﷺ would pacify them.

Once 'Umar ﷺ arrived to find his daughter Hafsah ﷺ speaking in a loud tone to her husband Nabee ﷺ. Aghast, 'Umar ﷺ reprimanded her, 'What, have you no fear? Imitating other women, you too have commenced talking loudly in front of Nabee ﷺ. Remember you will destroy yourself!' However, these noble Mothers of the Believers ﷺ knew full well that Nabee ﷺ would not be offended in the least, whereas for others to speak in such a tone was a major sin as described in the Glorious Qur'ãn:

> *'O you who believe! Raise not your voices above the voice of the Prophet (ﷺ), nor speak aloud to him in talk as you speak aloud to one another, lest your deeds should be rendered fruitless whilst you perceive not.' (49:2)*

Similarly, on another occasion Aboo Bakr Siddeeq ﷺ was just about to enter...when he overheard Ã'ishah ﷺ shouting at Nabee ﷺ. Infuriated, he entered and addressed his daughter, 'I have heard you shouting at Rasoolullah ﷺ.' (He was just about to strike her, when Nabee ﷺ stopped him). After his departure, Nabee ﷺ told Ã'ishah ﷺ 'Observe how I saved you, otherwise you would have been punished.'

Once Nabee ﷺ addressed Ã'ishah ﷺ, 'I know when you are

displeased with me.' She asked, 'Rasoolullah ﷺ, how?'

'When you are pleased, in your conversation you mention 'Never, by oath of the Creator of Muhammad ﷺ!' and when you are unhappy you say, 'Never, by oath of the Creator of Ibrãheem ﷺ!'

Ã'ishah ؓ replied, 'Quite true, but Rasoolullah ﷺ even in anger I only omit your name by mouth never by heart!' In the same way that Nabee ﷺ loved Ã'ishah ؓ, she too was equally in love with him ﷺ. She once recited a couplet:

'Had the ladies, who vilified Zulaikhah ﷺ, witnessed the Countenance of Nabee ﷺ, then instead of cutting fingers, without doubt, they would have torn their hearts out!'

Therefore, tantrums of wives when they become cross are merely an indirect expression of love, which the husband should be manly enough to accommodate. This too is a Sunnah. Remember, Nabee ﷺ once even ran a race with Ã'ishah ؓ...who was younger in age and lightly built. On this first occasion, she ran ahead and won. Some years later, they again ran...but this time Nabee ﷺ won, because now Ã'ishah ؓ was much heavier...ladies naturally put on weight much quicker...and when Nabee ﷺ ran ahead he called out, 'This is in return for the last time!'

Subhãn'Allah! What great behaviour and *tãleem* for the Ummah; that whatever the age difference between the couple, the husband should always take into consideration natural desires and wishes of his wife and be lofty enough to accommodate them within limits of the Sharee'ah.

Paradise at Home

haykh Ashraf 'Ali Thãnwi ﷺ narrates, 'There are (also) many worldly benefits in keeping one's wife happy and in comfort. Firstly, life becomes pleasing...both then sincerely appreciate the joys and concerns of each other. Mutual understanding, love and respect transforms this earthly existence into delight. What greater joy than for a fatigued husband to return home from a days toil and have his heart lifted by the sweet voice of his wife? She provides him with comfort; he should therefore constantly think of her well being. Once Aswar ﷺ requested Ã'ishah ﷺ, as to how Nabee ﷺ behaved at home. She replied:

> *'He would assist his wives in their housework...mending his shoes, sewing his clothing and undertaking housework as ordinary people amongst you do...He ﷺ did not act like a master at home. He would milk goats himself.'*

(Reported from Bukhãri & Tirmidhi in *Hayãtul Muslimeen*, p. 80)

Those who are fortunate to live such married lives are indeed experiencing Paradise in this world. This is the secret behind the *Awliya's* attempts to keep their wives happy...so that life becomes sweet. Commented Nabee ﷺ,

> *'When a man enters his home cheerfully, Allah creates, as a result of his happy attitude, an angel who engages in Istighfãr on behalf of the man until the Day of Qiyãmah.'* (Az-Zaujus Sãlih, p.52)

In whichever home there are disputes and quarrels daily, life becomes miserable. After the rigours of work, one returns home to worry and gloom: what kind of existence is this? But then this has become the order of the day...wisdom, nobility and good sense have disappeared.'

Noble Example of Nabee 🕌

*P*rophet Muhammad 🕌 commented, *'Four matters are such that whomsoever has been blessed with them has undoubtedly received the goodness of this world and the Hereafter:*

1) Such a heart which is grateful;

2) Such a tongue which makes thikr (remembers Allah 🕌);

3) Such a body which is patient upon difficulties;

4) Such a wife who is not a misfortune with regards to his heart and wealth.'   *(Mishkhāt)*

🕌haykh Maseehullah 🕌 commented, 'Nabee 🕌 taught us both Deen and *dunyā*. Ã'ishah 🕌 relates of how Nabee 🕌 would lie down with his head in her lap. He 🕌 would also share a drinking cup with her as well as eat from the same meat joint where she had eaten.' Shaykh Ashraf 'Ali Thānwi 🕌 commented, 'Whenever Nabee 🕌 visited the cemetery at night, he arose ever so slowly, put on his shoes and departed through the door without making noise. When Ã'ishah 🕌 inquired, he 🕌 replied, 'I left in this manner, thinking you might become frightened if awoken and finding yourself alone.' In complete contrast, when the need arises for 'modern man' to get up at night, the whole house will come to know that the 'giant' has awoken!

You should remember wives undertake great toil and worry in ensuring just your food and clothing alone. Without her, home management would crumble. I often say, 'Should your wives not undertake any of these tasks, merely 'supervise' the management of your home...this in itself would be worthy of a high salary.' If you doubt this claim, consider what high salaries and esteem is given to 'Government Ministers,' who externally themselves do not lift a finger...yet because they are responsible for the duty (of management) are paid huge salaries. Similarly, should wives undertake *only* the responsibility of 'supervising' home management, your mere provision of food and clothing for her would even then be insufficient as reward. In reality, they undertake much more, especially making great sacrifices in upbringing children and ensuring your comfort.'

The Value & Worth of Serving Your Family

Shaykh Ashraf 'Ali Thānwi ❀ narrated, 'Shaykh Junaid al-Baghdadi ❀ had a poor neighbour who toiled all day to support his family. Accordingly, he did not have much spare time for naf'l worship, nevertheless he refrained from sins and fulfilled the compulsory acts of Deen. Both neighbours passed-away. A pious person observed Shaykh Junaid ❀ in a dream and inquired as to how he had fared in the Hereafter, 'Alhamdulillah! I was forgiven and granted a high status in Paradise, but listen, my station is lower than that of my unknown neighbour who although not a prolific worshipper, nevertheless worked to serve halāl to his family!' (p152, Vol. 51, Majālis)

Personal Expenses of the Wife

$\mathcal{M}$any husbands will happily spend money on entertaining their friends and associates; donating large sums to charity; buying flashy cars with extras galore and horrendously expensive personalised number plates but are reluctant to gift even a small allowance to their wives...and when they do buy her anything, it is always grudgingly as if discharging a huge burden. Certain parents and relatives actually encourage and imbue such an attitude and outlook in their male offspring. This wrong notion and attitude in our society needs to be addressed.

$\mathcal{S}$haykh Ashraf 'Ali Thãnwi ☼ narrates, 'It is a moral right of the wife that she be regularly given a separate allowance to spend as she wishes. This 'personal allowance' is totally separate to whatever budget the husband gives to manage home affairs. This 'allowance' should be in accordance to the means of the couple. The husband should make a point of *gifting* this to his wife with love and happiness clearly stating, 'this is your personal allowance, your ownership to spend as you wish.'

Husbands should also appreciate that the amount they provide for managing home affairs (e.g. groceries, clothes, etc.,) is an *amãnat* (trust), whereas this 'personal allowance' is to be a separate gift. Understand well, there are many other expenses involved for a wife: should she not be given a generous personal allowance; she will be helpless to make use of some of these household expenses. This is both unfair, unreasonable and an injustice upon her. It is also worth remembering, that Zakāt upon jewellery owned by the wife is her responsibility, should she regularly receive a reasonable amount, she will be easily able to discharge these Wājibat (Sadaqah-e-Fitrah, Qurbāni).'

At times, a wife wishes to gift money to her juniors, etc. Having to ask her husband every time is embarrassing, accordingly, a personal allowance makes life easy for her.

Nowadays, the trend is for many Muslim ladies to go out to work. They therefore have access to large personal incomes, which they undoubtedly spend upon themselves. In contrast, many of the pious Muslim ladies who stay at home in *hijāb* do not have such large personal allowances at their disposal. The husband should therefore appreciate and acknowledge this dedication of his wife in staying at home by generously and wholeheartedly giving a 'personal allowance' to his wife. This will dispel any notion of being inferior or at a disadvantage in staying at home; for the 'Queen' of the home should be treated in accordance to her rank.

The husband should also refrain from mentioning this allowance whenever the topic of finances or expenditure arises. It should not be viewed as a 'top-up fund' or 'your money' from which the wife is expected to buy necessities for the home. Nor should the husband assume if he undertakes all the shopping, that because his wife does not complain or mention it, she does not require an allowance.

Spiritual Huqooq of Wives

A llah ﷻ says in the Glorious Qur'ān:
'O People of Imān! Save yourselves and your families (wives and children) from the Fire (of Jahannam)...' (66:6)

Q haykh Ashraf 'Ali Thānwi ﷫ narrates, 'In the same way it is necessary to see to the physical necessities of one's wife, children and juniors, similarly by means of Deeni Ilm and *Islāh* (reformation) it is even more important to ensure their spiritual development. Related Nabee ﷺ...

> *'Each person from amongst you is a ruler, overseer and responsible. On the Day of Qiyāmah each one of you will be questioned about your juniors.'* (p194. Islāh)

Nowadays many people regard this responsibility as irrelevant, i.e. they never bother to educate their families in Deeni matters, nor advise them to refrain from sins. Mere provision of food, clothing, housing, jewellery, luxuries, medical aid, etc., i.e. worldly needs, is considered sufficient. They never regard Deeni Huqooqs as their responsibility. For example, upon arriving home, the husband will ask and expect his meals ready and to his taste...if not, his wife will certainly receive his feelings in blunt terms. However, he will never enquire whether she has prayed Salāh or paid Zakāt...and if he does ask, it will be so light-heartedly as not to create any impact on his wife. In fact some husbands are totally uncaring whether their wives ever pray Salāh or pay

Zakãt. This advice does not advocate excess wrath, persecution or physical force. Initially, encourage with tenderness and love, should she not heed, display your unhappiness and sadness. Make available and advise her to read or listen to authentic Deeni material (literature and audio-cassettes by pious Ulamã, be it in English, Urdu or whatever language). Inshã'Allah, this wise approach will have its effects; her knowledge will increase, character improve and a Deeni awareness will dawn upon her.

Should she refuse to read (or listen), the next approach, which is tried and proven, is for you to sit down daily (preferably at a fixed time when the whole family is free) and commence reading aloud *Bahisti Zewar* (or other authentic Deeni literature recommended by Scholars). Try to read from cover to cover ~ a short portion each day. Do not insist upon your wife to sit down and listen...a few days of your self-recitation will prompt her (and others in the family) to come and listen of their own accord. Women are very easily influenced, should you remain steadfast on this approach, Inshã'Allah your wife will quickly reform...and many complaints within the home will end.

Many men complain of their wives lack of Deeni concern and ignorance, however they blissfully overlook their own shortcomings in this regard. Undoubtedly, women too are at fault, but do husbands display the same displeasure when their wives fail to uphold Deeni huqooqs as when they commit errors in cooking and housework? Should the wife cook something too salty a few times, will the husband just sit around and make a passing comment? Of course not, you will undoubtedly unleash such venom that the wife will readily come to know and correct her error. Brothers! Why have you never adopted this stance upon your wife's failure to perform say Salāh? Should she insist in being lax towards Deeni essentials, you may show your displeasure by temporarily:

- Stop sleeping with her, but still sleep in the same house.
- Stop eating the food she has cooked.
- Curtail talking with her to bare essentials.

Shaykh Maseehullah Khān ۞ narrates, 'It is not at all difficult for a husband to make his wife Deeni conscious if he truly wills. He should keep trying and be constant with du'aa. Understand well, one continuously comes across incidents contrary to one's temperament from the wife. Whenever any event takes place displeasing to you, pass it off with soft words,

> *'And say to My servants that they should (only) say kind words...' (17:53)*

> *'The good deed and the evil deed are not alike. Repel the evil deed with one which is better.' (41:34)*

Adopt forbearance; remember good character is a great quality. Nabee ۞ once asked the Sahābāh ۞...

> *'Shall I inform you of something which is better for a person than fasting the whole day and praying the whole night? Good character! It is much greater. Shall I inform you of something even better? To have good character with your wife...to treat her with mildness.'*

Anger & Apes of Wrath!

Allah ﷻ says in the Glorious Qur'ãn:

'Show forgiveness, enjoin what is good and turn away from the foolish. (7:199)

And if an evil whisper comes to you from Shaytãn, then seek refuge from Allah. Indeed, He is All-Hearer, All-Knowing.' (7:200)

Shaykh Maseehullah Khãn ﷫ often used to recite the couplet,

'She who shall be arriving (i.e. one's bride) heralds from the crooked rib (of Adam ﷤) and will speak irrationally. Therefore do not be surprised at her illogical talk; yes, the day she says something intelligent is the occasion to express wonder!'

When a person asked Rasoolullah ﷺ as to what would save him from the Wrath of Allah ﷻ. Nabee ﷺ replied, 'Do not become angry.' (p. 67, Tahzeeb Akhlaaq)

Shaykh Imdãdullah Makki ﷫ stated, 'There is good and bad in every entity...the difference is one of usage whereby it becomes either good or evil. Anger has been created by Allah ﷻ in order to frighten; it possesses the propensity to repel just like a firearm is made to injure. Whether you use the gun to shoot an enemy or friend...on both occasions it will kill. Accordingly, anger in itself is not evil, the fault lies entirely with the user (when he/she misuses it)...'

To Use Anger Correctly & Appropriately

*S*haykh Mufti Taqee Uthmāni *dāmat barakātuhum* relates, 'Allah ﷻ has created anger and a sense of honour whereby should anybody attempt any excess on your Deen, life, wife, children, relatives, friends, wealth, etc., then a person would make use of anger and honour to refute them. However, the Sharee'ah has stipulated limits and occasions for anger so that it is not misused. For example, a father reprimanding the incorrect behaviour of his child; a teacher correcting a student; a Shaykh training his disciple; on such occasions it is sometimes necessary to become angry, why? So that the junior is reformed and under such circumstances anger is praiseworthy...to not employ it would be wrong. The criteria with anger is to employ it within Sharee' limits and to refrain from using it beyond limits of decency.' (p42, Vol. 1, Islāhi)

This is where the services of a Shaykh are required. We all have anger within us, but to differentiate when to use and when to withhold it is only truly possible after establishing a true relationship with a Shaykh and following his treatment and prescription over some time. A general weakness amongst husbands nowadays is their tendency to become angry and scold their wives and children upon worldly trivialities; whereas when grave wrong of the Deen are committed by these very people they are able to bear it. The proof for this claim? Notice how a father is able to tolerate the entire household watching TV and sleeping at the time of Fajr Salāh, yet if they are late for work/school, see how his blood boils. This is the weakness and cowardness within us. Husbands should ponder upon this. Generally, a person will vent his anger only upon someone whom he considers to be weaker. Should a third person, higher in rank or stronger be present, one never displays wrath. Therefore remember, Allah ﷻ is Ever-present and always Supporter of the weak.

Treating Anger

Once a Saint asked Shaytãn, 'Where in the human body do you reside?' He replied, 'When man is happy I live in his heart but when he becomes angry I mount his head!' Consequently, the treatment showed to us by our beloved Nabee ﷺ is a perfect antidote. At times of anger, make ablution, an *ibãdah* whose water overcomes the fiery nature of wrath. Other suggested remedies to cure anger are:

- If standing, sit or preferably lie down, as contact with earth (its tranquil effect) produces calmness in a person.
- Recite *'Aaoozo Billahi*...(I seek protection of Allah from Shaytãn).'
- Drink cold water.
- Divert your attention by engaging in some other activity, especially reading which is very beneficial in eliminating anger.
- Withdraw from the presence of the person who is the target of your anger.
- Keep a sign somewhere prominent and visible in the house on which is written,
  'Remember Allah ﷻ has greater power and authority over you than what you have over anybody!'

Islāmic Outlook of
Middle-Aged Husbands

Allah ﷻ mentions in the Glorious Qur'ān

'Treat your wives with goodness.' *(4:19)*

Rasoolullah ﷺ related,

'The most chivalrous person is he who treats his wife with kindness and overlooks her indiscreetness's.'

(Jāme Sagheer)

Shaykh Ashraf 'Ali Thānwi ﷺ narrated, 'A labourer once purchased meat and other ingredients from his hard-earned income for his family meal. Unfortunately, his wife had added spices in such quantity as to make the dish uneatable. The labourer, a cultured and pious person, merely drank some water, arose and left without commenting thinking, 'if my daughter had mistakenly cooked such a meal I would never wish for my son-in-law to rebuke or display his displeasure. Accordingly, for the Sake of Allah I forgive her.' Many years after this incident, he passed-away, a Scholar observed him in a dream and inquired, 'Brother, how have you fared?' He replied, 'I had many sins but Allah ﷻ stated, 'One day you overlooked the indiscreetness of one of my servants, today, in return, I am Forgiving you.'

'...Do you not love that Allah should Forgive you? And Allah is Oft-Forgiving, Most Merciful.'

(Glorious Qur'ān, 24:22)

haykh Muhammad Hakeem Akhtar *hafizahullah* narrates, 'I wish to comment on a subject wherein we all are guilty of shortcomings; irrespective of whether one is a shaykh, scholar, professional, graduate, businessman or a lay person. The subject is chivalrous behaviour (*husne akhlāq*) with the Creation of Allah ﷻ.

'The perfect Mu'min is he from whose tongue and hands other Muslims (and by implication all of Creation) experience no inconvenience.'   (*Bukhāri*)

'All of creation are from amongst the household (ayal) of Allah, and the most beloved in the Gaze of Allah is he who acts with chivalry towards them.'
(*Mishkhāt, 425*)

The closest friend of Allah ﷻ is he who does not inconvenience creation; he remains sincere with creation; even those who are non-Muslims, i.e. he remains steadfast on the Commands of Allah ﷻ. It is not permissible to stare at or commit adultery with even non-Muslim women. The rights (*huqooq*) of the Creation of Allah ﷻ are binding upon a Muslim. Amongst *huqooq*, ones wife is amongst the foremost claimant. Irrespective of whether she is young, middle-aged, old or reduced to grey hair and wearing dentures, treat her with kindness. When she was young, you loved her immensely, now when she has aged and wrinkled, why hold her in contempt? You have aged together...yesteryear you were physically inclined to love her, now love her for the Sake and Command of Allah ﷻ. When she is tired, feeling down or ill, be of service and merciful unto her.

Whenever Shaykh Rasheed Ahmad Gangohi ﷺ ascertained during his lectures on Bukhãree Shareef that his audience of students had become weary, then to enliven them, he would, with a straight face, relate the same episode over and over again... 'Listen, an old childless couple used to live in Delhi; both affectionately shared a blanket at night. Whenever the old man wished to go to the bathroom, he would ask his wife... 'O Shaykha! I need to visit the toilet?' His wife would reply, 'Yes dear, go and relieve yourself.' Shaykh Gangohi ﷺ would maintain silence after relating this story whereas his students, who included people of the calibre of Shaykh Yahya Khandalvi ﷺ would laugh amusingly.

Some husbands in later years labour under the misgiving that our parents had erred in selecting this spouse for me...'she is not as pretty as she should be...what was my mother thinking about? Did she need an eye test?' He is bemoaning his mother, 'Did she wear the wrong spectacles!' I always claim, your partner has been predestined for you! Nothing happens without the Command of Allah ﷻ. Remain contented with whatever Allah ﷻ has decreed for you. These wives will be made more beautiful than the Damsels (*hür*) of Paradise. Allamah Ãloosee ﷺ writes in *Roohul Ma'ãni* of an occasion wherein *Umm al-Mu'mineen* Umm Salmah ﷺ inquired,

'O Rasoolullah ﷺ! In Paradise, who will be more prettier; damsels (of Jannah) or Muslim wives?'

An intelligent lady becomes aware the day her unfaithful

husband ogles at another female anywhere (what then to say of the daily staring on TV)? For the rest of that day he does not view his wife with the same outlook...his gaze (mood and libido) is always somewhat lowered (hence the ubiquitous need for sildenafil citrate). According to certain *Mashā'ikh*, a Muslim wife blessed with insight (*firāsate saadiqah*) is able to discern acts of betrayal such as ogling and staring at other women from the body odour of her husband and by looking into his eyes. Ample repercussion for the sin of wrongful observation. After viewing *biryani*, lentils (*daal*) appear quite mundane...

'On the day you prepare a dish of daal,

consider it for me a day of death (intiqaal).'

The question from Umm Salmah ♣ in reality was a query on behalf of all women. Rasoolullah ﷺ replied,

'O Umm Salmah! In Paradise, Muslim wives will be made more beautiful than maidens (hur).'

Umm Salmah ♣ inquired, 'Why will this be so?' Rasoolullah ﷺ replied,

'By virtue of their salāh, saum and on account of their acts of worship (ibaadah), Allah will shower His Light (nur) unto their faces.' (Roohul Ma'āni, 126)

The maidens have neither performed salāh, nor fasted, nor been of service to their husbands, nor undergone the pain of birth or the toil of upbringing children. Whilst Muslim women have prayed salāh, fasted, performed Hajj and been of immense service to their husbands, his children, relatives and guests.

This world is an abode of a few days. Ponder, tea at train stations is not of the best quality however it is sufficiently warm and wet to enliven the body and keep it alert. Real tea will be drunk upon arrival home. Similarly, this world is a train station; whichever wife has been destined for us here, persevere with her...in Paradise she will be made more resplendent than a *hur*. Should ones wife not be glamorously beautiful, then do not make it your preoccupation to taunt and belittle her. Ponder, if your daughter was not very pretty, or prone to tantrums, what would you desire? Would you like a son-in-law who disparages? Place your hand on your chest and answer! Would you prefer a son-in-law who abused her either emotionally or physically? 'From whither were you written in my destiny!'

Those of us who have daughters, especially an offspring with an obstinate or short-tempered nature, worry about their well-being before marriage. Friends! Our wives are also the daughters of somebody! If your son-in-law acts indiscreetly towards your daughter; scolds, rebukes or remains aloof from her over some matter...she wishes to talk, but you have retired in a corner with rosary in-hand...even Bayazeed Bustamee ﷺ or Baba Fareeduddeen ﷺ would be ashamed to see you...decide is this what we wish from our son-in-law and for our daughters?

Umm al-Mumineen Ã'ishãh ﷺ describes how whenever Rasoolullah ﷺ arrived home, he entered with a cheerful attitude...his eyes would not be closed in meditation and head lowered as if under the *Arsh*. He fulfilled the rights of those on earth despite responsibility of the Office of Prophethood and concern for the *Ummah.* To approach one's wife with a cheerful disposition is a forgotten Sunnah. Those who are far from Deen enter their homes as gangsters, red-eyes beaming with hostility and on the warpath. Those who are religiously inclined enter as if Khawajah Mueenuddeen Ajmeeri ۞, in deep contemplation residing on another plain unaware of worldly preoccupations. Both lifestyles are at variance with the Sunnah; enter your homes with a joyful outlook and converse with her...

'The most chivalrous person is he whose manners with his wife are the best.'

We laugh and are full of merriment with friends but stay with our wives in a state of woeful mourning, she is in shock, 'O Allah! I was in waiting for him all day, yet come night time he sits here like a stone statue.' Conversing, joking and laughing with her are also acts of worship. To worship all-night and not spend time with her is against even the Sunnah of the Sahābāh. Once a senior Sahābee ۞ visited a younger acquaintance. After a short while, the latter started to get up to pray optional salāh whereupon the senior Sahābee ۞ commented, 'Your guest has a haqq over you, I am your guest, accordingly converse with me.' Thereafter he commented, 'Your wife has a haqq over you, now go and spend time and talk with her.' (Riyadus Sāliheen)

Shaykh Ashraf 'Ali Thānwi ۞ commented, 'Those who vex their wives and do not behave with chivalry towards them and ignore the Command of Allah ﷻ are shameless men!' They are weaker and under your jurisdiction; her father and brothers are afar, after a few children she becomes even weaker. Whilst you, having feasted upon her cooking have become stouter and aggressive towards her. You blame your anger and lack of control when she fails to enact any service to your liking...did she arrive as your lifelong maid, laundrywoman or errand girl?' Accordingly, treat wives with chivalry. Tolerate the bitterness of their tongue, if you are unable to do so, then leave the house environment for a while. Shaykh S'ādee Sheerazi ﷺ advises, 'Whenever the wife speaks bitterly, then place a sweet in her mouth; even an offensive word will then appear pleasing.' Many misguided husbands wish to reform her by brute force, whereas this just is not possible. Rasoolullah ﷺ stated,

'A women is allegorical to a crooked rib.' *(Bukhāri)*

Should you wish to benefit from her uneven trait you may do so just like you benefit from your crooked ribs....or do you rush to the doctor in an attempt to straighten your ribs? You will find solace in her; your offspring will sprout from her; it is possible a pious person may spring from her lineage who will become the means of your forgiveness on the Day of Judgement...

'It may be that you dislike certain things whereas there is goodness in it.' (Surah Baqarah, Ayah 16)

You might consider her face, complexion and figure unappealing and desire a more glamorous lady, whereas it is possible she becomes the mother or grandmother of a pious hãfiz and scholar who will be of immense benefit to you in this world and the Hereafter. Therefore, do not let her colour deceive you; at times the soil is ash in colour, but it produces a very rich harvest; whilst from a fairer lady sometimes a wicked monster is born. Accordingly, do not consider your wife as mediocre, do not be dejected by her features, whatever her disposition, abide (*nibah*) with her. If you wish to benefit from her, you will have to tolerate her irregularities (in hadeeth terminology *Evajaa*). A hadeeth appears in *Roohul Ma'āni* wherein Rasoolullah 🕮 stated,

> *'The characteristic of women is they overcome a mild-mannered husband (yagleebna kareema).'*

The temperament of women is such that whichever husband is mild-mannered (*kareem*), cultured (*shareef*), unwilling to resort to revenge, vulgarity and violence, then wives will overcome and scold such husband's. However, uncouth husband's overpower their womenfolk by domestic violence and emotional abuse. Her father and brother are not present; she has no alternative but to maintain silence: the thought of narcissism (*naz*) does not even arise whereas this is her Sharee' right (*haqq*); to be pretentious and flirtatious in front of her husband.

When she resorts to tantrums and sulking, instead of coercion, place sweets and flowers around her. To place a morsel in her mouth is also Sunnah...by morsel is not implied a spiced pepper, but something succulent, charming and appealing. Always keep a box of her favourite chocolates or sweets in reserve.

Islām & Domestic Violence

A llah ﷻ Says in the Glorious Qur'ān:

'Indeed, there is for you in the Rasool of Allah, a beautiful model (character, way, style) - for him who has hope (in meeting) Allah and the Last Day.'

R asoolullah ﷺ commented,

'The Mu'min (husband) should not harbour enmity for his wife. If he dislikes something in her, then surely, he will be pleased with another quality in her.' (Muslim)

'A man who harms any Muslim and deceives him is accursed.' (Tirmidhi)

'(After many women had complained to the Mothers' of the Believers of their husbands' excesses, Nabee ﷺ commented, 'Many women are approaching and complaining of their husbands to the Wives of Muhammad (ﷺ)...these people (who hit their wives) are not the good from amongst you.' (p369, Mazāhir Haqq)

There is not a single case or incident of our Nabee ﷺ having either physically, emotionally or verbally harmed, abused or hurt any of his wives or servants even when they did anything against his temperament. It is against the honour and dignity of a Mu'min to behave in such a cowardly, uncivilised and ignorant manner with the person who performs so many acts of service for him and who is the mother of his children and in whom he fulfils his desires.

It is estimated that 1 in 4 wives in the UK suffer domestic violence at some time in their married life from husbands (and the majority of cases go unreported). Some husbands take out their anger, frustration and displeasure upon trivialities on wives because of the latter's physical weakness; inability to retaliate; reluctance to report to others and; upon the assumption that nobody is able to stop him. Complaints arrive of Muslim husbands, who after having fallen into drugs, alcohol and the company of lewd women coming home and taking out their wrath on the wife who faithfully stays at home to upbring their children.

The Moral Rights of a Wife being Abused

Nikãh is an ibãdah and Sunnah. It is not a license for the husband to do as he pleases. Accordingly, a Muslim wife has the moral right to report any excesses she is suffering to relatives (her husband's and her own and also pious, well-intentioned associates of her husband through their womenfolk). Moreover, the relatives and friends from the husband's side have a moral obligation to ensure that the daughter of another family who has arrived in the nikãh of their clan/friend is being treated with decorum. If they suspect or are informed of any misbehaviour, it is incumbent upon them to side with the 'innocent and wronged person' and not let family prejudices or loyalties sway their judgement. Almost all localities have an Imãm and elderly Ulamã who may be approached (by phone or letter) and a wife is quite within her rights to bring to sensible elders her 'genuine' predicament. They will be able to suggest to her the best response.

Marriage & the Significance of Family Ties

Based upon the Teachings

of

Shaykh Abul Laith Samarkandi 🌸

Shaykh Ashraf 'Ali Thānwi 🌸

Shaykh Abul Hasan Nadwi 🌸

Shaykh Manzoor Nu'maani 🌸

Shaykh Mufti Taqee Uthmãni

Shaykh Muhammad Saleem Dhorat

The Harmful Effects of Breaking Family Ties

haykh Abul Laith Samarkandi ☙ narrates,

'Aboo Ayub ☙ related, 'A villager appeared in the company of Rasoolullah ☙ and grabbing the reins of the latter's camel asked, 'O Rasoolullah ☙! Show me such a deed which takes me towards Paradise and distances me from Hell?' Rasoolullah ☙ replied, 'Worship Allah Ta'ala and do not associate anybody with Him; be punctual with salah, pay zakah and enjoin family ties (sila rahmi).'

(*Tanbeehul Ghafileen, p150*)

'Abdullah bin Abee Adnee ☙ related, 'We were sitting in the company of Rasoolullah ☙ on the evening of 'Arafah when he ☙ stated, 'The breaker of family ties (qata rahmi) should withdraw and not sit with us.' Upon this declaration only one person arose from a corner of the gathering and thereafter a short while returned. Rasoolullah ☙ inquired, 'What is the matter...nobody except you left from the entire gathering?' The person replied, 'O Rasoolullah ☙! When I listened to your auspicious announcement I proceeded to my Aunt who distances herself from me. She inquired, 'How come you have appeared today contrary to habit?' I related your statement to

*her whereupon she made repentance (istighfar) for
me and I made repentance for her.' Rasoolullah* 🌸
*commented, 'You did very well, sit down.
Remember, mercy does not descend upon such a
nation wherein there are those who break family
ties.'* (ibid)

Shaykh Abul Laith Samarkandi 🌸 comments, 'It is evident
from these Hadeeth that breaking family ties is a grave sin
which does not merely harm the persons involved but
deprives all those who associate with him of mercy also.'

Shaykh Abdul Hasan 'Ali Nadwi 🌸 relates, 'In this
era of Muslim decline wherein clear signs of our
failure are evident; our disgrace, humiliation, ignominy,
dishonour, degradation and lack of blessings, etc., etc., may
all be attributed and traced to internecine disputes and the
breaking up of relationships (*qata rahmi*) between family
members.

Our plunge has reached such depths that out of enmity we
go to great pains, cost and time to harm, disgrace and
dishonour our own to the extent families and clans are rent
asunder forever. Thousands of families, over trivial matters
such as heritage disputes, stay permanently aloof from one
another. Only on occasions of great sorrow, do we get
together momentarily and some are not even able to
manage this. For years and generations, such
disagreements and grudges are harboured; with energies
and resources employed in devising stratagems to disgrace
the other blood relative. No effort is spared to ruin the
other; any failure, harm or loss of a brother is viewed with

as much merriment as when, in bygone times, a fort or country had been annexed.

Those who are, somewhat aloof of such treachery and have not stooped to the lowest of low; those who appear and are considered religious; who have benefited from Deeni Uloom or the company of the pious; they too are lacking in healthy family relationships. They are indifferent of the virtues and apathetic to the importance placed upon *sila rahmi* by the Glorious Qur'ān and Hadeeth. Our lives are bereft of this Sunnah most beloved to Rasoolullah ﷺ and which was so prominent and evident in his life.

Our outlook has become so fickle that leave alone the concept of associating with the pious; or maintaining friendship with the acquaintances of one's parents - which is considered amongst the rights and service of parents; or preserving old relationships (*nibah*); or compassion upon juniors and respect for elders; we are unable to even sustain daily affiliations and fulfil our legal obligations.

The result of such petty selfish behaviour is clan's, neighbourhoods and finally households: instead of being reflections of Paradise and places of peace and tranquillity are ghettos of despair and woe. No traces of the gaiety of life, neighbourly camaraderie or the blessings of even an Islāmic lifestyle are noticeable. Ironically, we do not need a deep knowledge of the dire warnings sounded in the Glorious Qur'ān and Hadeeth of Rasoolullah ﷺ or an unbiased outlook to inform us of the reasons for such retributions and the lifting of blessings. The Glorious Qur'ān and Hadeeth are replete with the harms to society and oneself of disunity, *qata rahmi*, hatred, malice and revenge. Similarly, the benefits of redressing mutual relationships, tolerance and forgiveness, sacrifice and forbearance, to withdraw despite being on truth, *sila rahmi* with those who practise *qata rahmi* are mentioned repeatedly.

In this era, many activities of Deen have and are taking place. On worship and the virtues of practices, volumes upon volumes have been compiled; large publications on rulings (*masā'il*) have been edited and much attention has been expanded on politics and collective art. Each facet of these sciences has been highlighted and they are vibrant and visible amongst the lives of Muslims, however, with regards to mutual relationships very little work has been undertaken especially in a non-academic manner which would appeal to and be of benefit to all. Moreover, there is very little evidence of any improvement in our society.

Whereas the scourge of mutual and family disputes is so widespread that it is highly unlikely any neighbourhood, clan or family are free from it. The repercussions upon Muslim social interaction is grave: neither are our Deeni efforts and energies reaping full fruits nor the toils of political parties and groups proving beneficial. It is necessary this facet of life be fully highlighted, for without it, our existence is rudderless and our acts of worship and devotion devoid of strength and vigour. The efforts, resources and concern required to overcome this blight is just as great as the extent and severity of the problem facing us.'   *(Lectures of Ali Mia, Vol. 4, p .427)*

The Causes & Remedies To Family Disputes

age of this Ummah Aboo Dardah 🌸 relates,

*'Once Rasoolullah 🌸 asked his Companions 🌸,
'Why...should I not inform you of a rank which is
more virtuous than salah, sawm and sadaqah?'*

*The Companions replied, 'Indeed!' Rasoolullah 🌸
replied, 'Reconciliation between two people...for
mutual acrimony and disputes are means of
eradication.'*		*(Aboo Dawood)*

haykh Mufti Taqee Uthmāni *hafizahullah* comments, 'Whenever we think of worship, we consider salah, sawm, sadaqah, dhikr, recitation of the Glorious Qur'ān, etc., to be forms of veneration; which they indeed are. However, Rasoolullah 🌸 is informing us of a deed even higher in rank (to optional or *nafl* acts of worship): to initiate peace and concord between Muslims. Today, our society (*muasharah*) is so distanced from this teaching of Rasoolullah 🌸 that at every step there appears to be animosity, hatred, ill will and disputes; consequently life has become Hell. These underlying filthy character attributes are the means of obliterating Deen and the reason for our downfall and disgrace. Such disputes obliterate light from our hearts, replaces it with darkness and distances and alienates us from Deen.'

How To Be Saved From Disputes?

How do we save ourselves from internecine disputes and achieve mutual affection? Rasoolullah ﷺ has provided the Ummah with an extremely comprehensive set of advises; however before studying these one needs to appreciate a basic concept and core ingredient. Although amongst the Muslim community the clarion call is for unity, concord, and mutual empathy; nevertheless communal affection is still absent. Why? Study the opinion of the Pious Servants of Allah ﷻ, for He inspires the need of the times upon the hearts of His devotees. Haji Imdadullah Makki ﷺ stated:

'The root of unity and concord is to create two qualities within oneself; humility (tawadhu) and selflessness (iythaar). If any one of these two attributes is lacking then unity will not be possible.'

Islamic humility (*tawadhu*) is to regard oneself as being insignificant and, a servant of Allah ﷺ who is duty-bound to fulfil His Commands. Paradoxically, 'I have no excellences of my own, no automatic rights, accordingly if somebody does violate a right due to me (as specified by the Sharee'ah), then it does not matter for I am worthy of reproach.'

Unity is not present in our society because pride (*takkabur*) is present in our hearts. Each person regards himself to be greater: 'these are my rights; I am not being respected; my opinion is not being counted; I am greater.' When such egoistic, undeserving and fleeting standards of reverence for oneself are established in the mind; then whenever these absurd criteria's are not fulfilled, complaint, unhappiness and eventually animosity towards others arises in the heart and consequently disputes. The root cause of all such arguments is thus arrogance.

The Prescription For A Tranquil Life

Shaykh Ashraf Ali Thãnwi ❀ narrated, 'I will show you a prescription for a peaceful and tranquil life whereby *inshã'Allah* no complaint or disappointment towards anybody will arise. Firmly embed in your heart the concept this world is inherently bad and its original purpose is to vex; accordingly should any amongst creation irritate me then this is entirely in keeping with this worldly existence.

Should any benefit accrue from anybody then this is the occasion for surprise and to be thankful to Allah ❀. Accordingly, do not aspire from any acquaintance, relative, friend or associate any kind of hope or the thought of goodness: this person will give me benefit; or he will respect me; or he will aid me. Thereafter, should anybody be of benefit, you will be happy and express gratefulness to Allah ❀, 'O Allah! You have through Your Favours placed it in his heart as a consequence of which he has acted chivalrous towards me.'

Hope and aspirations should only be expected from One being; shun all expectation from everybody else. Rasoolullah ❀ used to recite this du'a:

'O Allah! Embed in my heart hope from only You and dispel anticipation from anybody except aspiration from only You.'

Pre-Requisites of Unity: Humility & Selflessness

When Islāmic humility is present in a person he will also not have any aspirations from anybody; subsequently there will not be any complaint towards another nor any grounds for disputes.

Therefore, the first pre-requisite is humility.

The second condition is to adopt selflessness (*iythaar*) towards creation. This is a concept of the heart whereby one's comfort is sacrificed for the benefit and preference of another Muslim...

'...And give them preference over themselves even though they were in need of that. And whomsoever is saved from his own covetousness, such are they who will be the successful.' (Glorious Qur'ān, 59:9)

Whomsoever is blessed by Allah ﷻ with this quality, is gifted with such ecstasy of faith (*iman*) that all delights of this world are insignificant. All bounties of this world are transitory, therefore inculcate *iythaar* through the blessings of which Allah ﷻ creates affection between hearts and endows his bounties upon the selfless one's.

The opposite of *iythaar* is selfishness (*hubbus zaat* or *khud garzee*): to forever wallow in fulfilling one's ego; 'how may I acquire extra wealth; extra fame; a higher rank etc., etc.' Night and day is spent in this egoistic preoccupation.

Similarly, the opposite of humility is arrogance.

Therefore when a person gives up pride and selfishness, he will inshā'Allah acquire affection and unity.

Banish Double Standards & Adopt One Criteria

The second concept which Rasoolullah ﷺ has stated in Hadeeth and which forms the root of all praiseworthy character traits (*akhlaaq faadhilah*) is...

'Desire for your brother what you desire for your self,

Detest for your brother what you detest for your self.'

Whenever dealing with anybody, then momentarily place him in your position, yourself in his place and consider what you would desire? Accordingly, whatever you desire for yourself should also form the basis of what you desire for another; similarly what you detest for your self, you should also detest for others.

One prominent illness in our society is the choice of double standards: a certain criterion for oneself and quite another for others. If everybody where to adopt the advise of Rasoolullah ﷺ in choosing for a brother the very same values one chooses for one self then all disputes and arguments would cease and a person would never undertake any course of action which would be detrimental to others.

Banish Habit of Complaining

Many Muslims, Alhamdulillah, living in prosperity in the West nevertheless have the habit of complaining about just everything (the victim mentality). Whenever they meet anybody, especially a relative or close acquaintance, a grievance is sure to follow, 'you said and did such-and-such.' A chain of complaints is unleashed and instead of affection increasing, animosity and hostility sets in.

Learn To Interpret Complaints Away

haykh Mufti Taqee Uthmāni *hafizahullah* comments, 'I speak from experience; today households upon households have crumbled over petty and trivial issues. O brethren! If somebody errs, learn to forgive and hand him over to Allah ﷻ. Rasoolullah ﷺ has placed so much emphasis on forgiving and forgetting, accordingly when you forgive, what do you have to lose? What mountain crashes or doomsday lands upon you? Learn to overlook and interpret events away with a big heart.'

Exemplary Behaviour of Mufti Azeez-ur-Rahman ﷺ

The Ustadh of my respected father, Shaykh Mufti 'Azeez ur Rahman ﷺ was an outstanding Scholar and writer. My father often used to relate, 'I never observed him rebutting anybody on their face...'you did this wrong.' Rather, even when somebody had erred, he would say, 'No doubt you meant this...' In this way he would interpret, redress and present the correct version in such a way the listener would be in no doubt as to his error but never forced into a confrontation or show down.

Similarly, whenever a spouse, brother, sister, child, relative or associate errs, then redress the error in a positive and mild manner and keep your heart clean. If you have to show your disapproval then say, 'Your such-and-such behaviour was displeasing to me.' If they present an excuse then learn to interpret it...do not make it the basis of an argument and dispute. This is why Rasoolullah ﷺ said,

'Do not dispute with your brother...'

Temporary Worldly Existence

This worldly existence is but for a few days and we have no guarantee to the length of our stay. In general, complaints and disputes are over trivial worldly matters: 'She said this to me; they did not invite us; or they did not respect or revere us; etc., etc.' All these are worldly preoccupations; material, wealth, fame, respect, rank, all are insignificant and perishable. No knowledge as to how long they will last or when they will be snatched away. Therefore fixate yourself with those matters which are Everlasting: 'What will happen there? How will I fare there? What answer will I present to Allah ﷻ there?' It appears in Hadeeth:

> *'Toil as much for this world as your stay in this world; toil as much for the Akhirah as your stay in the Akhirah.'*

Other common causes of disputes are to mock or jest at a person and make false promises. Jesting should not be confused with permissible light-hearted talk, jovialness or humour which is designed to cheer up others. Some people have a habit of ridiculing individuals, especially in front of others. This causes distress, rancour and disputes and is frowned upon...

> *'Do not dispute with any brother, do not jest or mock with him, nor undertake any promise which you are unable to fulfil.'*   (Tirmidhi)

Falsehood and false promises are frequent causes of disputes. Do not make them if you are unable to fulfil them and if you do promise, as far as possible honour them.

The Promise of a Heavenly Residence

Rasoolullah ﷺ narrated:

'I give guarantee of a residence in the middle of Jannah for the person, who despite being on truth (haqq), forgoes a dispute.' (Tirmidhi)

Shaykh Mufti Taqee Uthmāni *hafizahullah* comments, 'Our society has become so enveloped in disputes that loss of blessings and tyranny are evident everywhere to the extent spiritual light from worship is no longer visible. Arguments over trivial matters are rendering families, husband and wife, friends, siblings and relatives, scholars and people of Deen asunder. As a consequence, the Light (nur) of Deen has become extinguished.

We have witnessed our Respected Father, Shaykh Mufti Muhammad Shafee' ﷺ behaving throughout his life in accordance with the teaching of the above hadeeth. One incident, which people will find difficult to even comprehend comes to mind. Darul Uloom Korangi, which is located on the outskirts of Karachi, was initially sited in a prime city centre location, at a spacious place given by the government wherein is the present Islāmiyah College and the tomb of Allāmah Sayyid Ahmad Uthmāni ﷺ. This prime location came under the legal possession of the Darul Uloom and a building had been constructed, telephone line installed, when the time arrived for the official opening; eminent Scholars from throughout Pakistan arrived. However, a dispute was raised by some; 'This location should not have been given to the Darul Uloom, such-and-such institute was more deserving!' Some Scholars, revered by Mufti Shafee' ⌦, also became embroiled in this dispute. Initially, Mufti Shafee' ⌦ tried to resolve the dispute but it showed no sign of abetting. Finally, Mufti Shafee' ⌦ concluded, 'If the origin of a Madrassah is based on disputation, what hope is there of blessings?' Accordingly, he had it announced, 'I am forfeiting my right to this land.'

The Majlis Shura of Darul Uloom responded, 'Shaykh! What are you proposing? Such a large tract of land and, that too in a prime location; another example of which is difficult to find; you are the legal owner and you wish to forfeit it?' Mufti Shafee' ⌦ replied, 'I am not coercing the Majlis Shura to surrender this land, for indeed the Majlis Shura is the legal holder...if you wish construct the Madrassah but I will not participate in it: for whichever Madrassah is founded on a dispute, I see no blessings in it...' Thereafter, reciting the above hadeeth he commented, 'You might say a similar tract of land is unavailable elsewhere in the city centre, but Rasoolullah ⌦ has promised a residence in the middle of Jannah.'

Such examples of selflessness are difficult to find and only a person who has firm faith in ahadeeth of Rasoolullah ⌦ is able to act in this manner. Shortly thereafter, within a few months, through the Favours of Allah ⌦ an even larger plot of land was acquired; wherein today stands Darul Uloom Korangi. We people squabble over petty issues; such wrangling shears our Deen and wrecks destruction to our soul, therefore for the Sake of Allah ⌦ terminate disputes.'

(p82, The Rights & Duties of Society)

How To Seek Forgiveness For Previous Wrongs?

'Hereupon a question arises in the mind, 'If, from today we adopt the remedies shown by Rasoolullah ﷺ for preventing disputes, what of past mistakes? Of past backbiting, slander, hurt, etc?' Our past behaviour will show endless such errors with various people.' Seek forgiveness from Allah ﷻ for all wrong committed. If it is possible to genuinely locate and trace past acquaintances, we should do so and seek their forgiveness as well. However, as to those whom we are unable to locate, what to do? Make du'aa of clemency for them (even those still living). Rasoolullah ﷺ has shown us a very beautiful du'aa to make for those who we have wronged:

'O Allah! I am a mere human and in the same way other humans become enraged, I too become angry. In accordance with this wrath, if I have ever wronged anybody, or cursed him, or vilified him, then transform this into a du'aa for him.'

Our pious have shown a wonderful statement which encapsulate the spirit of this teaching, whenever departing from anybody say, 'Brother! Pardon my statements and listening.' If you ask a person for forgiveness and your request is refused, you have done your best.'

Similarly, whenever anybody seeks our clemency, learn to forgive. Resentment and bitterness, real and imagined, about what people did or said to us in the past are crippling to our body and injurious to our soul and enjoyment of life. Let it go. Clear it out of our heart. Forgive them.

Cardinal Way of Resolving Family Dispute

The best way of preventing and resolving family disputes is to adopt the measures shown by Rasoolullah 🌸 and our pious Scholars. The second secret is for family members to have a strong bond amongst themselves. With a true Islãmic outlook, love, respect and affection for each other, any dispute can be solved, no matter how serious. Most family disputes at home resolve around seniors setting rules and norms of behaviour (not necessary always confirming to Deen) and juniors breaking them to establish or display their free will and independence. Loyalty, faithfulness and true affection are sparse commodities in this era. Accordingly, seniors need to display correct intelligence and control their emotions and anger (no matter how outrageous the provocation or the behaviour):

1. The first rule to successful family ties in this era is to curb and manage anger:

   'Anyone can become angry - that is easy. But to be angry at the right person, to the right degree, at the right time, for the right purpose, and in the right way - that is not easy.'

2. Secondly, learn to analyse any dispute; trace the root causes of it; both inside and outside the family. Determine who actually is involved and who the instigator is and why. This takes time, patience and wisdom. Shaykh Hãfiz Dr. Suleiman 🌸 used to advise, *'Action, reaction, justification and motive behind the action.'*

3. Try to become a good role model, follow the Sunnah, both externally and spiritually and associate with the pious. Read their biographies and aphorisms to view how they handled situations.

Shaykh Mufti Taqee Uthmāni *hafizahullah* comments, 'It appears in Hadeeth:

'In reality, the preserver of family ties (sila rahmi) is he who, despite the antagonism (qata rahmi) of the other, does not reciprocate but answers with good interaction.'   *(Bukhāri)*

'One day some associates of Dr 'Abdul Hayy 'Arifee ❁ were sitting in his residence with him when, suddenly a relative of his appeared who had the appearance of an irreligious person. Immediately upon entry, he unleashed a volley of abuse and histrionics. Although, all those present found it difficult not to manhandle this person, surprisingly, Dr 'Abdul Hayy 'Arifee ❁ was replying, 'Brother, I have erred, excuse me, Inshā'Allah I shall recompense, we appeal to you, forgive me!'

Afterwards, when the relative had cooled down and departed, Dr 'Abdul Hayy 'Arifee ❁ commented, 'No doubt, this servant of Allah ﷻ was misinformed. In reality, I too could have replied or retaliated. But it was prudent to cool him down, because he is a relative and, they have rights over us. It is easy to break ties with relatives but to maintain them is, in reality the Sunnah of Rasoolullah ﷺ...

'Do not ward off iniquity with wickedness but with goodness.'

Lifemanship (Anthropology)

Most disputes arise not simply because of inappropriate statements or behaviour but also due to reactions to them. The Glorious Qur'ān teaches us:

'And the (faithful) slaves of the Most Gracious (Allah) are those who walk on the earth in humility and sedateness and, when the foolish address them (with bad words) they reply back with mild words of gentleness.' (25:63)

When somebody says or does anything inappropriate and you do not react (not through cowardice but to not allow anybody to lower you to their depth of depravity), most often the statement disappears into oblivion,

'There is peace in silence.'

Unnecessarily challenging a statement or act (especially that of an obstinate relative) turns it into an issue or scene which then blows out of all proportion. In the majority of cases, engaging in an argument is counter-productive and forces the other party to become more defensive and stubborn. How may one react to a unnecessary confrontation? Disengage; tarry the discussion for another time under any pretext and take the 'heat' out of the situation. An effective opt out is, 'I shall reflect on it,' or 'I shall inquire about it,' or 'I shall consult on it.' Undertake to ascertain both sides of the 'story.' An intelligent person never forms a judgement based on one version of events; no matter who the narrator; he always inquires. Established facts are always difficult to refute.

Modern Day Extremisms

In

Family Relationships

*S*haykh Muhammad Saleem Dhorat *hafizahullah* whilst solemnising a nikah mentioned, 'The Glorious Qur'ān is the Speech of Allah ﷻ, accordingly even a small portion of it contains great wisdom... I would like to comment on just one portion of the Verse recited at the time of Nikah...

وَ اتَّقُوا اللهَ الَّذِى تَسَآئَلُوْنَ بِهِ وَ الْأَرْحَامَ

'*...Fear Allah through Whom you demand (your mutual rights) and (do not cut the relations of) the womb (kinship)...*'

Herein, Allah ﷻ is addressing two specific realities. Firstly, fear Allah ﷻ through Whom we ask one another. Fear Allah ﷻ because He is our Creator and Nurturer. Our existence and possessions all are the Bestowal of Allah ﷻ. These occasions and days of happiness are also Gifts from Him. Accordingly, fear Allah ﷻ Who has Bestowed everything to you.

The Patronage of Allah ﷻ

In this world whenever we require anything of merit from one another we do so through the auspices and name of

Allah ﷻ. Ponder, whenever we Muslims have a crucial request to make, we employ the patronage (*wasta*) of Allah ﷻ. For example, when seeking forgiveness from a person who is obstinately refusing to pardon, we say, 'For the Sake of Allah ﷻ forgive me please!' Similarly, when in dire need of financial assistance, we say, 'For the Sake of Allah ﷻ lend me some money please?' Even the most hard-hearted person is forced to contemplate upon a request made in the Name of Allah ﷻ. Even in Hadeeth, we are advised,

'Should somebody request something from you with the Name or Patronage of Allah (and, there is no harm in giving), then you should do so.'

(Aboo Daawood, Nasaaii)

Although the emphasis is to support and aid whenever appropriate and possible, obviously, if a fraudster or cheat approaches and requests any amount of money or favour in the Name of Allah ﷻ, our *Sharee'ah* does not advise us to support or fall for his deceit.

Accordingly, when we fulfil and demand our needs in this world though the Patronage of Allah ﷻ, then one right of this reality is to fear and obey Allah ﷻ and not to disobey Him.

This is the teaching of *taqwa* which is repeatedly stressed in all three verses recited in the Nikah Sermon. Fearing Allah ﷻ does not imply the state of terror as when confronted by a lion, snake or sworn enemy, why? For the reason that Allah ﷻ is the most Merciful (*Raheem*), the One of Infinite Compassion. By fearing Allah ﷻ is implied the possibility of us erring, disobeying and incurring His

Displeasure and a consequential break-up of the intimate relationship which exists between us and our Creator.

Whenever there is a very cherished relationship between a couple, then the husband will fear...not the physical personality of his wife but the possibility of them ever becoming detached or distanced. This same concept is implied in Fearing Allah ﷻ, that your relationship with Him must not become impassive. Fear the possibility of sinning with the eyes, ears, tongue, etc. and differentiate between permissible (*halal*) and impermissible (*haram*).

This is the first command of *taqwa*, which is not restricted to *nikah* but to our entire existence. Literally, *taqwa* means to refrain from any deed wherein is the Displeasure of Allah ﷻ. To pray the five daily Salah, to pay Zakat, to perform Hajj, to be courteous and of service to neighbours - irrespective of their religion, to be kind to orphans, widows and the disabled, all these are compulsory facets of our Deen and the demand of *taqwa*. The second command mentioned in this Verse is that of...

وَ اتَّقُوْا اللهَ الَّذِىْ تَسَآءَلُوْنَ بِهٖ وَ الْاَرْحَامَ

'...Fear Allah through Whom you demand (your mutual rights) and (do not cut the relations of) the womb (kinship)...'

What is implied by fear in regards to family ties? Dread the possibility of them breaking! We are being warned of infringing two very necessary relationships; with Allah ﷻ and with family members. Why were these verses specifically recited at the time of *nikah* by Rasoolullah ﷺ?

A Bounty of Nikah ~ The Joining of Clans

Through the medium of *nikah*, a new relationship comes into existence. Two hitherto separate clans, through the blessings of this *Sunnah* enacted in a matter of moments, become entwined as one henceforth. Allah ﷻ has decreed this a very big favour (*nemat*). In Islām, after *nikah*, both clans belong to each other, whilst in other nations, even after marriage, there is no relationship or empathy between spouses and in-laws... 'I have got nothing to do with your family.' Islām's emphasis is on affection (*muhabbat*); the bride and bridegroom each regard the other's clan as their own. Why is this so emphasised on this occasion? The majority of couples, after *nikah*, become involved in extremes (*ifrat* and *tafreet*); some youngsters' are so enjoined to their parents that they are not prepared to have any relationship with their in-laws. Whilst some others, after *nikah*, align themselves so much towards their in-law's as not to maintain any relationship with their own family. These are the two extremes, whereas the Sharee'ah of Islām has enjoined rights (*huqooqs*) for parents and in-laws.

Our Sharee'ah, our Deen is so comprehensive that it has decreed rights for everybody. These are the rights of the wife, the husband, the father, the mother, the father-in-law, the mother-in-law, etc. etc. Our Religion is so perfect that whenever their appears any apparent clash or conflict, for example the parents demand a certain course of action whilst the in-laws desire an alternative avenue, our Sharee'ah will show us a solution as to which way to adopt and whose wishes should be favoured. If there is a clash between the wishes of the wife and mother, then our Sharee'ah will guide us as to whom to give preference to on any occasion. Our Sharee'ah has never said 'all rights belong to the mother with no rights for the wife.' Nor does it teach, 'All rights for the wife and nothing for the mother.' The rights of everybody has been ordained, if ever there is conflict, then incline towards the Scholars (*Mufti-yane-Kiram*) and seek clarification. This is not limited to marital disputes but wherever there is a dispute or disagreement: between brothers, between the imam and followers, between neighbours, etc., etc.

Modern-Day Extremisms

In our society (*mu'asharat*), we observe extremisms. The bride arrives at her husband's house and becomes completely forgetful of her own parents or despite living in his own house after marriage the husband becomes a cuckold (a *ghar jamai* ~ detaching himself completely from his own parents and clan). He takes his cue from the command and control centre of his in-laws. This is one extreme.

The other extreme, is the husband's allegiance to his own family to such an extent that he is unwilling to recognise or honour the rights of his in-laws. Another facet of this second extremism is the girl, despite having arrived at her husband's home still intransigently taking all her instructions from her parents and family and conducting her life in accordance to her parent's whims and fancies from afar.

The Sharee'ah has prohibited both forms of extremisms. The girl is being instructed not to forget her parents, siblings, uncles and aunts after marrying; whilst the husband is being commanded; all these people are the relatives of your wife, therefore you will have to support her in her endeavours to maintain a healthy relationship with them. Although they might not be directly related to you; they are very close to your wife. You might not wish to recognise her aunt; but she is her mother's sister. Her uncle may not be anybody in your view; but he is her father's brother.

Similarly, the husband is being instructed; after marrying, although a very big door is opening wherein there are brothers-in-law, sisters-in-law, uncles-in-law, aunts-in-law, etc., etc., nevertheless do not forget your own parents who nurtured you from birth. Do not forget your own grandparents, siblings, cousins, uncles and aunts...because nowadays people change overnight. Both the bridegroom and bride are being forewarned of extremism. Fulfil the rights of your parents and family and also those of your in-laws.

Breaking of Family Ties (Qata Rahmi)

This is the specific topic highlighted at the time of Nikah. However, there is the general subject of saving oneself from sins on all occasions...especially the calamity of breaking or weakening family ties.

Contemplate upon all such matters with an unbiased mind. Remember, nobody lives forever, accordingly, do not make this worldly existence the sole criteria for judgements and decisions. Ponder, a time is sure to arrive wherein our eyes will be closing as our soul departs for the Hereafter. One's spouse, wealth, position, business and friends will not avail, only Deen will be of use. Nobody will enter the grave with us or support us in the Court of Allah ﷻ on the Day of Judgement. When deciding matters, keep this reality at the forefront of your thinking process.

In our worldly existence, disagreements are bound to occur; however such relatively small differences of opinion should never be allowed to escalate to such abhorrent levels wherein relatives and associates are unwilling to look at each other until death and we leave this world in such conditions and so detached from the Mercy of Allah ﷻ.

Aboo Hurayrah ؓ relates that Rasoolullah ﷺ stated,

> *'When Allah ﷻ created this world, Sila Rahmi (family ties) appeared in the Court of Allah and pleaded, 'O Allah! On this occasion do I have permission to seek refuge from breakage (qata rahmi or breakdown of family ties)?'*
>
> *Allah ﷻ replied, 'Yes, why are you not happy upon this realism that whomsoever holds you in esteem I shall enjoin them to Me and, whomsoever disregards and breaks you I shall rent them asunder from Me?' Sila Rahmi replied, 'Yes, I am happy upon this (arrangement).' Allah ﷻ replied, 'This will be the feature of your reality...'*

> *(Bukhāri, Muslim)*

Family Ties ~ Means of Increase in Wealth & Age

Breaking of family ties is a grave peril. Seek protection and repent from disputes between brothers, between uncles and nephews, etc. In this era, this is a widespread malady, family relationships are either unhealthy and cold or non-existent. We should endeavour to live harmoniously with benevolence towards each other (family as well as with all creation). Rasoolullah ﷺ stated,

> *'Whomsoever desires in his heart for blessings in his wealth and life, then he should ensure he treats his relatives well.'*

> *(Bukhāri, Muslim)*

These are precisely the two most important bounties desired by everybody today; long life and wealth. A longer life is the opportunity to practise more good deeds and build capital for the Hereafter whilst blessings in wealth allows a person contentment and tranquillity.

Good & Bad Counsel of Elders

Accordingly, I make an earnest appeal to all married couples, especially those recently married, to foster a wholesome relationship with all family members on both sides. We should endeavour to train our children, boys as well as girls, to live with in-laws in a state of harmony. We should stress upon our daughter-in law and son-in-law to treat their own parents with due consideration, 'they have nurtured you from childhood.'

In bygone times, our elders would give good counsel, whereas nowadays elders give poor advise.

Before, parents would tell their daughters, 'We are bidding you farewell! Always come home with good news and a cheerful disposition...and your funeral bier (janazah) should leave from your husband's home.'

Contrast this with the behaviour of parents nowadays. I am involved in counselling with many youngsters and our daughters are complaining, 'I was living good-naturedly with patience, however my parents' would persistently probe into the behaviour of my mother-in-law, father-in-law and conditions at my husband's home to the extent some complaint or another would be revealed leading ultimately unto divorce (*talaq*)!'

Whereas before, even when a girl came and complained, her own parents would silence her, 'No dear! That is your home now, live with patience (*sabr*).'

It is the choice of parents; they should groom and train their children accordingly and give good counsel.

We should live in harmony with family members, fellow Muslims and non-Muslims. This is the ingredient for our progress and our advertisement of the benevolent nature of Islām.

Shaykh Muhammad Saleem Dhorat

hafizahullah

ഔൽ

Shaykh Muhammad Hakeem Akhtar hafizahullah comments, 'I have observed tyrannical husbands undergoing Divine Chastisement. One person, merely on the grounds that his wife was not so fair, divorced her despite her having mothered his six children! 'My mother had erred in selecting you...I am now unable to live with you.' His wife pleaded, 'If I was so unappealing to you then where have these six children come from? Why did you not divorce me from the beginning whereby I could have married elsewhere...now you have made me a mother of six and are divorcing me.' 'No, I am unable to tolerate any more...I shall marry a beautiful women...' So saying he blurted three talaqs. When she left with her six children, she looked up at the Heavens helplessly:

'To whom do our helplessness we show?

There remains nobody but the One in Heaven to observe our woe!'

Thereafter he married a very pretty woman, however within six months he became paralysed. For ten years he was bedridden; urinating and defecating on his bed; the beauty queen had left him immediately...'how can I live with him?' This is the repercussion of acquiring somebody's grief!

'Beware of the cry of the oppressed for there is no barrier between him and Allah.' (Bukhāri)

Chapter Twelve

The Harms of Talãq (Divorce)

odern surveys show in the UK for every three weddings there are two divorces. A necessary consequence of this appalling development is that approximately 150,000 children every year in the UK experience the tragedy, trauma and heartbreak of their parents either separating or divorcing. The UK has the highest proportion of lone parents in Europe; a quarter of children now live with a single mum.

Children from broken homes are more likely to have poorer health; to do worse at madrassah and school; less likely to attend the masãjid, become huffãz and scholars; more likely to commit crime, to smoke and take drugs; to be unemployed and to die earlier than children who live with married parents. By divorcing, parents have let loose a vicious cycle. Their children are more likely to repeat the cycle of unstable parenting which they had experienced and suffered.

haykh Qari Ãmir Hasan *dãmat barakãtuhum* related,

'When a husband remains patient upon the tantrums and indiscreetness of his wife, then in the Ãkhirah he will be awarded the reward of Prophet Ayyub ﷺ. *And when a wife remains patient upon the unreasonable behaviour and excesses of her husband she will be awarded the reward of Sayyidatina Ãasiãh* ﷺ *(the noble wife of Pharaoh).'*

haykh Mufti 'Abdur Raheem Lajpoori ﷺ comments, 'Nikãh is an act of worship and a bond between the husband and wife whereby they stay together with loving affection and beautifully pass their lives. Therefore, without a genuine Sharee' reason to pass *talãq* (divorce) is an act of gross injustice and tyranny. Should any feature of one's wife, e.g. appearance, habits, etc. be not to your liking and you wish to divorce her, always remember and ponder that she also possesses many good qualities. Allah ﷻ says in the Glorious Qur'ãn:

'Deal with women correctly and with kindness. If, then, you dislike them, then it is possible that you dislike something while Allah has created abundance of goodness in it.' (4:19)

Remember, it appears in Hadeeth that by proclaiming *talãq,* Allah ﷻ becomes displeased and the Divine *Arsh* shakes, moreover Shaytãn jumps with joy.' Nabee ﷺ commented,

'The most detestable of lawful things by Allah is talãq.' (Ma'ãriful Hadeeth, p.47, Vol. 7)

'A woman who asks her husband for divorce without a valid reason - on her the fragrance of Jannat is unlawful.' (ibid.)

Shaykh Ashraf 'Ali Thānwi ☼ comments, 'Issuing *talāq* without a genuine Sharee' reason causes the following:

1) Displays one's absolute stupidity and ungratefulness for the *nemat* (bounty) of Nikāh.

2) Deeply hurts one's wife, her family and emotionally harms the children.

3) Disgraces and degrades the wife, whereby she is now thought of as a person of bad character or unfaithful. This drastically reduces her chances of finding a good partner in the future and ruins her entire life.'

The last few years has seen a sharp rise in the divorce rate amongst Muslims. Our society is becoming corrupted by the abandonment of *purdah* (by both men and women). Muslim couples who co-indulge in excessive socialising: meals, parties, visits to the cinema, melas, shopping trips, holidays, barbecues and 'swinging' in the style of alien cultures should not be surprised when their own spouse appears boring and incompatible. Wherever there is free mingling between non-mahram people, then the nafs and Shaytān will spin their web of deceit and infidelity; for affairs usually take place between acquaintances; friends of spouses and co-workers. Disenchantment with one's spouse is the result of failure to remain loyal, dedicated, patient and contented upon what we have been blessed by Allah ﷻ.

haykh Ashraf 'Ali Thānwi ☙ narrated, 'The wise Luqmān ☙ was once forced to work as a farmhand. One day, his 'owner' came and requested him to bring a cucumber. Cutting it in half he offered one piece to Luqmān ☙ who happily ate it with relish. Thereafter, the owner took a big bite...when to his utter amazement it felt so bitter he immediately spit all of it out and remarked, 'O Luqmān! You were eating this cucumber with such relish as if it was sweet...but it is so awfully sour!' Luqmān ☙ replied, 'Yes, it is bitter.' 'Then why did you not say so and why did you eat it?' Luqmān ☙ replied, 'Why say anything? For the hand that has fed me sweet things a thousand times; if it should present something bitter occasionally, why should I mention it!'

This is such a beautiful concept, that if both the couple were to understand and act upon it, no disagreement or dispute would ever arise. The wife should remember, 'My husband has borne many tantrums of mine, an occasional 'broadside' is nothing to take to heart.' Similarly, the husband should vividly realize and appreciate the thousands of acts of service his wife has undertaken at the expense of her comfort; occasional 'lapses' are to be tolerated. Whilst some ladies are rude, husbands should remember they also have sterling qualities, one should always keep an eye on these and treat wives mercifully. They act as your servants untiringly providing you umpteen comforts night and day; therefore, the occasional error should be big-heartedly overlooked. Understand well, Islām's teaching is to make up...not break-up.'

Purpose of Nikāh is Not Talāq

haykh Mufti 'Abdur Ra'oof Sakhrawee *dāmat barakātuhum* relates, 'The ethos of Islām's teachings on nikāh is that it is a lifelong agreement (an ibaadah, institution and contract). The need to break or terminate nikāh should never arise because the ramifications or 'fall-out' are not restricted to just the husband and wife but profoundly affect and harm the offspring and sometimes becomes a means of anarchic dispute between families. Moreover, the fabric of our society is grossly affected.

Accordingly, all factors which contribute or lead towards the break up of nikāh have been discouraged by the teachings of the Glorious Qur'ān and Sunnah...'

'Although many incorrect factors of divorce have become entrenched in our society, the foremost, the most corrupted, the most wicked, the most damaging and the most unIslāmic is undoubtedly the evil practice of pronouncing three *talāqs* simultaneously. To compound the issue, out of pure ignorance, this totally incorrect method is considered the only way of issuing *talāq* as if divorce would not be valid without it.

Everybody, the lay and the learned, the wealthy and the poor, whether at the time of anger or after careful deliberation, whether by mouth or in writing will only give three simultaneous talāqs...never less. Occasionally, even if a husband was to issue one or two talāqs...the matter will not be allowed to rest here, for he will be either provoked, forced or goaded into issuing the remaining talãqs. Until the three have not been issued, the anger of the husband, wife and their respected families will not dissipate.

Moreover, before the final talãqs have been issued, nobody will take into consideration the plight of the children, the wife, the home and the families. Only after the three bullets have been fired will there be a return to sense and reality. Now, when the tearful, woeful, grief-stricken innocent faces of the small children appear does some form of sanity reappear and each party realises its folly. Now, both husband and wife are willing to forgive, forget and patch-up...however, after the floodwaters have dissipated, there is no point in building flood defences or shedding tears. Three talãqs are three talãqs.

Now, both parties take their plight to the Ulamã and Mufti's and crying profusely plead to be shown some leeway or loophole which would allow both of them to get together again if only for the sake of the young children. But, there is no way they may remarry, for all the options and methods shown by Allah ﷻ and His Rasool ﷺ have been instantly destroyed by one's own folly and stupidity.

The only possible way they may come together again is for the *mutallaqah* (divorced woman), after spending her *iddat* (period in waiting) to marry another man, have sexual intercourse with him and if he was to then divorce her with his freewill, again spend the *iddat* of that marriage and then remarry her first husband.

However, for the *mutallaqah* to insist at the time of her second nikāh that her second husband must divorce her has been cursed in the hadeeth. In some quarters, attempts and pressure are made upon the second husband to divorce the woman immediately after nikāh but *before* sexual intercourse. But under such circumstances, she just does not become halāl for her first husband...for sexual intercourse with the second husband is a condition...and which decent or cultured person could ever tolerate or bear such an event which is known as *halalah*?

The Impermissible Forms of Ruju' (Recall)

Some elders who try to superficially overcome this hurdle by marrying the *mutallaqah* to another person and then arrange for him to immediately divorce her before sexual intercourse are guilty of gross evil. Becoming oblivious to *athāb* (punishment) of the *qabr* (grave) and the Ākhirah, they soothe, appease and befool the couple by uttering nonsense like, 'talāq uttered in anger is not valid,' or 'talāq without witnesses is not valid,' or 'talāq without the wife's knowledge is not valid, etc.'

All this is the uttering of ignoramuses. Not only are the couple guilty of sin, those who arrange for them to live such an evil existence are also sinning.

Some husbands after issuing three talāqs approach a Mufti and then, blatantly lying, ask him for a verdict when only *two* talāqs have been given. The Mufti is not *'alim-ul-ghaib* (knower of the unseen), he issues Sharee' verdicts based upon the facts presented. However, the husband to befool the public will then go around showing the Mufti's ruling and justifying his wife's *ruju*. Such people may manage to fool the Mufti and the laity, but the wife forever remains harãm for him and nobody may protect them from the Punishment of Allah ﷻ.

When some people find no avenue for overcoming three talãqs in Hanafee Fiqh, they forgo its *taqleed* (following) and join the ranks of the *ghair-muqallideen* (freelancers). They are of the belief that if a person gives three simultaneous talãqs on one occasion they only count as one and he is able to make *ruju*...notwithstanding the fact that this verdict of theirs is in conflict with the Glorious Qur'ãn, Hadeeth, the rulings of the Sahãbãh ﷺ, Tãbi'een ﷺ, Imãm Shafi'ee, Imãm Mãlik and Imãm Ahmad ibn Hambal ﷺ and the 'Ulamã of the Ummah.

Three talãqs bring nothing but hardship and sin. Accordingly, if the *masã'eel* (commands) relating to divorce were learnt before or immediately after nikãh (when to learn the commands is compulsory) then such sad episodes would not come to the fore. Children and homes would remain intact and protected; peace and tranquillity would prevail; families would remain united.

Therefore, to refrain from issuing three simultaneous *talãqs* is *wãjib* (compulsory) and as far as possible one should not issue a talãq when in the state of anger. Heaven forbid, but if such an outcome does arise when in anger, leave the place. When anger has dissipated and one still feels talãq is the only option, even then study the commands of the Glorious Qur'ãn and Hadeeth on this matter and remain within the boundaries of the Sharee'ah.

Methods of Reforming an Intransigent Wife

Whenever a wife does not fulfil the rights of her husband; is being rebellious and does not appear to be living gracefully; then the Glorious Qur'ān has shown methods of reforming her which should be enacted before contemplating divorce.

Mild Persuasion~ The first step is for the husband to try and persuade her with mildness and dispel any wrong notions. If she is deliberately being intransigent then enlighten and encourage her of the correct mode of living. Should the matter be resolved at this stage then the wife will be saved from sinning and the husband from heartache and both will achieve tranquillity.

Display Displeasure ~ Should gentle persuasion fail to reform her, then the husband, to display his displeasure should separate from her bed and sleep on another bed in the same residence. This is a mild yet very effective rebuke. Should the wife heed, then the disagreement will end here. Shaykh Ashraf 'Ali Thānwi ﷺ has suggested a third form of rebuke. The husband should refuse to eat her cooking. This too affects the heart of a wife who has any sense of honour.

Zero Tolerance ~ Fourteen hundred years ago, Nabee ﷺ disapproved of physically assaulting one's wife...modern social reformers have now passed laws forbidding wife battering. Such vile behaviour is highly unbecoming of a Muslim. Moreover, husbands should not make a 'fuss' and 'confrontation' over small matters; discipline yourself to tolerate and make light of non-essential issues and as far as possible endeavour to maintain the bond.

Tolerance of the Pious

haykh Ashraf 'Ali Thãnwi ❀ relates, 'The great Saint Mirza Jãn Jãnah ❀ was a person of quite exquisite temperament: one unable to tolerate even a misplaced drinking cup; a student overeating; or crooked stitching in his quilt at night! Yet unto death, he patiently bore the curses, disrespect and wrath of his wife, never even thinking of harming or divorcing her. Daily, whilst lecturing, he would arrange for one of his students to call at his house and request his wife, from outside, whether she was okay or required anything. Everyday, this lady would unleash a torrent of foul abuse and insults directed at her husband, which the gloomy student would report back respectfully in these dry words, 'Shaykh, she is fine and sends her salãms!'

One day, unknowingly, Mirza Jãn Jãnah ❀ sent a hot-headed Afghan student to inquire. Unable to tolerate anybody insulting his Shaykh, the Afghan replied with vengeance and a large commotion was raised as both started shouting. This noise reached the Madrasah, from where Mirza Jãn Jãnah ❀ sent somebody else to find out what all the fuss was about. He returned with the student who commented, 'Shaykh, she was saying so many awful things about you...why, I could not just stand there and not say anything, anyhow Shaykh, why do you put up with such a woman?' Calmly, Mirza Jãn Jãnah ❀ replied, 'Brother, do not take offence at what she says, because she is your elder...as for me I accommodate her tantrums because she is my benefactor. All these excellences that I have been gifted is because of being patient upon her outbursts of anger and disrespect.' *Allahu Akbar!* A person with such a refined, delicate and elegant temperament, yet patiently bearing difficulties and vexing from his wife. It is a crying shame that whilst the *Awliya* would not even harm the hearts of their enemies, we people are unable to tolerate the indiscreetness of our best friend and 'neighbour,' our wife.

Shaykh Ashraf 'Ali Thānwi ﷺ continues, 'Whenever one is confronted by any displeasing behaviour or feature of the wife, regard it as a *kaffarah* (atonement) for one's sins. Accordingly, there was a Saint in Lucknow who was extremely pious whilst his wife was quite crude. People from afar would travel to him and derive *islaah* (training and education). One day out of frustration, he said to her, 'You unfortunate person, people from far away places come here and leave reformed, whilst you who have so much time with me remain just as ill-mannered and foolish!' His wife replied, 'Why, it is not I who is unfortunate, look how well-mannered a husband I have, in reality it is you who are wretched in having a crude wife such as me!' (Observe, who got the last word)!

Similarly, there was a Shaykh, both handsome in physique and character...however, his wife was hideously ugly. One day, whilst sitting together, he said to her, 'Dear, inshā'Allah we will both go to Paradise; for every time I look at you I make *sabr,* whilst when you look at me you are grateful. And, both the *sābir* (patient) and *shākir* (grateful) will enter Jannah!'

There was another Saint, whose wife greatly troubled him to the extent that people of the locality came to know of her ill-manners. Some friends approached this Saint and advised him to divorce such a wretched woman. The Saint replied, 'Indeed talãq is in my hands, however, do ponder what will happen to her if I should divorce her and she is unable to remarry, who will support her? She will be destroyed. Moreover, if she does remarry, in all probability she will vex her new husband, a brother Muslim as well. It is therefore best that until I am alive I undertake this difficulty and save other Muslims (especially her) from sorrow.' This is how the pious have convinced their hearts, and never have they divorced wives because of ugliness, vexing or ill-manners, always tolerating any difficulty. Accordingly, even when wives commit serious errors, one should as far as possible tolerate them. This patience brings great Deeni benefits and rewards.'

An Effective Method of Resolving Major Disputes

The measures outlined above are designed to resolve disagreements 'in-house.' However, at times disputes are of such magnitude, either because of the wife's temperament, rebellion or wickedness or because of the husbands' intransigence, excesses and faults that the domestic problem needs to be resolved with outside help. Nowadays when disputes reach such an ebb, outside people instead of resolving the dispute add further fuel by taking sides unnecessarily and flinging accusations and insults.

'He who brings the tales of others to you,
will take the tale of you to others.'

Hakam (Arbitration & Conciliation)

The Glorious Qur'ān has shown an extremely pure method of solving such major and acrimonious disputes. Two senior, experienced, wise and intelligent arbitrators; one from each side of the party should be appointed who have:

1) An adequate & competent level of religious knowledge.

2) Are trustworthy and upright.

3) Sincere and well-intentioned, truly desiring peace.

They should then endeavour to fully resolve the dispute. When such efforts to achieve peace and agreement are undertaken with sincerity, aid from Allah ﷻ will be forthcoming and the purpose will be achieved: Allah ﷻ will create affection and unity between the husband and wife. The advantage of this approach is that the matter still remains within the 'family.'

When Talāq is the Only Option

Shaykh Ashraf 'Ali Thānwi ﷫ comments, 'Some people go to such extremes as to regard *talāq* completely out of the question, regardless of whether there may be a genuine reason and now the only sensible option. Sometimes there may be total incompatibility between the couple; one of them may be avoiding *huqooqs* of the other; they may be so far away from Deen and unwilling to reform. In such cases of total marital breakdown with no hope of reconciliation, some families still insist on refraining from *talāq* so as to avoid staining their honour. All this achieves is to make lives of the couple wholly miserable.' When there is no real hope of reconciliation and the husband intelligently discerns (after seeking advice from pious Ulamã and sensible elders) that he will not be able to retain his wife correctly, whether because of his or her fault, then the honourable solution is to release her from his *nikãh* with kindness. Mutual recrimination and spite are most dishonourable and in conflict with the Glorious Qur'ãn,

'...*Either retention with beauty (and justice) or release with kindness.'*

The Best Method of Issuing Talãq

Whilst the Sharee'ah has given the husband the authority under such sad circumstances to issue talãq as a last resort and with great reluctance and reprehension, it has also shown a beautiful, civilised and cultured manner wherein are great worldly and spiritual benefits.

Shaykh Mufti Abdur Ra'oof Sakhrawee *dãmat barakãtuhum* continues, 'Accordingly, from the teachings of the Glorious Qur'ãn, the Sunnah and the statements of the Sahãbãh 🙵 and Tãbi'een 🙵 the method of issuing *talãq* when all other options have failed is: when the wife is free from menses (haidh) and in a period of purity during which the husband has not made love to her then the husband should in clear words issue only one *talãq* to his wife, for example, 'I am giving you one talãq.' Now let the *iddat* (period in waiting) pass. If they make *ruju* (reconcile and get together again) during the *iddat* then all the better. If not, then at the expiry of the *iddat*, the nikãh will automatically break and the wife will be totally separated from the husband and free to marry wherever she wishes. The Fuqaha (jurists) and the Sahãbãh ؏ have described this method of issuing divorce as *talãq ahsan.*

The Advantages of Talãq Ahsan

1) The biggest advantage is that out of all cases of Muslim divorce that come to the fore, in 99% of them, sooner or later, the husband/wife regret and become ashamed and wish for a reconciliation. However, because three talãqs were rashly and irresponsibly issued, remarriage is out of the question.

2) Shaykh Ahmad Sadiq Desai *dãmat barakãtuhum* relates, 'After *talãq ahsan,* the *iddat* for a non-pregnant wife (in the Hanafee Math-hab is a time period of three haidh (monthly periods) and according to the Shãfee Math-hab a period of three *thurs,* i.e. periods of purity ~ where *thur* is the period of purity between periods).'* Shaykh 'Abdur Ra'oof Sakhrawee *dãmat barakãtuhum* continues, 'If the wife is pregnant, the iddat is until childbirth. During *iddat* the husband and wife both have ample time to reflect, ponder and experience the reality and repercussions of separation. Moreover, they have time to decide upon future issues. During this period, if they both reach a conclusion that divorce is not good and they become remorseful: the wife wishes to obey the husband and promises to overcome her shortcomings; the husband realising the hardships and pain to the tarbiyyah of his children and understands the peace and well-being to his home in coming

together...then nothing has been undone yet. They may come together again as husband and wife...*ruju* has been enacted. Both should endeavour to fulfil each other's rights. However, it would be more prudent if the husband was to say, 'I am retaking my wife again into my nikāh,' in front of either two males or one male and two females. This is the best way of *ruju* and dispels any wrong notion and allows people to become aware of the reconciliation just as they became aware of the *talāq*.

3) If during *iddat* the husband did not make *ruju* and the *iddat* finishes, then the *mutallaqah* (divorcee) is now completely free from his nikāh and may marry wherever she wishes, her former husband has no say or influence over her. Both are strangers.

4) The second advantage in this method of *talāq ahsan* is that even after a considerable time as individuals, if memory of each begins to haunt them, or the acrimony and grief of separating is gradually replaced with awareness and longing for the comfort, service and joy of each other...even now, if both wish, they may, without *halalah*, remarry instantly.

There are no 'instant or quick' steps in the method of *talāq ahsan* for hastiness in worldly affairs is from Shaytān. At every stage and thereafter in *talāq ahsan*, the emphasis of Islām is on granting an occasion to reflect, on making up, on avoiding divorce and if it is absolutely necessary to separate, to issue *talāq* in as small numbers as possible thereby leaving the opportunity open to reconcile and remarry. (*Refer to p37, Az-Zaujus Sālih ~ The Pious Husband)

Hadeeth Narrations Chastising Three Talāqs

Imām Nasāee ❀ narrates,

'Rasoolullah ❀ was informed of a person who had given three simultaneous talāqs to his wife. Rasoolullah ❀ arose in anger and commented, 'What? Allah's Kitab is being played (flouted or belittled) whereas I am still present amongst you!' Another person present asked, 'O Rasoolullah ❀! Should I kill him?' (Nasaee, Kitab Talāq, p98, Vol. 2, ibid.)

'Ubaadah bin Thāmit ❀ narrates,

'A person gave one thousand (1,000) talāqs to his wife upon which Rasoolullah ❀ commented, 'Three talāqs have materialised, the remaining 997 he has oppressed. If Allah wills, He will punish him, or if He will's He may forgive him.' (p248, Vol. 1, Islāhi Lectures)

In the final analysis, nikāh is such an important Sharee' institution that preparations for it commence for a very long time and involve a lot of soul searching. Moreover, it is conducted in accordance to the method shown by the Sharee'ah. Similarly, if in some respects more so, talāq is an extremely sensitive matter for which the Sharee'ah has laid down beautiful guidelines. To follow these rules is *wājib* (compulsory); to ignore them and to rashly pronounce three simultaneous *talāqs* in anger considering oneself absolutely free and independent is not only sinful and impermissible but generates great destruction in our society. Peace and comfort lies in following the teachings of Prophet Muhammad ❀ the greatest benefactor of mankind.' (Vol. 1, Islāhi Lectures)

Error of Husband & Wife

haykh Maseehullah Khãn ﷺ relates, 'When evening approaches, Shaytãn spreads his 'throne' upon the sea and seats himself. His off-springs, fellow Shayãteen, who have been roaming around since morning spreading evil, return to give their reports. Shaytãn listens to all and comments indifferently and impatiently at each: 'Yes, yes, well done. Yes, yes, well done.' Thereafter, one Shaytãn gets up and says, 'Listen to my report. Today I created friction between husband and wife, with the result that both flew into a rage...I then goaded them on until a stage was reached whereby the husband gave his wife three *talãqs*.' Upon hearing this, Shaytãn stands up in ecstasy and rushes to pat his junior Shaytãn, 'Bravo! Bravo! You have really done marvellous work, bravo!'

haykh Ashraf 'Ali Thãnwi ﷺ narrates, 'Generally, women fail to recognize the demands of a situation. Many a times the husband is in anger...whereupon the wife will not quieten down but will aggravate the argument...until in anger he blurts out *talãq*. Such episodes are quite common...where talãq was given in anger...now there remains nothing but remorse for both the couple and their families - who become lifelong enemies.

Many women are so uncouth as to blurt out to their husband during a row, 'Yeah, go ahead and give talãq, what else can you do?' Both husband and wife should remember never ever to bring the word *talãq* unto one's lips, whether in jest or anger. This word is so dangerous that it is synonymous to a bullet in a revolver (pointed at your head). Irrespective of whether you pull the trigger in jest or anger, the bullet of a surety will strike you. Being angry is no excuse in the Sharee'ah...keep your wrath under control...for there is nobody who has ever pronounced three talãq's in anger who did not live to regret the consequences of his rashness. May Allah ﷻ protect us.'

Advice for Wives & Mothers-in-law

Shaykh Ashraf 'Ali Thãnwi ﷺ narrates, 'Many women demand *talãq* upon the slightest pretext. Severe warnings have been sounded in the Hadeeth regarding such behaviour. Rasoolullah ﷺ commented:

'A woman who asks her husband for divorce without a valid reason - on her the fragrance of Jannat is unlawful.' (Ma'ãriful Hadeeth, p.47, Vol. 7)

Shaykh Maseehullah Khãn ﷺ often recited the couplet of Muslim ladies of yesteryear,

'In the husband's home that arrived I at marriage, should also leave my funeral carriage.'

Muslim sisters should understand that divorce is not a simple matter. It is a smirch on their honour and reputation, irrespective of whether they are at fault or not. They stand to lose and suffer more in case of *talãq*. They should not be misled by the behaviour of some other cultures, whose 1 in 3 marriages end in divorce. Nor should they allow the promise of free legal aid, state welfare benefits for lone parents and the provision of local authority housing ~ sometimes dinned into their ears by ignorant and selfish mothers ~ guile them into pressing and commencing unfair court proceedings for divorce. Remember that although victory in divorce proceedings may bring temporary material gain, your return to your mother's home will not be welcomed by your family and neighbours. It is infinitely better and more honourable to stay (even unhappily) with one's husband and survive on bread and water in a simple barrenly furnished residence, than dine upon exquisite dishes in your mother's mansion as a divorcee.

Husbands Especially Should Control Anger

haykh Ashraf 'Ali Thãnwi ﷺ narrates, 'Many men regret their folly of pronouncing three simultaneous *talãqs* by saying, 'I said it in anger, I did not mean it in reality.' People should remember nobody says *talãq* out of happiness; *talãq* is always pronounced because of displeasure and anger! Therefore keep your wrath under control, learn and adopt those methods which pacify anger...not for nothing has the Sharee'ah taught us these methods.

Importance & Benefit of Consulting Pious Scholars

mãm 'Ãmash ﷺ (684-771CE) is considered amongst the leading *Muhadditheen* capable of relating 4,000 Hadeeth from memory. His appearance was not very handsome ('Ãmash refers to a dim-eyed), in complete contrast to his wife, who was outstanding in beauty and somewhat proud of it. She detested her husband; always looking for an argument and excuse to be separated from him. One night, their bouts of wrangling reached such heights that she refused to speak henceforth; Imãm 'Ãmash ﷺ lost his temper and blurted out, 'If you do not speak by morning, you are divorced!' After calming down, he realized his folly and the plight of his young children should their mother continue to refuse to speak with him that night. He pleaded and cajoled with her, but to no avail. In desperation, he sought the opinion and advice of elders but nobody could show a solution. Finally, he visited Imãm Aboo Haneefah ﷺ who suggested a strategy, 'Not to fear, keep calm, we shall arrange for the Azãn this morning to be recited before *Sub'a Sãdiq.*' Thereafter, the Great Imãm personally approached the Mu'azzin of the local Masjid during the night and persuaded him to recite one Azãn before *Sub'a Sãdiq.* Now, the wife of Imãm 'Ãmash had packed her bags and was just waiting for the Fajr Azãn...as soon as she heard *'Allahu Akbar!'* she exclaimed in delight. 'All thanks to Allah! Now I am separated and free from this old-man!' Imãm 'Ãmash ﷺ replied, 'All thanks to Allah ﷻ, that the Mu'azzin, through the ingenuity of Imãm Aboo Haneefah, recited the Azãn before *Sub'a Sãdiq* thus preventing our marriage from breaking up!'

Such incidents wherein talãq is blurted out highlights the need for the husband especially to seek the advice of pious scholars before even contemplating issuing talãq. The Sharee'ah has vested this authority and right to the husband so that he may act rationally and unemotionally.

The Consequences of Divorce on Children

A llah ﷻ bestows children to parents whereby both lovingly, correctly and faithfully nurture them so they become pious and responsible citizens who are of service to Him, His Deen, humanity, creation and society. There are numerous rights of the children upon parents. When a father issues *talāq* to his wife, obvious though it may sound, he should fully understand he is also divorcing the mother of his children and the grandmother of his grandchildren for all of whom it is a mind shattering, painful, distressing and heartbreaking experience. The repercussions will be felt for generations well after he has died.

Even if the father remarries and gains custody of his children, in the overwhelming majority of cases, his new wife will never treat her stepchildren in the way she treats her own. Even if he marries a lady with a very big heart who genuinely wishes to treat her stepchildren like her own, it will be very difficult for her. Why? Because in this era of selfishness and disrespect, the majority of children are just as ungrateful and will never accept the *maqām* (rank) of their stepmother. Let neither party delude themselves that all will be well when they separate and remarry. The father by divorcing has doomed his children, his grandchildren, his new wife (if he remarries), former wife and himself to a life of separation, anxiety, grief, instability and turmoil:

1) The foremost disadvantage experienced by a 'divorced' child is the physical absence of the father (most often

because of the way the courts apportion custody). Consequently, the love, support, stability, discipline and tarbiyyah associated with fatherhood is lacking with a detrimental effect. Generally, children who have no paternal role model to aspire to suffer from an inferiority complex and either lack or have insufficiently developed ideologies, discipline, maturity and positive outlook in life.

2) Children feel bitter and insecure when parents separate: physically and emotionally the other parent is no longer immediately available to turn to for support, love and guidance. The normal family routine of a child is disrupted and their 'innocent' outlook on life is disorientated. Additional responsibilities are hoisted upon the child at too young an age as his/her childhood is almost taken away. The demand for instant maturity sets in and the overwhelming number of children are not able to cope, as a consequence they rebel, misbehave and fail.

3) Many mothers delude themselves into thinking that by keeping the children with them, their 'new' stepfather (if she remarries) or maternal male relatives will serve as an adequate substitute for the father. The love, concern and affection of paternal and maternal relatives, no matter how genuine and sincere is entirely different. Maternal grandparents and uncles have a natural tendency to be over lenient. This is quite normal, acceptable and proper when the parents of the child are together; however, when they separate and the mother gains custody, such softness and excessive mildness inculcates immaturity and emotionalism in the child.

4) The 'divorced' children's bond with their other paternal relatives especially grandparents, uncles and cousins is severely affected. This too pains a child and puts him at a disadvantage. Generally, paternal relatives demand and expect higher standards of achievement and behaviour in all spheres of life from 'their' offspring.

5) A great number of children lacking the physical presence of their father fail to develop spiritually and fall prey to the *nafs* (lowly desires). Many drift far from Deen, especially as they reach the formative years during adolescence, when they are somewhat 'independent' and beyond the physical control of the mother. Without the 'watchful' and at times 'stern' gaze of the father the child is more prone to rebel against his mother, teachers, elders, society and religion.

6) The majority of young people who proceed to become successful in their lives; studies, careers and business are often those from family backgrounds where both parents strive to upbring them. Research shows how children whose parents have separated are more likely to underachieve academically in secular studies. Whilst in the field of Deeni Uloom also, very few children whose parents have divorced have the opportunity, encouragement, discipline, confidence, financial support and steadfastness to complete Hifz of the Glorious Qur'ān or the Ãlim course. Make an appraisal of the youngsters attending salāh, conferences, *majālis*, lectures of the Ulamā and Jamā'at activities at the Masājid and one will note the majority of those present will be from 'united' families and attend because of encouragement by both parents.

Chapter Thirteen

Pregnancy, Childbirth & Infant Care

Based upon the Teachings

of

Shaykh Ashraf 'Ali Thãnwi ﷭,

Shaykh-ul-Hadeeth Ibrãheem Palanpoori ﷭,

Shaykh Manzoor Nu'maani ﷭,

Shaykh Muhammad Saleem Dhorat

$\mathcal{A}$llah 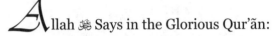 Says in the Glorious Qur'ãn:

> 'And We have enjoined on man (to be dutiful and good) to his parents. His mother bore him with much difficulty and delivered him with much difficulty, and his weaning is in two years - give thanks to Me and to your parents. Unto Me is the final destination.' (31:14)

$\mathcal{R}$asoolullah ﷺ commented (upon seeing a mother approaching with one child in her lap and another holding her hands),

> 'These women first of all bear these children in their womb. They then give birth to them; thereafter they lovingly and kindly rear them. Those amongst them who have (good, i.e. not bad) relationships with their husbands and whom are steadfast upon Salãh will go straight into Jannah!'

(Ma'ãriful Hadeeth)

Pregnancy

_A_llah ﷻ says in the Glorious Qur'ãn:

> 'To Allah belongs the kingdom of the Heavens and the earth, He creates what He wills. He bestows female (children) upon whom He wills, and bestows male (children) upon whom He wills. Or He bestows both males and females, and He renders barren whom He wills. Indeed, He is the All-Knower and is able to do all things.' (43:49-50)

_Sh_aykh-ul-Hadeeth Ibrãheem Palanpoori ﷫ comments, 'After marrying, most couples have a natural desire to be blessed with children from Allah ﷻ. Consequently, with their union, children start to arrive. However, sometimes, despite all efforts by the couple, Allah ﷻ out of His infinite Wisdom withholds offspring. There is no need to become saddened, depressed or lose hope...nor should the husband become displeased with his wife for not bearing children.'

Both should keep trying, continuously pray to Allah ﷻ and should there be a need, seek reliable medical advice and treatment. Do remember this must be in accordance to limits of the Sharee'ah. It is possible one of the couple may be ill or require treatment...correct and _halãl_ methods will, Inshã'Allah yield results. Always comprehend that there will be some _Hikmat_ (Divine Wisdom) behind any delay.

R asoolullah 🙼 said:
'When a woman becomes pregnant by her husband and he is pleased with her, she obtains the thawāb (reward) of a person engaging in fasting for Allah and for spending the night in Ibādah.'

When Allah 🙼 bestows a child, the first stage will commence with pregnancy which is, of course, discernable from various symptoms; stopping of monthly periods, 'morning sickness,' etc.

Shaykh-ul-Hadeeth Ibrāheem Palanpoori 🙼 advises, 'During pregnancy, ladies should take their health into full consideration. In accordance with medical advice (they should eat nourishing foods). As many pregnant ladies suffer from nausea, vomiting and a craving to eat salty, spicy items, they should exercise caution and only eat foodstuff which is beneficial to health. They should avoid all harmful and over spicy, sour foods.'

A suggested cure for 'morning sickness and nausea' is coconut and sugar candy whilst Nabee 🙼 is reported to have advised the eating of sweet melons, dates and grapefruit for the benefit of both mother and her unborn child. However, pregnant mothers' should appreciate that although nausea and sickness usually starts after six weeks and lasts up to the third month of pregnancy, they receive tremendous reward for bearing it patiently. Therefore, one should not unnecessarily resort to medicines and any medicine during pregnancy should only be taken upon your GP's advice.

Halāl Diet & Pregnancy

llah ﷻ addresses all the Prophets ﷺ (and thereby their followers) in the Glorious Qur'ān:

'O (you) Messengers! Eat of the Tayyib (halāl, pure & wholesome) and perform righteous deeds...' (23:51)

We are what we eat. Today we complain our children are disobedient towards us, but why the surprise? If we feed our children harām (even when they are in the womb) then the thoughts that will be bred in their minds (later in life) will be harām. Understand well, halāl food breeds halāl thoughts and halāl actions whilst harām food breeds harām thoughts and harām actions.

haykh Ashraf 'Ali Thānwi ﷺ narrates, 'If before birth of the child, parents were to reform themselves and adopt piety, then there is no reason why the child born too should not be pious. The actions of parents during pregnancy have a profound effect on the unborn child. Accordingly, the son of a Saint was quite mischievous. Somebody queried the Saint; 'It is indeed strange; you are so pious yet your son is so naughty?' The Saint replied, 'One evening I was invited to meals by a rich person (whose income was doubtful). After eating, my *nafs* became excited and I made love to my wife who became pregnant. This child is the effect of the doubtful food.'

Therefore, during pregnancy (especially) it is of the utmost importance to eat a varied 'halāl' diet brought from 'halāl' income. If in doubt regarding ingredients, leave it out. Rasoolullah 🌸 has related in a lengthy hadeeth...

> *'Undoubtedly Allah Ta'ālā is Pure and He only accepts that which is pure (deeds, statements and items). Undoubtedly the Command (to eat only halāl) which Allah ﷻ has ordained for the Prophets ﷺ is incumbent upon the Mu'min also...'* (p86, *Virtues of Du'aa*)

The pregnant mother does not need to overeat. Today our problem is that we eat too much and drink too little water. During the first six months of pregnancy, the majority of ladies do not need to 'increase' their food intake; merely ensure it is tayyib (pure), sensible, varied and contains adequate amount of nutrients and energy.

Milk ~ Best food for a Pregnant & Nursing Mother

Milk is such a blessing from Allah ﷻ for which Rasoolullah 🌸 recited a specific du'aa:

$$\text{اَللّٰهُمَّ بَارِكْ لَنَا فِيْهِ وَ زِدْنَا مِنْهُ}$$

'O Allah! Grant us blessings in this and increase it for us.'

Milk especially (and dairy produce in general) should be consumed by pregnant and lactating mothers as we receive two-thirds of our calcium from these sources (if worried about weight gain use semi-skimmed or low-fat-type). Should plain milk appear unappetising during pregnancy, one may supplement it into breakfast cereals; custards; rice puddings; milk shakes; yoghurt and lassi. Being a healthy weight is important before and during pregnancy both for the mother and unborn child.

Accordingly a balanced halāl diet is one, which includes sensible portions from:

- Milk & Dairy Products (eggs should be well-cooked)
- Fruit and vegetables
- Starchy Foods (such as chapatti, bread, rice, pasta, cereals)
- Lean (white) Meat ~ such as chicken, fish
- Nuts and pulses

All over-spicy, sour and bitter foods as well as those that cause constipation should be avoided. If the stomach feels heavy, resort to nutritious soups and broth.

Spiritual, Physical and Emotional Preparation

Just as important is to stay calm, composed, happy, free from worries and gloom. A Muslim mother-to-be should always be optimistic, positive and display a beautiful character under all circumstances, whether pleasing or (Allah ﷻ forbid) displeasing. She should stay clean, both physically and spiritually; i.e. not commit sins; watch TV, read novels, listen to music or view harām objects. All these have a harmful effect on one's unborn child. Accordingly, the pregnant mother should be punctual with Salāh and recitation of even a small portion of the Glorious Qur'ān.

Pregnant ladies should not rest to such an extent that they become lazy. Neither should they over exert themselves, by jumping, running or lifting heavy objects...for there is the very real danger of bleeding or miscarriage. However, they should try and walk a reasonable amount everyday.

Lovemaking During Pregnancy

$\mathcal{S}$haykh Ashraf 'Ali Thãnwi ﷺ narrates, 'Understand well, pregnant women are not always able to make love especially during the (first and third trimesters). It is necessary during these times, for the health and well-being of the mother and unborn child, that she rests and refrains from lovemaking. This situation remains for quite some time even after birth. (One should remember, even when *nifaas* (post-natal bleeding) finishes early, the womb, vagina and body are still recovering from the traumas of childbirth).

Therefore from a health point of view, pregnant and recently delivered mothers should abstain from lovemaking until their strength returns. Although this advice to refrain from lovemaking is primarily for health reasons, one should appreciate that excess force and passion by an irresponsible husband could cause miscarriage. Another reason for not making love during pregnancy is that excess force has a detrimental effect on the *akhlãq* of the unborn child.'

Although it is advisable to avoid lovemaking during pregnancy in order to protect the long-term health of the mother and child, nevertheless, it is quite proper for the couple to indulge in 'foreplay' and be intimate with each other. The couple may use other (permissible) parts of their bodies to arouse and satisfy themselves. It is self-masturbation which is impermissible.

Childbirth

R asoolullah ﷺ commented:

'Whenever a woman undergoes labour pains, then nobody in the Heavens and earth is aware of the glorious eye-soothing rewards in store for her. When the child is born, before a drop of milk appears from her breast; and for every gulp of milk the child takes; she receives reward for every mouthful and sucking. Moreover, if she has to awaken during the night because of her child, she receives the reward equivalent to emancipating 70 slaves in the Path of Allah!' (Kanzul Ummal, *Tarbiyyah Awlaad*, p.19)

Shaykh-ul-Hadeeth Ibrãheem Palanpoori ﷺ narrates, 'When the time approaches for childbirth, it is best if this takes place in the pure confines of the home under the supervision of a competently (qualified) midwife. This will ensure correct treatment and procedures. Nowadays, the trend is to take one's wife into hospital to give birth, but because...scant regard is given to *hijãb*, it is not wise to forgo the pure Islãmic environment of one's home...yes, should there be some medical reason or a midwife be not available then there is permission to enter hospital.'

Muslim women in the UK have a legal right, if they so wish, to give birth at home. As long as you stay within the law and consults with your GP, this cannot be termed radical as many non-muslim ladies also make use of this legal option.

Choice of Pregnancy Care & Childbirth in the UK

Under the provisions of the Government's (tax-funded) National Health Service, the following options are available to UK pregnant women notwithstanding the emphasis placed by local NHS Trusts on births and care at hospitals.

Midwife Only ~ This is where midwives (usually part of a NHS team) attend to the pregnant lady at home.

Midwife/General Practitioner ~ This is where supervision of the pregnancy is shared between the GP and NHS midwives at the doctors ante natal surgery. One still has an option to give birth at home or at the hospital.

Shared (Midwife/General Practitioner/Hospital) ~ This is when the ante natal supervision is shared between the midwives either at the doctors surgery and/or hospital under the supervision of a Consultant. Here assumption is made that the pregnant lady will enter hospital for the birth though she is at liberty to discuss with her GP and Consultant all the options available including home birth.

Hospital ~ This is where supervision is provided at the Ante Natal Clinic of a local hospital by NHS midwives and doctors under a consultant. Again, the assumption is made that birth will take place at the hospital.

Private Options ~ For a fraction of the expenditure incurred at weddings nowadays, Muslims have the option (and moral duty) to arrange for all aspects of Ante-Natal supervision and birth to be carried out by qualified female practitioners; independent midwives, doctors and consultants.　　(For further information visit www.aims.org.uk)

The Rise & Rise of Caesarean Births

ince the time of Prophet Adam عليه السلام and Mother Hawwā عليها السلام, births have and are taking place the 'natural way' through the vaginal canal. Nowadays, an unnecessary worry for many pregnant Muslim ladies in the west (but not so epidemically in the east...yet) is the phenomenal and alarming increase in the number of caesarean sections (so-much-so that a Parliamentary Select Committee was formed in early 2003 to undertake an inquiry). It is estimated that almost 30% (the official figure is 23%) of all births in the UK are now by surgical operation and half of these could have been easily prevented with appropriate 'care.'

Undoubtedly, some caesarean are life-saving and necessary, nevertheless the majority of births could be normal. There is a belief that authorities (despite the costs involved) are resorting to and pressurising mothers into caesarean too often for the sake of convenience. What mothers fail to realise is that although a caesarean birth 'without strain and pain' may appear modern, trendy, quick, clinical and easy; it will take two months thereafter, at least, to recover (the time when the baby needs the most attention). Moreover, women who have a caesarean, which is major surgery, are more likely to be readmitted to hospital for complications; wound and uterine infections, hysterectomy, appendicitis, cardio-pulmonary, gallbladder problems and postnatal depression. Sceptics claim all these unnecessary caesareans are in fact an indirect form of birth control.

In complete contrast, despite the energy and labour involved in giving birth the natural way (for which the mother receives great *thawāb*), most are back on their feet quickly (within hours) and are able to return to their normal routine very soon (within days). In fact, childbirth the 'natural way' without intervention and unnecessary 'painkillers' and medicines is best for both mother and child. Alhamdulillah, passage and 'massage' of the new born baby through the vaginal canal provides it with a wonderful 'wake-up call' to all of its body organs and senses, considerably reducing the chances of respiratory problems and agitation. The baby after a normal 'natural birth' appears more at ease and tranquil...as are mothers.

How to Avoid A Caesarean

Until there is a genuine overriding medical condition and need, Muslim parents-to-be should politely, wisely yet positively avoid opting for or 'request' a caesarean. The parents task will be made much easier if they are well-read on legal rights, hospital procedures and policies concerning pregnancy/childbirth. A Muslim father should also take the time to read the many excellent publications prepared by midwifery, child birth and consumer organisations and not be ashamed to accompany and support his wife at all stages except for the actual act of childbirth which he should leave in the hands of qualified midwives. Even here, he should be 'on hand' and available to physically and emotionally support and comfort his wife. Hospitals are more likely to listen and cooperate with a couple who are well-informed, diplomatic, polite yet determined.

Throughout pregnancy, the mother should eat a well-balanced diet rich in proteins and vitamins. The body should be prepared for the rigours of pregnancy and labour. Such an approach contributes towards a healthy baby and easier birth.

Avoid having to go to the hospital for childbirth unnecessarily early. Walk around during the early stages of labour instead of lying on the back; throughout childbirth, as far as possible work with and not against gravity. Avoid (unless absolutely necessary) 'epidurals,' non-vital pain killers, medicines and electronic foetal-monitoring equipment as many actually prolong labour, increase 'after pains' and the chances of caesarean. By going into hospital, the expectant mother does not lose her rights and privileges, she is at liberty to decline and refuse any form of unnecessary 'treatment.'

Shaykh Ashraf 'Ali Thānwi ﷺ suggests, 'Write the following Qur'ānic Verse and wrap it around the right thigh of the mother in labour. Upon childbirth, immediately remove. Inshā'Allah, birth will become easy:

اِذَا السَّمَآءُ انْشَقَّتْ، و اَذِنَتْ لِرَبِّهَا و حُقَّتْ،

و اِذَا الْاَرْضُ مُدَّتْ، و اَلْقَتْ مَا فِيْهَا و تَخَلَّتْ،

'When the heaven is split asunder. And listens to and obeys its Lord - and it must do so. And when the earth is stretched forth. And has cast out all that was in it and became empty.' (84:1-4)

Masnûn Acts upon Childbirth

Ghusl (Bathing)

Bathe the baby as soon as practicable after birth. Although midwives clean the baby with 'baby wipes;' at the first opportunity (if necessary upon return home) give a complete *Sharee' ghusl* (there is no need to create a commotion if hospital authorities do not allow bathing of the baby). Of course, no gargling or placing of water up the babe's nostrils is necessary (as for adults) nor should the baby be taken outside afterwards and do remember to wrap up the baby well and ensure a warm environment.

Azãn & Iqaamah

Aboo Rãfee' ﷺ relates he witnessed,

'Rasoolullah ﷺ recited the same Azãn (as for Salãh) into the ears of Hasan bin 'Ali ﷺ, when he was born at the home of daughter Fãtimah ﷺ.'

(Ma'ãriful Hadeeth, p. 19, Vol. 6)

After bathing the child, ask some pious Ãlim (if possible) or a pious family elder to give Azãn softly into the right ear and *iqaamah* into the left ear. Pious elders have mentioned that one *hikmat* behind the recitation of *Azãn* is to make the baby aware that both *Azãn* and *iqãmah* have been called, now await your *janãzãh* (funeral) Salãh. Another *hikmat* is to strengthen the capacity of *Imãn* in the baby by making them aware of the 'Greatness of Allah ﷻ,' which is repeated constantly in both *Azãn* and *iqãmah*. This also serves to distance Shaytãn.

Some Masnûn Du'aa's ~ For girls recite:

اَللّٰهُمَّ اِنِّیْ اُعِیْذُهَا بِکَ وَ ذُرِّیَّتِهَا مِنَ الشَّیْطَانِ الرَّجِیْمِ، اَللّٰهُـــمَّ

اجْعَلْهَا بَرَّةً تَقِیَّةً وَّ اَنْبِتْهَا فِی الْاِسْلَامِ نَبَاتًا حَسَنًا، اَللّٰهُمَّ عَلِّمْهَـــا

الْکِتَابَ وَ الْحِکْمَةَ وَ فَقِّهْهَا فِی الدِّیْنِ،

'O Allah! I seek Your protection for her and her descendents from the accursed Shaytãn. O Allah! make her pious and God fearing and let her grow up in Islãm to her excellent strength. O Allah! Teach her the Glorious Qur'ãn and Wisdom and grant her the understanding of Deen.'

For boys recite:

اَللّٰهُمَّ اِنِّیْ اُعِیْذُهُ بِکَ وَ ذُرِّیَّتِه مِنَ الشَّیْطَانِ الرَّجِیْمِ، اَللّٰهُمَّ اجْعَلْهُ

بَرًّا تَقِیًّا وَّ اَنْبِتْهُ فِی الْاِسْلَامِ نَبَاتًا حَسَنًا، اَللّٰهُمَّ عَلِّمْهُ الْکِتَابَ وَ

الْحِکْمَةَ وَ فَقِّهْهُ فِی الدِّیْنِ،

Burial of After-Birth/Placenta

As every portion of the human body is sacrosanct, parents of the newborn should ensure they 'collect' the placenta and arrange for it to be buried somewhere. Shaykh Dr. 'Abdul Hayy Ãrifee ﷺ states, 'If some part of the body of a living person is cut off or removed in an operation, it does not require any bathing...it should be simply wrapped in a piece of cloth and buried.'   (Ahqãme Mayyat, p.128)

Most hospital authorities are only too willing to allow the father to collect the after-birth in an airtight container. One merely needs to request politely at the appropriate time.

Tahneek

A smā' binte Aboo Bakr ﷺ relates, *'When 'Abdullah bin Zubair ﷺ was born, (we) presented him into the lap of Nabee ﷺ, who requested a date and after chewing it, placed a small amount onto the palate of 'Abdullah bin Zubair, making du'aa for goodness & blessings.'* (Uswai Rasool-e-Akram, p. 545)

Therefore, request some pious person to chew and completely soften a piece of date. Thereafter, place an extremely small amount (the purpose is to taste (not feed) sweetness of the date and saliva of some pious) upon the palate of the babe for the purpose of benediction. This is known as *tahneek* - a Sunnah of Nabee ﷺ and practised by the Sahābāh ﷺ. Our Ulamā state that this chewed date; its sweetness and the saliva of some pious entering the child's stomach, will Inshā'Allah assist the baby in acquiring *taqwā*. Although any Muslim may carry out these acts, it is best if the person performing the *Azān* and *tahneek* be a pious person. Somebody once asked Shaykh Rasheed Ahmad Gangohi ﷺ, 'What is the ruling regarding *tahneek*? He replied, 'Should the *tahneek* be from a pious Ālim, then it is *masnûn*, otherwise what benefit is there in tasting the saliva of some sinner!' Nevertheless, should a pious person not be available, then the parents themselves (even the mother) should perform *tahneek* with the niyyat of sunnah.

Breast-feeding (Radhā'at)

R asoolullah ﷺ commented:
"*When a woman breastfeeds her baby, then for every gulp of milk sucked by the baby, she receives thawāb equivalent to the reward of reviving a dead person. When she weans her baby, a (special angel) congratulates her (on the successful execution of the holy obligation of breast-feeding). And he says: 'All your past (minor) sins are forgiven.*"

(Al Mar'atus Sālihah, p. 42)

Breast-feeding is an *ibaadah* which earns tremendous reward and enhances the physical and spiritual bond between mother and child. Before, Muslim mothers used to always breastfeed their babies whilst in the state of *wudhu* and after reciting *Bismillah*. This is one reason why great personalities knew by heart large portions of the Glorious Qur'ān even before weaning. Even today, there are many servants of Allah ﷻ who breastfeed their children in the state of wudhu through the blessings of which their children become Huffāz at a very young age. Even from a purely health point of view, every Muslim mother should breast-feed. Dr Jack Newman, MD, FRCPC advises,

The vast majority of mothers are perfectly capable of breastfeeding their babies exclusively for four to six months. In fact, most mothers produce more than enough milk. Breastfeeding is the natural, physiologic way of feeding infants and young

children milk, and human milk is the milk made specifically for human infants. Formulas made from cow's milk or soy beans (most of them) are only superficially similar, and advertising which states otherwise is misleading. Here are a few ways breastfeeding can be made easy:

1) *The baby should be at the breast immediately after birth.*

2) *The mother and baby should stay in the same room.*

3) *Artificial nipples should not be given to the baby.*

4) *Supplements of water, sugar water, or formula are rarely needed.'*

Breastfeeding protects babies against gastro-enteritis, constipation, ear and chest infections, eczema, wheezing and childhood diabetes. Anti-bodies are passed from the mother into her breast milk, protecting the baby against illnesses for up to a year if the infant is breastfed for three to four months. The composition of breast milk changes as the baby grows, adjusting to give the nutrients the baby needs. Moreover, mothers who breastfeed are at a lower risk of pre-menopausal breast cancer ~ the risk can be reduced by up to 25% by breastfeeding. Breastfeeding mothers also have less chances of ovarian cancer and hip fractures later in life and they get their 'figure' back more quickly than those who bottle-feed because breastfeeding helps the womb to contract and by using 400 calories a day also helps to lose the excess weight gained during pregnancy.

The Spiritual Benefits of Breastfeeding

One benefit of *tayyib* (pure wholesome) food is the creation of bravery, courage and resolution within a person's heart. In complete contrast, *harām* or unwholesome food produces cowardice. It is related that in Khorashan, the Governor of Kabul, Ameer 'Abdur Rahman Khan's grandfather was Ameer Dawst Muhammad Khan (c. 1850 CE). He had appointed one of his sons as his successor. Some years later, an enemy invaded Khorashan and overran large areas. Ameer Dawst Muhammad Khan dispatched his son as head of an army to drive out the enemy and reclaim the pure land of Khorashan for Islām.

Accordingly, the son achieved this task and was returning home victorious...when false reports reached Ameer Dawst Muhammad Khan that his son had been defeated and fled home in disgrace. Saddened and grief stricken, Ameer Dawst Muhammad Khan slowly walked home and notified his wife of their son's behaviour...

'Our son has disgraced us...in the prime of his youth when he should have displayed his strength and courage, he fled from the battlefield and failed to drive out the enemy...what am I to do? People will say, you appointed a coward to be your successor!'

His wife immediately replied, 'This information is incorrect, it just is not possible that our son would suffer defeat!' Ameer Dawst Muhammad Khan retorted, 'But my informants have told me, he has suffered defeat and, here you are sitting within these four walls telling me the reports are wrong!' After a short while, a second report arrived confirming reality, that the Afghans had won, the enemy had been driven out and the son was indeed returning home victorious. Overjoyed and abashed, Ameer Dawst Muhammad Khan rushed to his wife and informed her that the first report was false and queried, 'Tell me, living within these four walls, how were you able to be so certain that our son had not been defeated?' His noble wife replied,

'I did not wish to relate this to anybody, however upon your insistence I will inform you. When our son was in my womb, I had decided, leave aside harãm I shall never eat anything doubtful, because I knew harãm sustenance creates weakness and cowardice within a person, whereas, halãl produces courage and boldness. I maintained this even after he was born; moreover I only breastfed him whilst in the state of wudhu and reciting Surah Yãseen. Even during this time, I protected my throat from harãm and doubtful, in order to strengthen the internal abilities and strength of our son. Accordingly, I was confident that he would never be a coward and when he had gone to fight the enemy, he will return victorious Inshã'Allah. This is why I said, 'Your report is incorrect.' (p106, Islaahi...)

A similar incident is reported of Sultan Teepu ☀ (1759-1799 CE) of how at a young age he single-handedly confronted a lion in the jungle. When his father informed his mother, she too replied of how she had always breastfed him whilst in the state of *wudhu*.

Common Misconceptions

*T*hough instinctive, successful breastfeeding is an art which needs to be learnt from experienced mothers. Parents also need to overcome the 'yuk' factor ~ where anything to do with human lactation is considered outdated and unhygienic. We have no problem drinking cow's milk prepared in a parlour and transported in tankers; therefore there is no reason to consider breastfeeding as uncivilised, in fact, it is the best form of nutrition for infants according to Islām and modern medical science.

Many mothers lose courage when their breasts become heavy, swollen and sometimes painful within a day or two of giving birth and preceding the flow of milk. Recite *Bismillah* and allow the baby to suck each breast for a few minutes until the milk flows freely. Some mothers become despondent and give-up because the baby appears to be losing weight. This is normal; the weight loss is in actual fact loss of body water. Rest assured, the baby will drink milk from the breasts as much as is needed. Dr Jack Newman, MD, FRCPC advises, 'The best treatment of nipple soreness is prevention. The best prevention is an early start to breastfeeding and a good latch. More than minimal nipple pain in the first two or three days after your baby's birth is due to a poor latch, no matter who tells you the latch is fine. Sometimes nipple ointments (which should be prescribed by your GP/Health Visitor) can be very useful for mild to moderate pain, but fixing the latch is still the best treatment.'

Misfortune of Bottles & Dummy's

*O*nce a Sahãbee 🕮 came into the company of Nabee 🕮 and inquired, 'O Rasoolullah 🕮, the faculty and eloquence of speech which you possess is not present in any of us!' Nabee 🕮 replied,

'Are you aware of which ladies' milk I have drunk? A blessed lady from the Banu S'ãd by the name of Haleemah as-Sã'deeÿah 🕮. I have drunk her milk. This is the effect of her milk that Allah has bestowed this excellence to me.' (p159, Lectures...)

From this we may conclude that the drops of milk, which spring from the mothers' bosom, bring with it the character of the mother. If she is pious, spiritual light will flow from her milk and descend into the child's heart.

Nowadays, the trend is for even Muslim mothers to unnecessarily place a milk bottle or rubber dummy/soother into the baby's mouth every time he cries, needs to be fed or lulled to sleep. This allows the mother 'freedom' from the responsibilities of motherhood: allows her to drive; go to work; go shopping; designate the task to another; socialise with friends; watch TV or undertake other activities. Motherhood is not so cheap and certain homeopathic doctors claim that babies who are given bottles, dummy's and soothers are more prone to illnesses, weakness and coughs notwithstanding the sterilisation undertaken. They are also deprived of the natural immunisation received by a breastfed baby from its mother.

haykh Ashraf 'Ali Thānwi ❀ related, 'There was a couple who made an agreement, 'Come, we shall perform *taubah* and make a promise to refrain from all sins so that all our children are born pious.' Sometime thereafter she became pregnant and a pious *Sāleh* child was born to them. One day, this child stole some fruit from a shop and ate it. The infuriated father asked his wife, 'Tell me the truth, where did this effect come from?' The mother replied, 'One day whilst he was in my womb, I picked and ate fruit from the branch of our neighbour's tree which is overhanging in our garden.' Her husband replied, 'The effect of that act has surfaced today!'

A similar episode is related of the great Saint Junaid Baghdādi ❀. He was in the habit of spending 40 days every year, all alone, in some remote location engaging in spiritual exercises and the remembrance of Allah ﷻ. On one occasion, upon his return after 40 days he did not notice the usual *anwārāt* (spiritual light and progress) in his *quloob* (heart). Disappointed, he related his worry and concern to his mother, 'Dear mother! I have returned after 40 days of fasting, spiritual exercises and ibādāt. Yet, I am not noticing the usual spiritual progress. My food, clothing, everything was halāl, in fact, I was fortunate to make greater effort than usual, yet the spiritual upliftment is lacking! What could be the possible reason?' His mother replied, 'Dear son, it is my fault! When you were in my womb, one day I broke and ate fruit from the branch of a neighbours tree overhanging our garden. We are now witnessing the consequences of my deed. Wait, let me go and apologize for this action of mine.' Consequently, the mother departed for next door and explaining her act requested she be forgiven. Immediately, spiritual light showered upon the *quloob* of Shaykh Junaid Baghdadi ﷻ. Remember, the first condition for pious children is for parents themselves to become pious.'

Removal of Babe's Hair & 'Aqeeqah

B areerah ؊ relates, *'During the (pre-Islāmic) days of ignorance, we had the custom whereby when a child was born an animal would be slaughtered and thereafter its blood would be used to colour the clean-shaven head of the baby. With the advent of Islām (and Nabee ﷺ) we would slaughter the 'aqeeqah animal and clean shave the babe's head on the seventh day. Thereafter we would rub some saffron upon the child's head.'* (Ma'ariful Hadeeth, p. 23, Vol. 6)

S haykh Manzoor Nu'maani ﷻ narrates, 'It is a well-established practice amongst all nations and cultures of the world to regard the birth of a child as an occasion of joy and to display this happiness in some form or another. Islam has enjoined only two specific acts upon this occasion. Firstly, the shaving of the hair of the head and secondly 'aqeeqah. Both deeds are closely related to the distinguished way of Prophet Ibrāheem ﷺ and are synonymous with the rites of Hajj. Moreover, through 'aqeeqah, the father is publicly accepting the child as his and closing the door for anybody to point even a finger of guilt or doubt towards his wife.' (p22, Vol. 6, Ma'āriful Hadeeth) haykh Ashraf 'Ali Thãnwi ☸ narrates, 'By performing *'aqeeqah* (slaughtering of an animal) the child is saved from misfortunes and mishaps. One should note the following:

1) Whenever a boy or girl is born, it is preferable to name the child and perform *'aqeeqah* on the seventh day.

2) For *'aqeeqah,* two sheep or goats should be slaughtered for a boy and one sheep or goat for a girl. Alternatively, these shares may be incorporated in one of the seven shares in a cow or camel.

3) Hair of the head should be clean shaven on the seventh day and its weight equivalent in silver (our Ulamã suggest £5) should be donated to the 'poor' in charity. Remember to bury the hair.

4) If unable to afford two *'aqeeqah* animals for a boy, one animal too is sufficient. Should this also be beyond one's means, then there is absolutely no harm in not performing *'aqeeqah.*

5) If *'aqeeqah* was not performed on the seventh day, whenever this act is carried out, try to make it on a 'seventh' day, e.g. the child was born on a Friday, try to perform *'aqeeqah* on any Thursday.

6) The *'aqeeqah* meat may be distributed both raw and cooked to whomsoever one wishes: relatives, friends, poor and the affluent.

7) The animal which is fit for *qurbaani* is also fit for *'aqeeqah.'*

Tasmeeyah

(Naming the Muslim Child)

A llah ﷻ Says in the Glorious Qur'ān:

'He is Allah, the Creator, the Inventor of all things, the Bestower of forms. To Him belong the Best Names. All that is in the heavens and the earth glorify Him. And He is the All-Mighty, the All-Wise.' (60:24)

R asoolullah ﷺ commented:

'It is a child's haqq (right) upon his father that he (or she) be given a good (Islāmic) name and be adorned with good manners and habits.'

'A man's first gift to his child is his name, therefore he should choose a good (Islāmic) name.'

'On the Day of Qiyāmah you will be called by your own names and that of your forefathers...therefore keep good (Islāmic) names.'

'Keep the names of Prophets (عليهم السلام)...'

'Amongst your names, the most beloved and pleasing to Allah are 'Abdullah and 'Abdur Rahmān.'

(Ma'āriful Hadeeth, p. 29-30, Vol. 6)

S haykh Manzoor Nu'maani ﷺ narrates, 'To choose a good (Islāmic) name is one of the rights of the child. The reason why the names 'Abdullah and 'Abdur Rahmān have been highlighted is the intrinsic feature of

submission to the Creator which is very Pleasing to Allah
ﷻ. Similarly, the names of the Prophets ﷺ are also very
desirable as they reflect and portray a relationship with
them. Rasoolullah ﷺ himself chose the name Ibrāheem for
his son. In a hadeeth it appears,

'Base your names upon the names of the Prophets ﷺ.'

Rasoolullah ﷺ also used other good names when naming
children, for example Hasan and Hussain for his ﷺ
grandchildren ﵁. It is evident that this was the way of
Rasoolullah ﷺ, accordingly parents should either select a
good appropriate name or preferably request a pious
scholar to select one.' (p31, ibid.)

This latter advice is most appropriate nowadays as many
'modern Muslims' select names with a westernised flavour
or resort to westernising names by shortening them.
Remember well, names (and the true intention behind
them) greatly influence a person's life. Our Nabee ﷺ often
changed name's which were displeasing. If in doubt,
approach your local Ulamā and inquire.

Shaykh Muhammad Saleem Dhorat *dāmat
barakātuhum* narrates, 'Addressing somebody by
their correct Islāmic name is akin to making a du'aa for
them and has a profound effect. This is why in Arabia,
unknown persons were addressed as 'O Saleh (pious)!' or 'O
Sa'eed (fortunate)!' or 'O Muhammad (praiseworthy)!' All
these are commendable terms of address and supplication.
Allah ﷻ alone knows at what moment a person's du'aa is
accepted, accordingly always call a person by their full
Islāmic name.'

Some Names of Prophets ﷺ

Muhammad (ﷺ), Ãdam, Ilyaas, Ayyûb, Dãwûd, Hãrûn, Hûd, Ibrãheem, Idrees, 'Easaa, Ishãq, Ismã'eel, Lût, Mûsã, Nûh, Sãleh, Shu'ayb, Sulaymãn, 'Uzair, Ya'qûb, Yahyã, Yûnus, Yûsuf, Zakariyyã (ﷺ)

The Ten 'Asharah Mubassharah ﷺ

Aboo Bakr, 'Umar, 'Uthmãn, 'Ali, Talhah, Zubayr, 'Abdur Rahmãn, Sa'd, Sa'eed, Aboo 'Ubaydah.

Some Other Male Sahãbãh ﷺ

Abbãs, Hamzah, Qãsim, Ja'far, Fadhl, Hasan, Husayn, Aboo Hurayrah, Anas, Ammãr, Aboo Ayyûb, Usamãh, Bilãl, Thaabit, Hishãm, Hudhayfah, Khãlid, Khabbãb, Zayd, Sufyaan, Safwãn, Salmãn, Suhayl, 'Umayr, 'Utbah, 'Uqbah, 'Amr, Mas'ood, Mu'aawiyah, Mu'ãdh, Mus'ab, Nu'aym.

Some Famous Scholars & Saints

Aboo Haneefah, Mãlik, Shafi'ee, Ahmad, Junaid, Ashraf Ali

The Daughters of our Nabee ﷺ

Zaynab, Ruqayyah, Umme Kulthoom, Fãtimah (ﷺ)

Mothers of the Believers ﷺ

Khadeejah, Ã'ishah, Hafsah, Sawdah, Umme Salamah, Zaynab, Juwayriyyah, Umme Habeebah, Maymoonah, Safiyyah (ﷺ).

Some Other Female Sahãbeeyã' & Pious Ladies ﷺ

Ãsiyah, Ãminah, Asmã', Aneesah, Bilqees, Haleemah, Hassaanah, Hãmidah, Humairaa', Hawwaa, Khaalidah, Khawlah, Durrah, Rãbi'ah, Zubaydah, Zahrã', Zaybun Nisaa, Zulaikah, Sa'diyah, Sa'eedah, Saarah, Sumaiyah, Shaahidah, Sughraa, Sulaym, Safoora, Safeera, Taahirah, Tayyibah, Ammaarah, Mu'minah, Maryam, Naseerah, Haajarah, Naa'ilah, Mãriyah, Rayhãnah, Rãbiyah.

Circumcision

haykh Ashraf 'Ali Thãnwi ۞ narrates, 'When one notices the ability of the child to be able to tolerate, perform circumcision without any formality. It is preferable (*mustahab*) to perform it before 7 years of age and compulsory by the time the child reaches 12 years. Experienced and pious Doctors too recommend 'early' circumcision as Allah ۞ has created very rapid healing ability in the new born.'

Baseless Customs & Birthday Parties

Our beloved Nabee ۞ has exhorted the Ummah from refraining and imitating others in every respect... '*He who imitates a nation becomes of them.*' With regards to birthday parties, parents should realize that on every birthday, their beloved child is closer to his death. In the narrow confines of the grave, only good deeds will be of any benefit, therefore, if you truly desire goodness for your child; adorn him with noble character and piety. Balloons, party hats, cakes, cards and presents all end up as garbage.

haykh Muhammad Saleem Dhorat *dãmat barakãtuhum* narrates,

'Heed should be taken by those who attend or celebrate (unIslãmic) ceremonies and festivals for recreational reasons. Consequences will have to be paid (in the Ãkhirah) whatever the reasons for participation. Our (religious) ceremonies too should be free from alien customs that have crept in from other communities and religions...'

Birth Control & Abortion

llah ﷻ Says in the Glorious Qur'ān:

Say (O Muhammad ﷺ): Come, I will recite what your Lord has prohibited from: join not anything in worship with Him; be good and dutiful to your parents; kill not your children because of poverty ~ We provide sustenance for you and for them...' (6:151)

asoolullah ﷺ commented:

'Marry such women who love their husband and give birth in abundance so that I may be proud of your greater number over (previous) Ummahs.'

(Aboo Dāwood, Mazāhir Haqq, p249, Vol. 3)

Nowadays Muslim couples are opening Kitab-un-Nikah at a time when they should be referring to Kitab-ul-Janāiz. Despite acknowledging Allah ﷻ as our Creator and Sustainer, Muslims have allowed foreign ideologies to convince them that it is inappropriate, ignorant, uncivilised, foolish and a burden on the world's resources, one's career, freedom and health to have more than two children or to become pregnant too early or too often.

Shaykh Mufti Ibrāheem Desai *dāmat barakātuhum* comments, 'Reversible contraception is permissible on a limited scale for valid Sharee' reasons...' Amongst these is physical weakness; sickness; couple being on a journey or distant land; etc. For specific fiqh rulings, seek the advice of a qualified Ãlim. Permanent contraception is only permissible when the wife's life or health is in danger:

Birth Control Due to Ill-Health

Q haykh Mufti 'Abdur-Raheem Lajpoori ﷺ was asked the following question...

Question: *'My wife has been ill for the past several years. She is getting weaker and is unable to even undertake domestic chores. Despite receiving medical treatment, her health continues to deteriorate. If she were to conceive, her condition and illness would seriously worsen. Homeopathic and Medical Doctors suggest she undergoes sterilization. Should we do so and is it permissible in our case?*

Answer: *'Because of ill-health and weakness, your wife is unable to bear the rigours of pregnancy, you should therefore firstly try some form of contraception. If this is not suitable, then upon the advice of a qualified pious Muslim Doctor your wife may resort to an operation. However, a non-muslim doctor's advice is not valid.'*

Fatāwā Raheemeeyah (Vol 3, p. 148)

Abortion (Killing of the Innocent)

In Islām, the human body and life are viewed as an trust from Allah ﷺ. In the UK alone, a staggering 540 abortions (of innocent unborn children) are committed daily (almost 1 in 3 pregnancies)! According to the Jurists of Islām, the *ruh* (soul) enters the foetus on the 120th. day; upon which it is not permissible, under any circumstances, to abort. Even before 120 days, it is only permissible under certain circumstances: rape; incest; severe foetal deformity; etc. Therefore, one must consult a Mufti first.

Miscarriage & Stillbirth

R asoolullah ﷺ commented:

'Whenever a pregnant women suffers miscarriage, the unborn foetus will drag its mother into Jannah if she maintains sabr (patience) with the hope of acquiring thawāb (reward).

'Whichever lady passes away in her virginity, or during childbirth or nifaas (post natal bleeding period), will attain the rank of a Shaheed (martyr).'

(Quoted from *Tarbiyyah Awlaad*, p.18)

Shaykh Ashraf 'Ali Thānwi ﷺ related, 'There was once a Saint who remained a bachelor. One night, he abruptly awoke and called out 'Quickly, I wish to marry.' An associate, who was in attendance, was the father of a virgin maiden. Immediately, he departed home and awakening his household explained the golden opportunity. His daughter willingly agreed and accompanied her father to the Madrasah where *nikāh* was performed that very night in the presence of other students! After some time, a child was born but, unfortunately this child died shortly after birth. The Saint thereafter addressed his wife,

'My purpose in getting married has been fulfilled. Now you have a choice. If you are desirous of dunyā I shall divorce you and, you may marry some other. However, if you wish to spend your life in the obedience and remembrance of Allah ﷻ you may happily continue to live with me.'

Because the lady had enjoyed the companionship of her husband, she wisely replied, 'I shall go to no other!' Accordingly, both husband and wife continued to happily live together. Some intimate associates enquired from the Saint, 'Shaykh! We fail to understand. With great speed did you marry in the middle of the night. And, now that your child has passed away, you are offering her the chance to separate?' The Saint replied,

'Fact of the matter is, whilst I was asleep that night, I dreamt Qiyāmah had arrived and, on the Plain of Reckoning people were crossing the Pûl (Bridge) of Sir'āt. I noticed one particular person undergoing great difficulty in crossing: slipping and swaying. The Angels arrived to drag him towards Hell. Suddenly, a baby appeared and began to pull this man towards Jannah. A great tussle and commotion took place between the Angels and child over this man, upon which Allah ﷻ Commanded, 'He is a mere child who just will not understand and obstinately persist. Therefore allow him to take his father to Jannah!' In the twinkling of an eye, the child dragged his father into Jannah. I enquired, 'Who is this child?' A voice replied, 'He is the child of that man and, passed away in infancy. Here the child has become the medium of his parents' salvation!' At this point my eyes opened and I pondered, 'Why should I be deprived of this opportunity lest a child be the medium of my salvation.' This is why I married.'

Example of Umme Sulaym ﷺ

Shaykh Ashraf 'Ali Thānwi ﷺ relates, 'The noble behaviour of Umme Sulaym ﷺ, wife of the eminent Sahābee Aboo Talha ﷺ and mother of Anas ﷺ is related in hadeeth. Another child of theirs had fallen ill, and Aboo Talha ﷺ would ask of his health every day upon his return from work. One day the child passed away.

When Aboo Talha ﷺ came home that evening, Umme Sulaym ﷺ did not inform him of their son's death so as not to upset him immediately upon his return. He again queried 'How is our son?' Mustering courage, the grieved mother replied, 'He is in a much better and tranquil state now.' (In reality this was no lie, for there is no greater tranquillity for a Mu'min than *death*). After her husband had eaten, he expressed a desire to make love...which Umme Sulaym ﷺ bravely fulfilled.

After *ghusl*, she asked her husband, 'I would like to pose a question, If somebody had given us an item to keep as *amānat* (trust), what should we do if he wishes to reclaim it?' Aboo Talha ﷺ replied, 'Why, we should of course return the owner's item back to him with happiness.' Umme Sulaym ﷺ commented, 'Well, make *sabr* upon your son's death and happily make preparation for his burial, for Allah ﷺ has reclaimed His *amānat*.'

Aboo Talha ﷺ became furious, 'What! Why did you not inform me last night?' Calmly, Umme Sulaym ﷺ replied,

'Why? What difference would it have made, you would not have eaten (after a day's fasting) and spent the whole night in grief...this is why I did not inform you upon your return.' After Fajr Salāh, Aboo Talha ⚬ related the whole episode to Nabee ⚬ who commented, 'Allah Ta'ālā approves and is pleased with Umme Sulaym's behaviour, and I have great hopes that Allah Ta'ālā will bless you with a *mubarak* child from this night's union.' Indeed, a son named 'Abdullah ⚬ was born, whose *tahneek* was performed by Nabee ⚬ and this child went on to become the father of nine son's, all *Qari's* (expert reciters by heart) of the Glorious Qur'ān!

Umme Sulaym ⚬ stated a reality. Children are an *amānah* from Allah ⚬, whenever He wishes to reclaim them, we should happily return them to Him. This begs the question; 'If they be an *amānah,* then why has Allah ⚬ created so much love for children in their parents' hearts?' The reply is this, 'Such love has been created so as to ensure their correct upbringing, because without *muhabbat* who would clean the child's urine, faeces and vomit? Just ponder how difficult it is to look after somebody else's child...'

'When one's own child is crying the heart aches,

but when somebody else's child cries, the head aches!'

'Also remember, when a child is grown up...love for that child naturally decreases. This is the reason for greater love of one's younger child compared to the eldest. Therefore, regard children as the property of Allah ⚬, whose *amānah* we hold but for a few days. This contemplation will ensure sorrow in moderation upon their loss, because grief occurs when one considers the child as one's sole ownership.'

Nifaas (Post-Natal Bleeding)

haykh Ashraf 'Ali Thãnwi ☺ relates in 'Heavenly Ornaments,'

Mas'alah 1: The blood which emerges from the front opening (vagina) after childbirth is known as *nifaas*.

Mas'alah 2: The maximum duration of *nifaas* is forty (40) days...whilst there is no minimum period. Even if bleeding stops after a few moments, it is still classified as *nifaas*.

Mas'alah 3: If somebody does not bleed at all after childbirth, even then it is *wãjib* (compulsory) to bathe.

Mas'alah 4: If more than half the baby emerges (but not completely) then the blood which flows is also *nifaas*. Prior to half the body emerging, the bleeding is known as *istihãdhã* during which time, if one's senses are present, it is incumbent to pray salãh (even if by means of only gestures) and not let it become *qadhã*. If in praying salãh, there is genuine danger (to the mother or baby), then forgo salãh (and make qadhã later).

Mas'alah 5: Should a lady suffer miscarriage and half an limb is formed, then the blood after miscarriage is also *nifaas*. However, if no limbs were formed...merely flesh, then the accompanying bleeding is not *nifaas*. If it could be classified as *haidh* (monthly periods ~ bleeding for a minimum of three days and with a duration of 15 pure days in-between) then it is *haidh*, otherwise *istihãdhã*.

Mas'alah 6: Should bleeding continue beyond forty (40) days and this is the first birth, then the nifaas is for 40 days, the remaining days of bleeding are *istihādhā.* Accordingly, after 40 days, the mother should bathe and commence Salāh and not wait for (the *istihādhā)* bleeding to stop. However, should this be a subsequent birth and a previous nifaas is established then even on this occasion those set days are nifaas, the additional days (from habit past 40 days) will be known as *istihādhā.*

Mas'alah 7: If somebody has a habit of thirty (30) days nifaas and on a new occasion bleeding surpasses 30 days then she should wait (for her final bath). If the bleeding stops up to the 40th. day, then all the days are of nifaas; but if the bleeding continues even after the 40th. day, then only the 30 days will be known as nifaas, the remaining 10 days will be *istihādhā.* Immediately, upon the 40th. day, bathe and make qadhā Salāh of the extra 10 days.

Mas'alah 8: If bleeding stops before 40 days, immediately bathe and commence Salāh. Should bathing be injurious, then make tayammum and perform Salāh. Never ever miss Salāh.

Mas'alah 9: During nifaas, it is not permissible to perform Salāh or Saum. The only difference is that Salāh is waived completely but not so Saum (of Ramadhān); qadhā will have to be made of missed fasts upon acquiring purity. It is also not permissible to recite or touch the Glorious Qur'ān.

Mas'alah 10: During nifaas, it is impermissible to make love or for the husband to either view or touch any portion of the body between the navel and knees. Besides this, all else is permissible; living, sleeping, eating together, etc.

(Heavenly Ornaments, p179 & 182, Vol.2)

Ibaadah & Time During Nifaas

During times of nifaas and haidh (monthly periods), although it is not permissible to pray Salāh, keep Saum or recite the Glorious Qur'ān because of the state of greater impurity, it is also not a time to be neglectful of the remembrance of Allah ﷻ.

At the time of each Salāh, as normal, one should make ablution, spread the prayer mat and engage in some form of *thikr,* du'aa's, durood, Istighfār and the reading of authentic kitabs for the time it normally takes to perform Salāh. This will, Inshā'Allah, dispel any inclination towards Deeni negligence or grant the nafs (self) an opportunity to rebel. It is perfectly reasonable to even engage in such spiritual activities whilst breastfeeding the baby. During nifaas, make a point of bathing regularly and staying meticulously clean.

Shaykh Ashraf 'Ali Thānwi ﷺ narrates, 'As soon as the nifaas bleeding stops, bathe immediately and commence the performance of Salāh. To miss even one Salāh without a genuine Sharee' excuse is a grave sin...'

'There is also absolutely no need for other ladies of the family to gather at the end of nifaas and bathe the nursing mother three (or any other number of) times. In certain quarters, meals are prepared and various special dishes served. These are all unfounded, silly and stupid fanfares and customs which need to be ended...'   (Tarbiyyah Awlaad)

When Couples Cannot Conceive

llah ﷻ says in the Glorious Qur'ān:
'To Allah belongs the kingdom of the Heavens
and the earth, He creates what He wills. He bestows
female (children) upon whom He wills, and bestows
male (children) upon whom He wills. Or He bestows
both males and females, and He renders barren
whom He wills. Indeed, He is the All-Knower and is
able to do all things.' (43:49-50)

Couples who are unable to conceive should not become
depressed, pine away their life in worry or grief, blame each
other nor allow it to sour their relationship or even
remotely consider the possibility of remarrying. Firstly,
remain happy and accept the choice of Allah ﷻ for the
delay in being blessed with children. Thereafter, after a
reasonable time (at least a few years during which the
couple themselves should make du'aa after every Fardh
Salāh), seek the services of your own GP and make use of
only halāl methods and treatments. The malpractices and
harām taking place at infertility clinics are too well
documented to warrant comment. The following Qur'ānic
du'aa's after every Salāh are very beneficial:

رَبِّ لاَ تَذَرْنِيْ فَرْدًا وَّ اَنْتَ خَيْرُ الْوَارِثِيْنَ، رَبِّ هَبْ لِيْ مِـنْ

لَّدُنْكَ ذُرِّيَّةً طَيِّبَةً ۚ اِنَّكَ سَمِيْعُ الدُّعَآءِ،

Shaykh Ashraf 'Ali Thānwi ۝ narrates, 'My tutor Shaykh Sayyed Ahmad Dehlwi ۝ once observed his uncle, another scholar, sitting despondently. Upon query, he replied, 'Old-age has arrived and I still have no children.' My tutor commented, 'Subhān'Allah! Is this a matter of sorrow or happiness?' Uncle replied, 'How may it be a means of happiness?' Shaykh Sayyed Ahmad Dehlwi ۝ commented, 'It is indeed a cause of happiness; because in your lineage you were the intended person; all your forefathers were means; in contrast to those with children; they are not the intended ones; they were created for sorrow. Observe, how cereal seeds are of two kind; one which is used for eating; the other for replanting. The intention is to eat...therefore the seed which is eaten is superior. Similarly, those who have no children, from the time of Prophet Adam ۝ to their parents, all their forefathers were means to their final existence...just like the seeds replanted for final fruition.'

Although, this is a philosophical approach, nevertheless it is the way couples without children should overcome their sorrow. Moreover, should grief still remain, then just observe the behaviour of the majority of children of this era. They are a medium of worry and unhappiness for their parents. Should even this reasoning fail to sooth one's conscience, then accept the fact that whatever Allah ۝ has decreed is best for us. And, should you be unable to do this...then at the very least appreciate that your wife has done no wrong. Why blame her?'

(p32, Tarbiyyah Awlaad)

Chapter Fifteen

Tarbiyyah
(Correct Training)
of
Muslim Children

Based upon the Teachings of

Shaykh Ashraf 'Ali Thãnwi ﷺ

Shaykh Maseehullah Khan ﷺ *&*

Shaykh Muhammad Saleem Dhorat

ow may the babe acquire husne akhlãq (good character), when both its milk and its tarbiyyah sprouts from boxes (powdered milk & TV)?

The State of Our Muaasharat

*U*qbah bin 'Amir ﷺ once requested, 'O Rasoolullah ﷺ! What is the method of saviour and salvation? Rasoolullah ﷺ replied:

'Keep your tongue under control and your home should be spacious for you, i.e. without necessity, do not come out of your houses: moreover, weep upon your shortcomings.' (Islāh Khwāteen)

*OS*haykh Ashraf 'Ali Thānwi ﷺ commented,

'Concord (salāmati) is present in pre-occupation; whether this be of a Deeni or permissible worldly nature. In all conditions, pre-occupation is better than inactivity. Experience shows that whenever a person (especially a child) remains unoccupied, Shaytan prevails over him. And amongst activities, the company of the pious (scholars or their publications) is best...' (Malfoozāts, Vol.6, p46)

*OS*haykh Muhammad Saleem Dhorat *hafizahullah* narrates, 'Make an appraisal of our *Muaasharat* (society) and two 'forms' of parenthood will be noticeable. The first approach is of those parents who are totally neglectful of the true *tarbiyyah* of their children; whether they pray, swear, misbehave or adopt the company of the pious...all religious matters and activities of their offspring are irrelevant. Such parents are drowned in their own 'problems' and contented with their own religious performances. They are completely indifferent to the spiritual and moral well-being of their children and this is the case of the majority of Muslim homes; total negligence!

The second group of parents are those who genuinely wish their children to be religious and pious...but through shortcuts, i.e. threats, scolding, physical punishment and without any effort on their part. Who has the time to sit down with children and affectionately make them understand who Allah ﷻ is; how many favours and bounties of His we enjoy throughout the day; the importance of Salāh and how we only have to perform it five times a day, etc., etc? Therefore, although wishing our children to be pious, nevertheless we are only able to threaten. Instead of creating the awareness, attention and greatness of Allah ﷻ, by threatening violence, we create our awe in their hearts!

As far as the first group of parents are concerned, any possibility of *tarbiyyah* and reformation of the child is annihilated from the very beginning by apathy and indifference. The children from such households grow up with Muslim names...but alas, upon maturity; doubts and ridicule regarding the basic tenets of Deen arise in their minds and appear on their tongue whereby they leave the fold of Islām notwithstanding the occasional salāh and fast in Ramadhān.

The second group of parents who resort to threats and force to compel children to perform religious duties have failed to inculcate Deeni, spiritual and moral awareness amongst the child. There is a stark absence of *muhabbat* (true love). As long as the father's ability to dominate and overawe the child are present, he/she will comply, live and eat together, yet without true respect, affection, real eye contact and openness with the parent. Each loath the other. The father soothes his conscience by thinking, 'I am being very religious and rewarded in keeping the children under my awe.' However, ask yourself the question whether this ignorant approach is for the sake of Allah ﷻ or to pacify one's ego that the child is under my control?

Another Misunderstanding

Up to about nine years of age, the child will happily walk along and accompany his parents...even holding their hands. However, upon reaching his teens, the same child will become rebellious. Where has this sudden irreligiousness come from?

What we need to understand is that because correct affection, tarbiyyah and Deeni awareness was not created during infancy, the child has always been irreligious but the parents failed to realise this because the disobediences to Allah ﷻ that he carried out were not important. When the adolescent child missed Salāh; watched TV; abandoned purdah; departed to work in an unIslāmic environment; we did not consider it to be wrong. But when the same child started arriving late; became entangled in an illicit relationship with girls or enacted something which dented our honour, we started to get worried about the *religious* aspects of his life.

In reality, we are not worried about Deen at all, it is only when he/she does something that stains our honour that we become anxious and perplexed. We are blissfully unconcerned about their open violation of the *ahqāms* (commands) of Allah ﷻ, we are only worried and hurt when they disobey us. Our daughters spend up to six hours and more every day at institutions without *purdah,* with hair of the head uncovered. Upon returning home, children view TV, video and the Internet...but parents are unconcerned, because in their sight, she is not off-track or irreligious.

However, two or three years later, when the parents advise their daughter to marry her cousin, she openly refuses, 'I have no intention of marrying him! Tell me, is it *fardh, wājib, sunnah* or *mustahab* to marry him? What is the ruling according to the Sharee'ah?' Obviously, the Sharee'ah does not make it incumbent to marry one's cousin...nevertheless, because she is now going against your wishes, you will go around telling everybody how disobedient your daughter has become! When she failed to perform salāh, intermingled, travelled to college and work with non-mahram men, listened to music, watched TV...in essence, enacted every form of disobedience to Allah ﷻ, even then she was good in your books because she lived in accordance to your wishes. However, the minute you realised she no longer listened, you concluded 'she has rebelled.' In the final analysis, our judgement and decisions are not based upon our children's faithfulness to the *ahqāms* of Allah ﷻ, rather they are decided upon whether our wishes and desires are being fulfilled.'

The Two Responsibilities of Parenthood

Understand well, parents have two responsibilities. Firstly, to make themselves 100% religious and secondly, to also make those for whom they are responsible 100% religious. Remember, the time to make our children Deeni conscious is not when they reach puberty, rather it starts from the time they are born.

Does a child suddenly go 'off-track' at 14 or 15 years of age? Does a person become disorientated overnight? Are *taqwā* and *deendaree* so fickle as to allow such a dramatic revolution and corruption within a matter of hours? No, even before puberty, from a very young age, we had failed to ingrain correct religion into the child. The Deeni consciousness of the heart was missing all the time, the only difference is that before the age of 13 or 14 years, he was unaware of these promiscuous evils which he now enacts with relish. A boy of 8 years will not incline towards girls, only after 14 years of age will his interests arise. Why? Because, daily you had served a diet of immoral relationships between semi-nude men and women on TV. Foolishly, naively and stupidly you had hoped his brain would fail to be influenced from this poison. Think rationally, intelligently and correctly, how is this possible?

One must prepare the child's temperament from birth. Save children from inappropriate friendship and evil environments. From birth, apply your full efforts, energies and resources to create such a deeni temperament in the child, that when he reaches puberty and enters any environment, he will not be influenced by its evil.

Remember, the whole world has become corrupted...for how long will you be able to shield your children away from its influences? They will attend school, college, universities, city and shopping centres, factories, offices and foreign countries. These are all realities and necessities of modern-day life, therefore during childhood, spend all your energies to ingrain into their minds and hearts that,

'I am a servant of Allah ﷻ and my life must exist in accordance to His Wishes. Should I deviate in the least, I shall be in mortal danger; both in this world and in the Hereafter.'

Should Parental Affection or Awe Dominate?

The majority of parents commit the error of over imposing their awe upon their children and subjugating their *muhabbat*. Whereas the first and foremost demand of *tarbiyyah* is for a child to understand in his mind and heart that, 'although my parents sometimes display their displeasure at my misbehaviour, nevertheless there is nobody on the face of this earth more benevolent, affectionate and loving towards me.'

When this concept is ingrained in the child and the need does arise to reprimand and discipline, the child himself will become abashed to see his parents changing their affectionate tone towards one of displeasure. But this is only possible when love is dominant and awe remains latent. Now, the child will feel so much loyalty for its parents instead of loathing and despising them. All children crave for affection, love and parental attention.'

Caring for the Young

Allah ﷻ Says in the Glorious Qur'ān:

'O People of Imān! Save yourselves and your families (wives and children) from the Fire (of Hell).'

(66:6)

Rasoolullah ﷺ commented,

'Everyone of you is a shepherd and everyone of you will be questioned about his flock.'

(Ma'āriful Hadeeth, p. 30, Vol. 6)

Shaykh Ashraf 'Ali Thānwi ﷺ relates, 'An experienced person stated, 'The time for a child's character reformation is up to five years of age, by this period, whatever habits are to be ingrained become grounded.' From this we may conclude that the general assumption of infancy being a period of low understanding is false; for children digest and take influence from their environment. This is why our *Akābir* have stressed the easiest way of character building is for parents' to devote their full energy in developing and training the first child. Like sheep, all subsequent children will follow and imitate every trait and habit. Remember, infants grow up in their mother's lap, therefore the mothers *akhlāq* and habits greatly influence them. The wise suggest that although infants are unable to speak, every action and expression registers a picture onto their pure minds. Upon maturity, this picture serves as a 'blueprint' dictating their behaviour and footsteps.

This is why parents' should not even undress or commit any uncivilized or sinful act in their presence. Some *akābir* advise that even during pregnancy, the mother's behaviour and thought's influence the foetus. Hence the Sharee'ah's emphasis on *taqwā* and *tahārat* (physical purity) during pregnancy. As the child grows, adorn him with *Deeni Tāleem* and reprimand him upon sins with *hikmat*. Ensure he only associates with the pious and keeps far away from immoral and bad company.'

Just as important is to censor what the child reads, views and hears. Nowadays with the convergence of TV, computers and *Internet* under the banner of education: parents' should be extra vigilant and ensure their children stay far, far away from the evil of TV and music.

- It is best to sleep the young child on his own bed (or cot) as there is the real danger of being inadvertently injured by sleeping parents. (Nevertheless, for the first few years the young child should sleep in the same room as the parents or a responsible mature sibling/close relative so that a constant eye be kept on the child. It is not enough to place a baby monitor).

- Try to create in the child the habit of being confident with the company of others (cultured, reliable and pious relatives). This will dispel total dependency upon one person whose sudden death, Allah ﷻ Forbid, may then prove unbearable for the child.

- Wash and clean the child daily...this will save him from many diseases.

- Immediately change nappies when a child soils them and clean surrounding areas well with water and then dry.

- When the time arrives to leave milk and wean the child, do not give him very hard foods; these damage and weaken gums and teeth.

- When the child appears to understand, teach him to wash and eat with his right hand after reciting *Bismillah*. Teach him to eat less, this will prevent greed, avarice (and many diseases in life).

- Instead of feeding just one type of food, inculcate in your child the habit of eating a variety of *tayyib* nutritious foods...especially fruits in season. Never feed him something until the previous meal has been digested. Do not allow too many sweets or sour foods and always make them rinse and clean their teeth after eating.

- Emphasize upon the child to first come home and seek permission from parents' before eating anything given by other's. Stress upon the child never to ask of anybody except his immediate elders or to take property of other's without their permission. Do not spoil the child by over pampering or fulfilling his every whim, fancy & tantrum.

- A common error nowadays is for parents to buy ludicrous animated and musical toys/electronic gadgets which 'lullaby' the child to sleep. True love and devotion is not so cheap...it requires parents to spend hours cradling, soothing and rhyming Islāmic prayers, du'aa's, nazams and stories. Only then does a strong Imān and sense of right and wrong become embedded in the child.

Shortcomings of Parents

'Today we are unable to bring even 10% of our teenagers into the Masjid for Salāh; consequently thousands of our youth are turning away from Deen...'   Shaykh Asad Hussain Ahmad Madanee

Shaykh Ashraf 'Ali Thānwi ﷺ narrates, 'Nowadays parents' rear their children in the same manner as a beef farmer. Like him, they fully feed and nourish them until they are bloated all-round...however his objective is to slit a knife across the animals' throat. Similarly people laud comfort and luxuries upon their children to the extent they become fodder for Hell Fire. In consequence, these *stockmen* (parents) are running a knife across their own throats; because of indifference towards their children's lack of Salāt, Saum and Deen in general. Many parents' are happy because of their punctual performance of Salāt; but blissfully unaware that they too will accompany their offspring because of failure to make them pray.'

It is not sufficient to send a child to Madrasah only as not much thought is given to moral reform. Whilst an Ālim will impart the Sunnah du'aa's at Madrasah, it is the parents who must oversee whether the child puts this *tāleem* into practice. Nowadays, parents pour water over whatever efforts the Madrasah Teacher's make by means of their neglect, apathy and by creating a totally unIslāmic environment at home. The most destructive factors are undoubtedly TV and the corrupt company befriended in pursuing secular education.

The Forgotten Art of True Family Conversation

Allah ﷻ says in the Glorious Qur'ān:

'O you who believe! Let not a group scoff at another group; it may be that the latter are better than the former. Nor let (some) women scoff at other women, it may be that the latter are better than the former. Nor defame one another, nor insult one another by nicknames. How awful it is to insult one's brother after accepting Imān. And whosoever does not repent, then such are indeed the repentant.' (49:11)

In an era of phenomenal scientific, social, moral and spiritual change, the art of true, meaningful and compassionate conversation and tāleem between members of the family is fast declining. Contemporary Muslim families live separate detached existences. We 'relish' communicating with people on the other side of the ocean, continent, country and town but not to our kith and kin on the other side of the room. We communicate (not converse) with our own in short sharp bursts in the style of text messages. Remember a good talker is also a good listener and a good observer. Islām teaches us to reflect first, talk afterwards when necessary or appropriate; however with our dear one's even permissible informal talk is encouraged and rewarded. This is the meaning of the home being an allegorical *Khanqāh* (spiritual training centre).

However, a recent survey estimated that over 40% of children under the age of four have a TV in their own bedrooms and the number is rising. Children are withdrawing into unIslāmic values by staring into TFT screens of all sizes (game consoles, mobile phones, etc.). Those who are able to make our children believe in absurdities are also able to control them to commit profanities. Such is the power of corporate propaganda. Do we really control the keypad or are our children being 'remotely' programmed and controlled by others?

When the Muslim child does not have the opportunity to venerate, converse, communicate and listen to his parents, siblings and sincere elders in a wholesome loving (*tayyib*) environment and atmosphere away from ubiquitous technological distractions, his *nafs* (self) loses direction, rebels and directs its energies in a spiritually destructive manner. Children become detached, distracted, inattentive and ultimately deprived and alienated. Whatever happened to the gaiety and innocence of youth?

It is the parents' values, outlook and ideals, related in behaviour and conversations, which form the blueprint of success or otherwise on our children's minds. When the day our child is able to walk independently arrives, and arrive it surely will, this mental blueprint will dictate the direction his feet will take him. If he was given a good loving Islāmic upbringing (*tarbiyyah*) free from gossip, backbiting and alien values, *Inshā'Allah* no environment or group of insincere 'friends' or peers will be able to permanently deviate him...even an occasional phase of disorientation or 'teenage madness' will *Inshã'Allah* be overcome. However, he who was deprived of true Islãmic parental love and values, will sooner or later, feel alienated and disorientated. It is either Deeni talk-talk in childhood or rebellious walk-walk in adulthood.

Parents should daily make a point of finding quality time to sit and converse with their children; this could be in various forms: for example, after the Fajr or Esha *salãh,* at the end of family meals, after the family tãleem session, over a night-time warm drink; who said it has to be boring or dead serious? Share a smile, a hug, a cuddle, a pat or stroke on the head, a decent joke, a story or anecdote of the pious, a masa'eel, an event or tale, even the practise of exchanging *salams* when awakening, leaving and arriving home and when retiring to sleep. Daily, keep the channels of family conversation open; even when tired, upset or when the child appears to be forever moody. Refrain from *gheebat* and the TV.

The benefits of relating the teachings of Islãm to our family members, is that constant hearing of the advices of our pious predecessors (*aslãf*) over a period of time enables the *tãleem* to became second-nature and remembered at the opportune occasion; sometimes long after the demise of the parents. Even if children do not become fully pious, the fact that correct Deeni values were related to them by their parents will, *Inshã'Allah,* make them civilised and cultured: qualities which will save them from many destructive vices and self-harm to ensure they go onto to become assets to society. Rest assured, when parents' carry out their share of the trust (*amānah*), Allah ﷻ will carry out His Share...

Shaykh Mufti Taqee 'Uthmāni *hafizahullah* relates,

'My Shaykh Dr. 'Abdul Hayy 'Arifee ﷯ *narrated, 'Whenever I used to attend the Majālises of Shaykh Ashraf 'Ali Thānwi* ﷯ *I too harboured the desire to either memorise or write down the statements (malfoozat) that were related but could not do so because I could neither remember nor write them down quickly enough.*

Once I mentioned this dilemma to my Shaykh ﷯ *who replied, 'What need is there for you to write them down...why do you not become a person of statements?'*

I was astonished at this suggestion, whereupon Shaykh Thānwi ﷯ *commented, 'In reality, whenever and whatever is related, if it is truthful (haqq) based upon correct understanding (fahm saleem) and concern (fikr), when such matters reach your ears and you accept them with your heart, then they become yours. Now, regardless of whether or not you recall them verbatim, whenever the occasion arises, inshā'Allah the advice will come to mind...and you will receive the tawfeeq (from Allah* ﷻ*) to act thereupon.'* (p46, Irshādāt Akābir)

Deeni Tarbiyyah Program

Shaykh Ashraf 'Ali Thānwi ﷺ narrated, 'The first words to be taught to a child should be 'Kaleemah Tawheed,' *Lãillaha Illallãh*...thereafter teach them necessary *Ãdabs* (etiquettes).

- Always keep the child clean, neat and tidy in simple Sharee' clothes devoid of animated pictures (designer-wear logo's) and do not overdress or pamper them.

- Keep hair of boys short (and do not cut the hair of girls). Also, do not adorn girls with jewellery until they remain in *hijãb*.

- Instruct them to make *salãm* (and reply to the salãms of others) whenever they meet any Muslim.

- Explain to them the sin and vulgarity of lying.

- Incline children towards Allah ﷻ by constantly reminding them, for example, 'Allah ﷻ grants us *rizq* (food, clothing, home);' 'Allah ﷻ Sees everything,' 'Allah ﷻ Created the universe,' etc.

- Whenever the child misbehaves, tell him Allah ﷻ is aware of everything and will get angry. Such constant reminders, especially by the mother will create a vivid awareness of Allah ﷻ.

- Thereafter teach them the short Sûrahs of the Glorious Qur'ãn and daily Sunnah du'aa's (audio Qira'aat, *naz'ms* without music, and Deeni lectures are also beneficial).

- By the time a child reaches 7 years of age, teach him to

perform Salāh and inculcate the habit of making du'aa for all worldly needs and the *Ākhirah*. At 10 years, the Sharee'ah emphasizes the adoption of sternness in making children perform Salāh (for boys with Jamaat). Nowadays most parents are apathetic with their children's *Deeni* obligations...yet in fulfilling worldly needs they go to extremes. Islām is crying and asks such parents,'

'Shame! Have you forgotten me completely...why, do you expect the non-Muslims to save your child?'

- When the child reaches the age of 'learning,' try and enrol him in a Madrasah where the Scholars are qualified, pious and caring. Girls too should be taught at a Madrasah where full cognition is taken of Sharee' *hijāb*.

- As soon as the child has learnt the rules of correct Arabic recitation and short Surah's...proceed with learning the Glorious Qur'ān from an expert. Should the child show good intelligence and memory it is best to commence *Hifz* (memorization) of Qur'ān, otherwise complete by *nāzirah* (visual recitation).

- After completion of either *Hifz* or *nāzirah*, arrange for the systematic *Tāleem* of Deen. Also ensure the child learns beneficial worldly education (in a *Tayyib* environment, this means nowadays, English, Math's, Sciences, IT, Geography - *translator*). For girls ensure Sharee' *Hijāb* from an early age as well as Home Economics.

- If Allah ﷻ has granted the means and opportunity, let the child study the *Alim-Faadhil* course (at an authentic

Darul Uloom) as there is need for such persons nowadays. Otherwise, guide him towards some *tayyib* profession, trade or skill, whereby he is able to support himself and his wife and children in life.

- Endeavour to take along mature children with you into the company of *Ulamã* and *Mashã-ikh* (Saints). Through their blessings and association, Deen and Imãn develop.

- Regarding Deeni education, do not impose unbearable burden upon the child. Gradually increase studies from say, one hour to two, three and so on. Always take into account the child's health and capacity: as overwork dulls intelligence and memory as well as dampening enthusiasm. At the same time do not allow the child to take 'time-off' from Deeni studies on mere and trivial pretext's, e.g., weddings, shopping, sports, day-trips, etc.

- Remember to make your child learn the main lesson early in the morning when his mind is fresh: leaving secondary lessons until later when the body is tired.

- From beginning, inculcate into the child esteem for fellow Muslims and aversion for the styles and fashion of other nations and culture. Advise him never to hold the poor in contempt.

- Daily arrange a time at home, wherein you read out aloud some authentic Deeni *Kitaab*. Try to provide a mixture of *masã'eel* (rules), *fadhã'eel* (virtues) and episodes. Do not fear or worry if nobody listens, you continue your daily recital...even if it be one or two pages only. Consider it as incumbent as recitation of the Glorious Qur'ãn and as necessary as worldly duties.

• Couple all this with constant supervision of your child's actions and behaviour. For example, should he make *gheebat* (backbite) of anyone, correct him, 'this is wrong,' and outline the harms and evil of this sin. Similarly, should he display arrogance, point out the vulgarity of *takkabur*. Should he miss Salāh with *jamā'at,* admonish him. Whenever he lies or steals, correct and reprimand him...always with *hikmat,* never with *zulm.* Accordingly, it appears in Hadeeth that Allah ﷻ curses a person who steals even one egg and orders punishment for this person. Why such sternness on an apparently trivial act? Because these small steps open the door for future sins and destruction...'

There was once a thief, who eventually got caught, imprisoned and was about to be hanged. He requested a final meeting with his mother...who appeared at the prison in a distressed state. Sitting behind bars in the visiting room, he asked his mother to come close as he wished to whisper something. As she placed her ear between the bars...her son (the thief) bit it so ferociously as to cause severe bleeding. The mother yelled out and asked, 'Why did you do that for?' Her son replied,

'Mother! From when I was young and began lying, deceiving and stealing...you never reprimanded or punished me. Had you done so, you would not be witnessing this day when your son is about to be hanged. You by your carelessness and indifference have shown that you are my enemy manifest!'

Character Development

$\mathcal{S}$haykh Ashraf 'Ali Thãnwi ☀ narrated, 'To prevent bad habits and greed developing in one's children ensure the following:

• Whenever children observe something desirable, then do not let them become avaricious; rather in accordance with your means arrange for purchase of a (halãl) object to their liking. However, should they become obstinate (demanding something, which you had declined for a valid reason), never 'give-in,' such weak behaviour will only serve to increase their tantrums and obstinacy.

• Emphasise upon children never to eat secretly on their own, rather share it amongst the family children. This applies when the object is not the child's property. Therefore, whenever you wish to distribute anything amongst the children, whether it be money, sweets, etc. ask children to share it amongst themselves (under your supervision). This will develop big-heartedness, mutual love, compassion, responsibility and generosity whilst saving them from stinginess and petty-mindedness.

• Similarly, prevent children from doing anything secretly, because they will carry out in secret only that which they consider bad. Should you appease; the child will develop this habit.

• Whenever truth in any matter is revealed by anybody, ingrain into your child the humbleness and good-sense to accept. Develop humility; purge out self-glory and pride.

- Should the child commit any error, especially when another's *huqqoq* is involved, ensure they fully apologise and accept their wrong even to juniors. This is very important, as it ensures safety for one's Deen as well as worldly peace and respect. To make excuses, create a smokescreen or scenario to cover one's fault is a sign of arrogance, disgrace and humiliation.

- From infancy a child should be taught the vulgarity of over eating. Remember it appears in Hadeeth, 'The stomach is the fountain of good health.' This applies to both physical and spiritual health as overeating causes greed and obesity. Therefore, kindly but constantly, instruct the child to wash his hands and recite *Bismillah* before eating; to eat with the right hand and the food closest to him; to chew food properly without gobbling and to drink in more than three gulps; to recite *Alhamdulillah* during meals; to attribute food as having arrived from Allah ﷻ and not to pick faults; to not stare or take another's share; to clean the plate; recite the Sunnah du'aa and thoroughly wash mouth and hands. Also, ensure the child is not accustomed to always eating freshly cooked bread and (take-away) dishes, occasionally serve simple meals. Point out the harms and ills of overeating and without naming anybody inform them that such people are uncouth and uncivilized.

- Do not allow the child to shout, especially girls, otherwise they will grow up loud-mouthed and vulgar.

- As far as possible, do not allow the child to associate with children who are ill disciplined, ill-mannered, over pampered and who dislike learning. Otherwise their bad qualities and values will corrupt your child's temperament and breed: arrogance, lying, jealousy, pettiness, self-glory, love for dunyā and fame.

- Constantly make them aware of the harms of anger, deceiving, hatred, greed, stealing, backbiting, boasting, excess and inappropriate laughter, over-talking. Reprimand them when they speak without thinking.

- Should they break, damage something, hit anybody, etc. discipline them with an appropriate and measured response so they do not repeat such actions. Overlooking such misbehaviour is to destroy one's children.

- Do not let them go to sleep very early and inculcate the habit of waking early but ensure they sleep at least 8 hours daily.

- Upon return from Madrasah and study allow children time to play with other good children so that their mind refreshes. However, the play must be such wherein no sin, vulgarity or lying is involved.

- Do not allow children to waste money on fireworks or to attend *kuffar* sporting arenas and venues.

- Develop in children the habit of performing their own task's with their own hands: making bedding; tidying, placing clothes in their places and in the wash room when soiled; minor repairs to clothing, etc. Stress upon them to return all items to their original place and not to leave objects lying around. This will, Inshā'Allah, create order and methodology in their temperament and lives.

- Stress upon girls to observe keenly and master all domestic duties. Do not allow girls to play with any boys except their brother's...otherwise the morals of both will suffer. Whenever, other boys (even if they be toddlers) do come to your house, arrange for your daughters to go into another private room.

- Whenever a child performs a good act, lovingly compliment her well and reward her so that her courage increases.

- Should the child commit any error, firstly bring it to his attention in private, 'Look that was wrong, whatever will anybody say, good children never behave in such a manner, woe betide such behaviour in future!' Should he repeat such action, punish him accordingly.

- Impose some form of responsibility upon the child wherein he becomes occupied, so that his health and courage develop and laziness be kept at bay. For example, boys could be asked to walk or jog half a mile daily (in a safe respectable location). Instruct them to walk at moderate pace; not too fast. Girls too should be required to carry out physical exercises within the home environment (e.g. fitness bike).

- Inculcate humility and gentleness into the child so that boasting, harshness, airs and arrogance do not drip from his gait, walk, talk or behaviour. Stress upon them never to 'brag' even amongst fellow children of their wealth, house, possessions, family, cars, mobile, clothes, etc.

- At appropriate intervals, grant the child moderate pocket money: neither too much (as is the norm nowadays) so as to provide him leeway to squander it on undesirables; nor too little so as to make him feel avaricious and inferior to other children.

• Teach him manners and etiquette's of sitting, talking, eating and behaving in the company of others.

• Teach your children name's of parents, uncles and aunts: also their addresses (and telephone numbers. Instruct them how to use the telephone in cases of emergency and at other times only with your permission. Also, demonstrate to them how to answer the phone and not to give away any clues as to who is in the house, etc.)

Summary of Children's Huqooqs

haykh Ashraf 'Ali Thãnwi ※ commented, '...the rights of children are:

1) A man should marry a good pious lady so that noble children are born.

2) Children, especially girls, should be treated with love, compassion and kindness. The correct upbringing of daughters guarantees Paradise!

3) To ensure a child receives his milk from a noble pious lady as this has a great effect upon his character.

4) To teach the child *Ilm* of Deen and *ãdãb* (manners).

5) When they reach the age of marriage to marry them to a noble person.

6) Should one's daughter become widowed (or divorced), to maintain her with compassion and kindness until she remarries and to happily bear her maintenance.

Disciplining Children

haykh Ashraf 'Ali Thãnwi ❁ narrates, 'Teachers and parents both give *naseehat* (advice) to children. However, there is a big difference in their approach. The teacher's advise will be formal and curt, but parents will adopt such a tone and attitude whereby *naseehat* becomes ingrained. Although this may appear harsher, their heartfelt aim is to truly reform and correct the child for all time. This is true *shaffqat* (love and devotion) and why, sometimes, their behaviour, tone and speech appears irrational. For example, over meals the father 'lectures' to his children to keep away from bad company...all of a sudden his gaze falls upon his son taking too big a morsel. Immediately, he will stop the first topic and ask sternly, 'What are you doing? One never takes such large mouthfuls, it is uncivilized and harmful to health, take small portions and chew your food slowly and thoroughly!' Thereafter, he will recommence his early topic. An inexperienced person (or ungrateful child would mumble), 'what is the connection between the two issues?' However, any parent will immediately appreciate that this 'disassociation' is appropriate and a sign of the father's affection and true concern for his child.'

Forms of Disciplinary Action

haykh Ashraf 'Ali Thãnwi ❁ narrates, 'Tã'zeer is an Arabic term describing the punishment meted out (within Sharee') limits in order to reform, reprimand

and discipline. This may be in various forms:

- Rebuke or employing stern (though not foul) language, that is a 'ticking-off.'
- To threaten (e.g. a family boycott).
- To 'imprison,' for example, sending the child into his bedroom and forbidding him the opportunity to play.
- Imposing financial penalty, e.g. withholding pocket money.

Another possible disciplinary measure is to impose some menial physical task, e.g., writing out lines, cleaning-out driveway, etc. Remember, the motive is not punishment but *islaah* (reformation). Whenever mild persuasion is adequate, this should be used. However, this approach requires tact and much patience. You will have noticed the mischievous child who is always physically punished...he becomes bold and rebellious not fearing anyone. Other harms of physical punishment are:

- The physique of the child, which is already fragile, deteriorates.
- Due to fear, he begins to forget previous lessons and studies.
- A negative effect upon *tãleem* and *tarbiyyah*.
- Lack of shame becomes second nature and a life long calamity.

Parents' should remember never to commit *zulm* (tyranny) upon their children; they are an *amãnat* about whom Allah ﷻ will demand a reckoning. Allah ﷻ has granted parents' a superior rank in order to make *tarbiyyah* of their children and grant them comfort. Yes, accepted, in order to grant life-long comfort it is sometimes necessary and permissible to discipline and penalize, but never when in the state of anger. Remember as far as possible curb anger. During anger, one's judgement is never correct, therefore do not punish when angry, rather adopt the following:

1) Ask the child who is the target of your anger to leave (send him to his bedroom) or you leave so as to cool down. Before speaking or taking any further action, ponder three times (three separate occasions) *after* your anger has cooled as to what is the best response.

2) Remember Allah ﷻ has greater right over us and we too are disobedient to Him; if He too should adopt the same wrathful attitude as we adopt with our juniors, what will be our condition?

Should any injustice be committed upon one's child, apologize and make recompense, e.g. present a gift and humour him until he becomes happy.'

Shaykh Mufti Muhammad Shafee' ﷭ was exemplary in this matter. His mode of tarbiyyah was not to rebuke at every step. Yes, he noted *everything*, then every month he would summon the child in private and without being emotional highlight his every error; their harms and the advantages of avoiding such behaviour. In this way, the self-esteem and respect of the child is preserved; true affection is displayed; correct tarbiyyah is achieved and most importantly the child himself realises the value and purpose behind his training.

Parental Mannerism

Shaykh Mufti Abdur Ra'oof Sakhrawee *dāmat barakātuhum* relates, 'Today our behaviour towards children has transformed our homes into law-courts. Children are hauled and dragged like prisoners; sworn at; slapped on the face; harshly rebuked and insulted and threatened with being 'thrown-out-the-house.' When you belittle and tell your teenage child 'to-pack-up-and-go' every time he enacts something contrary to your wishes...then the day the tables are reversed and you become old...he/she will tell you to leave the home!'

Shaykh Mufti Mahmood-ul-Hasan Gangohi ۞ narrated, 'I was once in the company of Shaykh Maseehullah Khãn ۞ when he commented, 'Nowadays, parents should behave towards their children as children: father should act as a son; not with the awe and fear of yesteryear. He should deal with love, tenderness and affection...'Son, it is time for meals...son, it is time for bed, etc.' These are all requests: as if one brother was talking to another; for the era of dictating and commanding are over. Similarly, husbands too should live with their wives as partners and friends...not as dictatorial rulers issuing orders all the time. Teachers should behave towards their students as fellow students. In brief, one shall have to make *tarbiyyah* in accordance with the conditions and atmosphere of the time.' Shaykh Maseehullah ۞ added, 'Parents should understand *tarbiyyah* is a life-long process.

This is why parents must 'indiscreetly supervise' and keep an eye even upon their newly married children for a minimum of one year after they marry: not even undertaking a journey which entails their absence. In this way, any trivial argument or incident between the couple will be 'nibbed in the bud' before it proves detrimental. My grandmother would often reproach my uncle. When anybody remonstrated with her, 'O nanny, he is grown-up and has children, surely you should not rebuke him now that he is married!' Grandmother would reply, 'Whatever he might be, he is still my baby!'

Shaykh Sa'ādee ﷺ relates this reality very beautifully, 'Once during the prime of my youth I scoffed a reply to my beloved mother, who naturally took offence and departed to fetch a small shawl from the cupboard. Holding it up in front of me, she spoke,

'O darling! Today you are a strong youth with great airs upon your strength and intelligence. However, this was not always the case. At one time, you used to lie in this shawl helplessly; those arms of yours did not have enough strength to swat a fly sitting upon your nose. You couldn't even turn sides. Therefore, son, never forget the fact that one day death will snatch away the light of your eyes. Once again, you will return to your original helpless condition, wherein worms will eat away at your brain and you shall be unable to move them away. Do not consider the strength and power you posses to be your own achievements, rather regard these as gifts from Allah ﷻ!'

Three Major Huqooqs of Children

haykh Ashraf 'Ali Thānwi ❀ narrated: 'Once during the time of Ameerul Mu'mineen 'Umar ❀, a father came to the state court and lodged a complaint against his son, 'He does not uphold my rights.' Umar ❀ summoned and asked the son for an explanation. The son replied, 'O Ameerul Mu'mineen! Is it only the father who has rights' over his children or do they enjoy any *huqooqs* over him?' 'Umar ❀ replied,

'Undoubtedly, children too have rights.' The son requested, 'Would you kindly inform us what these huqooqs are?' Umar ❀ replied, 'Their rights are:

1) To choose a noble lady as mother for one's children.

2) When the child is born, to choose a good Islāmic name for blessings.

3) When children begin to understand; to adorn them with Deeni 'Ilm and good manners.'

The son commented, 'My father has failed to fulfil a single one of these *huqooqs*. Firstly, he chose and married a lewd women for my mother; secondly, he named me *Jo'al* (a revolting name meaning faeces 'bug'); thirdly, he failed to teach me a single letter or Command of Deen!' Hearing this reply, 'Umar ❀ became infuriated at the father and threw his case out saying,

'Tyrant! First of all address your own shortcomings and thereafter come and complain about your son!

In reality, you have committed greater wrong and injustice. Go, never ever behave in such a manner with one's children!'

Shaykh Muhammad Saleem Dhorat *dāmat barakātuhum* narrates, 'Nowadays, when youngsters wish to marry, they neither look at family background, wealth or piety. Their sole criteria for selecting a spouse is beauty. Nobody is denying the importance of attractiveness and Nabee ﷺ himself instructed us to 'view' a prospective spouse before deciding whether to marry in order to ascertain whether they are pleasing or displeasing to us. However, to make beauty the only factor and to ignore the Deeni inclination of the spouse is against the Teachings of Islām. Muslim youngsters have reached such an ebb, that even when they find the beauty of a non-Muslim heart-pleasing; they are prepared to marry her.

1) Pious Spouse

Piety should be the foremost quality, if this is present, then the spouse will forever remain contented and in a state of bliss...as will the children born, parents, in-laws, other relatives, neighbours, friends and associates, etc. If the mother is pious, the newborn child will, Inshā'Allah, go on to become the Hāfiz, Ālim and Shaykh of his era. If you doubt this claim, study the lives of any great Deeni Personality. The undisputed Imām of Hadeeth, Imām Bukhāree ﷺ, his father passed-away during childhood. He was brought up by his mother. Similarly, the tarbiyyah of Imām Shāfi'ee ﷺ was carried out by his mother.

Today, the state of our *muaasharat* is that whilst beauty is the criteria when selecting a girl; parents and girls when choosing a boy, instead of viewing his Deen and Akhlãq as instructed by Nabee ﷺ, are more concerned about his employment, salary, house, car and the brand of his mobile phone! Allah ﷻ alone help us and our children when these are the features sought in spouses. If you doubt this claim, ponder why an attractive young maiden from a good Deeni family receives so few proposals comparatively? Her only 'fault' is living in hijãb, not watching TV and being conscious and punctual with Salãh and the ahqãms of the Sharee'ah. Accordingly, when the father-to-be and mother-to-be fail to select a correct spouse, tomorrow, on the Day of Qiyãmah they will have to stand in the Court of Allah ﷻ and answer for their behaviour when their 'off-track' children complain.

2) Proper Islãmic Name

The second major *huqooq* of the child over the father (not over the paternal aunt as has become the norm) is his selection of an Islãmic name. Understand well, to choose the name is the haqq of the father and to choose a good Islãmic name is the haqq of the child. We are all aware of the excesses in this arena nowadays. Parents opt for the names of film and sports personalities. Even in choosing names of Prophets عليه السلام, Scholars and pious ladies...the intention appears to be to find a name which appears acceptable to western ears. For example, many parents opt for the name Sarah for girls (ostensibly because it is the name of the Wife عليها السلام of Prophet Ibrãheem عليه السلام). When this name kept appearing, I realised that Sarah is also an English name. Another common selection is Māriyya, (again ostensibly because it was the name of the Wife ﷺ of Rasoolullah ﷺ), whereas the reality is, it is also a name kept by the Europeans. These are the traits of our muaasharat.

3) Deeni Knowledge & Tarbiyyah

The third major huqooq incumbent upon the father is to provide his children with knowledge of the Glorious Qur'ān and Sunnah. Teach them the importance and difference of halāl and harām, between right and wrong. Undoubtedly, for this it is necessary to also seek a pious, dedicated, affectionate and well-intentioned Ustadh...somebody who will achieve and ingrain these objectives. Moreover, the parents themselves must aid, support and reinforce the teachings of such teachers...for the prime responsibility is the father's! On the Day of Qiyāmah, every parent will be questioned as to what tāleem they imparted to their children.

It is not sufficient to only teach Deeni Knowledge, we have to also impart Deeni Adab (etiquettes). Tāleem and tarbiyyah, although separate entities, are both compulsory, complimentary and must go hand-in-hand. In bygone times, there were two facets to Madārises: in one session the *muallimeen* (teachers) would teach Deeni Knowledge; whilst in the second session the *mu'addabeen* (training tutors) would develop the character of the children. Such was the emphasis and importance of *tāleem* and *tarbiyyah* that when the great Caliph Haroon al-Rasheed ﷺ entrusted his two sons (Prince Mamoon and Prince Ameen to their

Ustadh, he requested him, 'In the matter of tāleem, be firm and do not allow laxity or the thought that 'they are prince's' to determine your approach."

One day the Caliph was passing the Madrasah unannounced, when he noticed the Ustadh leaving and the two Prince's vying with each other to carry and present their teacher's shoes. Finally, they took and placed a shoe each. The Ustadh wore his shoes and emerged outside to be met by the Caliph. After exchanging greetings, the Caliph asked his son's teacher, 'Who is the most fortunate person on the surface of this earth?' The Ustadh replied, 'Sir, only Allah ﷻ knows this, however He has placed the responsibility of the entire Muslim Ummah upon your shoulders, therefore in my estimation there is nobody more fortunate than you.' The Caliph replied, 'Incorrect! Upon this entire surface the most fortunate person is he for whom the Caliph's two son's vie with each other to align his shoes.' This was the esteem, respect and veneration of the Ustadh in the Caliph's heart, why? Because whomsoever respects his teachers acquires a tremendous portion of 'Ilm.

Today, when a Ustadh says something contrary to our or our children's whims, airs and fancy...immediately, we are prepared to barge-in to the Madrasah, confront and dispute with him right in front of all the children. However, with secular teachers, we are very 'civilised,' never ever storming into their classrooms...why? Because, we suffer from a massive inferiority complex, whereas we do have a legal right to approach the Head teacher and the Board of Governors at School and air our grievance or opinion. Very few people are prepared to approach them and the minority that do will behave very politely. Yet, when it comes to Madrasah; because we have paid a nominal fee, we consider it our own property, to be entered at will and the Ustadh, our assumed employee, to be sworn, reprimanded and belittled at our leisure. Be under no illusion, if we continue with this ignorant attitude of ours, our children and Muslim Society will continue with their descent into Hell.' To emphasise the importance of Deeni Knowledge and tarbiyyah we relate an episode which should serve as an eye opener for every parent and child.

Shaykh Maseehullah Khān ﷫ related, 'Once a man passed-away. After burial, his wife observed him in dreams on numerous occasions, suffering punishment in Hell-Fire. This saddened and pained her immensely. Within a short while, the mother admitted their only toddler into Madrasah for basic Deeni Tāleem commencing with *Bismillah*.

That very night, the mother observed her late husband again in a dream, this time happily strolling through Paradise. Puzzled, she asked, 'How did you manage to escape from Hell?' Her husband replied, 'When you admitted our child into the Maktab and his Ustadh made him recite *Bismillah*...Allah ﷻ announced to the Angels, 'Remove his father from Hell-Fire, for My Mercy is abashed to see the father of a child who attributes My Name to *Rahmān* and *Raheem* burning in Hell-Fire.' This is how I entered Paradise, through recitation of *Bismillah* by our child!'

*S*ayyidina 'Ali ibn Abi Talib ﷺ advised an associate: 'O Kameel, 'ilm is better than wealth, for 'ilm protects you whilst you have to safeguard wealth. 'Ilm is sovereign whilst wealth is subservient. In consuming wealth, it decreases and in employing 'ilm it increases.' *(p18, Successful Taalib Ilm)*

*S*haykh Maseehullah Khan ﷺ used to say, 'The two institutions Maktab and nikah originate from the Heavens; the first Maktab was wherein Allah ﷻ taught Prophet Adam ﷺ and the first nikah was between Prophet Adam ﷺ and Mother Hawwa ﷺ.'

*S*haykh Hussain Ahmad Madanee ﷺ used to say, 'These Makātib of Deen and Madāris of Islām are the backbone of the Muslim Ummah.'

*A*llamah Iqbal ﷺ used to say, 'Leave these traditional Makātib of our land in their original states, otherwise the condition of our nation will be that of Andalus (Spain); despite Muslim rule of over 700 years, not a single Masjid in operation!'

*S*haykh Abdul Hassan Ali Nadwi ﷺ used to say, 'To whichever country the people of Gujarat migrate to, they take along four items: Masājid, Makātib, Papodums & Samoosas! The Ahl-e-Gujarat are recipient of 'original' Islām from the Sahābāh ﷺ who came to India via the ports of Gujarat...'

(Lectures, Shaykh 'Abdullah Kapodrawee)

Chapter Seventeen

Muslim Children & Importance of Deeni Makatib

haykh Saleem Ullah Khan hafizahullah comments, 'The Scholar's perception is that our duty is to solely teach the Glorious Qur'ān, Hadeeth and Fiqh. Who is asking you to stop these activities? I insist you preoccupy yourself in these noble endeavours!

However I advise you to also supervise the establishment of separate academies wherein professionals impart expertise in temporal fields (to Muslim youth); you should sponsor, guide and advice such institutes wherein true understanding of Deen predominates. This is the need of the hour to create such experts who are conscientious, steadfast, philanthropic, devoted and dedicated to only Deen; who work with intellect and far-sightedness. We need to create such talented Deeni assiduous young Muslims who serve society and their country in all fields for the betterment of humanity...'

(Al Balagh, Vol 43, No. 10, p599)

*A*llah ﷻ mentions in the Glorious Qur'ãn:

'...*And verily, it (reads): In the Name of Allah, the Most Gracious, the Most Merciful.'*   *(27:30)*

*R*asoolullah ﷺ narrated,

'*That person is the best amongst you who learns and teaches the Qur'ãn.'*   *(Bukhãri)*

'*Whichever community, assembles at a place from amongst the abodes of Allah ﷻ to recite and revise the Glorious Qur'ãn, then tranquillity (Sakeenah) descends upon and mercy (Rahmat) envelopes them. The Angels of Mercy surround them and Allah ﷻ mentions them in the gathering of the Angels.'*

(Aboo Dãwood)

'*Paradise lies under the feet of your mother.'*

Mother's Lap ~ The First Maktab of Islãm

*OS*haykh Ihtisham-ul-Haqq Thãnwi ﷺ related, 'For a Muslim child, his mother's lap is the first *Maktab* wherein although no formal syllabus is followed nevertheless, the priceless upbringing therein determines the foundation and direction of the child's future. If the mother is pious the *tarbiyyah* will be Islãmic; if Deen is lacking from the mother's lap how and from where will the child acquire teachings of Islãm? During days of colonialism, the imperialist mercenaries undertook a scheme to remove faith from the hearts and minds of Muslims. Although they succeeded in imposing their institutions, education, culture, language, clothing and values nevertheless the *iman* of Muslims remained intact.

At a loss for an explanation, an experienced psychologist suggested, 'The primary reason for this is the laps of their true Muslim mothers. During their upbringing these ladies make them of such stout faith that even if you were to cut the child to shreds they will not forgo their *iman*. Therefore if you desire these children to leave the fold of Islām then remove Deen from their mothers' laps.'

Those blessed ladies who used to teach us the values of Islām and *Bismillah, Inshā'Allah, Mashā'Allah, Subhan'Allah and Surah Al-Fātihah* in childhood are fast disappearing; from where will our grandchildren acquire these teachings? This is why we daily hear of Muslims reneging their faith. Why? Because although Muslims are still being raised, our foundations are no longer indestructible. The mother's lap was the base and the first Maktab, whilst the Madrassah associated with the local Masjid is the second Maktab.' (Vol.2, p112, Lectures Ihtisham)

Prime Minister William Ewart Gladstone (1809-1898) is famous for telling the English Parliament in 1882, 'As long as this Qur'ān exists, Europe will never be able to (overcome Islām).' Similarly, the French Colonial Governor of Algeria said in 1932, 'It is a must to remove the Arabic Qur'ān from their presence and to remove the Arabic language from their tongues in order for us to have victory over them.'

What is the purpose of a Maktab?

haykh Abul Hasan 'Ali Nadwee ﷺ asks, 'What is the rank and purpose of a Maktab? They are the biggest studios wherein the clerics, servants and followers of Islãm are prepared. Makãtib are the powerhouses of the world of Islãm, from wherein spiritual life and energy is transmitted and distributed to Muslims and mankind. Makãtib are those places from where the mind, soul, vision, hearts and all human existence is aligned. Its ordinance is binding on the entire universe, yet no worldly decree is binding upon it.

The Maktab is not subservient to any era, civilisation, culture, language or protocol whereby the possibility exists of any rise or fall over time. It is directly connected and takes its nourishment from the Office of Prophet Muhammad ﷺ which is universal, living and forever vibrant. They are such places wherein the exemplary life, piety and mission of Prophet Muhammad ﷺ are found. Allah ﷻ forbid, but should they cease to exist human existence would shrivel and perish...' (Vol.1, p46, Lectures Ali Mia)

Origin & Root of Maktab

haykh Maseehullah Khan ﷺ used to say, 'The two institutions *Maktab* and *nikah* originate from Heaven; the first *Maktab* was wherein Allah ﷻ taught Prophet Adam ﷺ and the first *nikah* was between Adam ﷺ and Mother Hawwa ﷺ.' The second *Maktab* of Islãm was the barren Cave of *Hira*, wherein Jibra'eel ﷺ arrived to instruct Prophet Muhammad ﷺ to recite the Glorious

Qur'ãn. The Arabic word *Maktab* originates from the root word *kataba* (to write), because a Muslim child first learns to formally read and write the language of the Glorious Qur'ãn here. Shaykh Ashraf 'Ali Thãnwi ۝ often used to narrate:

> *'Study the Qã'eedah (elementary Arabic alphabet and method of pronunciation) from me (a qualified Qãri); go and read the Glorious Qur'ãn thereafter from somebody else.'*

A necessary (*wãjib*) facet of a *Maktab* is *tarbiyyah* and *adab* (development of character and comportment). For any *Maktab* to be successful four core ingredients are necessary:

- A dedicated, sincere and qualified teacher (*Mu'allim*).
- A dedicated, sincere and respectful *tãlib-ul-ilm* (student).
- Parents who respect the *Mu'allim, Ahl-e-'Ilm* (Scholars) and *Maktab* and who encourage their child.
- Punctuality and standard of teaching.

Buildings to house the *Maktab,* a syllabus, library and resources although useful and helpful are all secondary.

The Goal (*Maqsad*) of Makãtib

Shaykh Mufti Muhammad Shafee' used to say, 'Nowadays, our Makãtib have become barren.' We should firmly understand that the goal of our *Deeni Makãtib* is not only the teaching and learning of a syllabus (Darse Nizam), but also to ensure we act accordingly and thereby produce pious graduates who become Huffaz,

Scholars of Deen and responsible Muslims. For centuries we have been imparting knowledge of the Qur'ãn, Hadeeth and associated skills, however...the need is there for us to turn our gaze away from funding bodies and the affluent; adopt austerity and for the Sake of Allah ﷻ and the protection of His Deen form Deeni Makãtib which are also academies of character reformation.

Shaykh Ahmad Desai *hafizahullah* states, 'The goal of the *Maktab* consists of the following attainments:

- Strengthening of the *Iman* of the growing-up children of Islãm to enable them to withstand the onslaughts of disbelief and influences of an unIslãmic environment.

- Correct recitation of the Glorious Qur'ãn with Tajweed.

- Memorisation (*Hifz*) of Surah Fatiha, Juz Amm, Surah Yãseen, Surah Wãqiah & Surah Mulk. Also Hifz of Aayatul Kursi and the last Ruku' of Surah Baqarah.

- Memorisation of the Kalimahs and all necessary *Masnoon* du'aa's.

- Practical knowledge as opposed to mere theory of purity and Salãh.

- Brief and simple explanation of the fundamentals of Islãm.

- Moral character which the *Mu'allim* must teach and try to inculcate by reading or relating the episodes of Prophets ﷺ and Saints (Awliya) ﷺ.

(Vol. 16, No. 11, p8, The Majlis)

Etiquette's (Ãdab) of Maktab

Parent's and students wishing to successfully acquire *'ilm* should remember some fundamentals:

1. Respect all the teachers from whom you acquire *'ilm*. Never speak ill or bad of any Ustadh or the Maktab even if they are in the wrong otherwise you will be deprived. Respect the kitabs which you study.

2. Pay special attention towards the rules of Maktab. Parent's admit their child for studying not for purpose of interfering in the Maktab's operation.

3. Ensure the child wears clean appropriate Islãmic clothes and attends Maktab punctually and diligently; do not take leave for trivial reasons (holidays, weddings, visits, sporting events, minor illnesses, etc).

4. Place shoes/coats neatly in designated areas. Keep ablution/toilet areas, corridors and classrooms tidy.

5. Carry your kitabs and stationary to-and-from Maktab in a suitable bag held in your hand against the chest.

6. Do not write or lean on kitabs, books, benches & walls and do not enter other classrooms without permission.

7. Enter your classroom with *salam* and sit in the place designated by your Ustadh. Behave with decorum. Do not stretch your legs. Always address your Ustadh with respectful titles.

8. During tuition, when sitting in front of your Ustadh, concentrate, do not look hither-thither and do not interrupt when he/she is speaking or explaining. If you need to ask a question, obtain permission first.

Noble Sunnahs of Our Beloved Nabee ﷺ

llah ﷻ mentions in the Glorious Qur'ān:

'Say (O Muhammad ﷺ to mankind), 'If you (truly) love Allah, then follow me (my Sunnah); Allah will love and forgive you of your sins. And Allah is Oft-Forgiving, Most Merciful.' (3:31)

asoolullah ﷺ commented,

'None amongst you can be a perfect Believer until he/she subordinates his desires to that which I have brought.'   *(Mishkhāt)*

'One who turns away from my Sunnah has no connection with me.'   *(Bukhāri & Muslim)*

Understand well, until and unless Muslim parents teach and ingrain within their children the Sunnah way of living, then they have failed to fulfil the rights of tarbiyyah and to equip them for true success in this world and the Ãkhirah.

haykh Mufti 'Abdur Ra'oof Sakhrawee *dāmat barakātuhum* relates, 'For correct tarbiyyah of children, from an early age relate episodes from the Seerah (life) of Prophet Muhammad ﷺ at home. Children should be aware of when he was born; how he grew up; how and when he received prophethood; the difficulties he undertook in propagating Deen; his services for humanity; how details of his entire life have been preserved, etc. Secondly, relate details and stories of the Ahl-e-Bayt ﷺ (his

immediate family); his Companions ﷺ. This was precisely
the method adopted by the Sahābāh ﷺ; they would teach
the Seerah of Prophet Muhammad ﷺ to their children at
home in the same way we teach the small Surahs from the
Glorious Qur'ān. Now ponder, reflect and contrast this with
our behaviour; in most Muslim households nowadays even
the blessed name of Nabee ﷺ is never mentioned!'

Shaykh Qāri Ãmir Hasan *dāmat barakātuhum*
relates, There are three rights of Nabee ﷺ upon us:

1) *Muhabbat* (love and affection);

2) *Azmat* (respect and reverence);

3) *Mutāba'at* (to follow, imitate and obey).'

From birth, even in all aspects of infant and childcare, we
have to follow the Sunnah, which is the method,
mannerism and mode of living of Nabee ﷺ. By adopting
these Sunnahs from an early age, they will become
instinctive, second-nature and entirely in keeping with the
tab'ee (natural) temperament of a Muslim child.

Shaykh Mufti 'Abdur Ra'oof Sakhrawee *dāmat
barakātuhum* relates, 'Understand well, tarbiyyah
of children is not an easy-task. Firstly, we should make
du'aa to Allah ﷻ for Divine Aid, because when the blessings
and favours of Allah ﷻ arrives our task becomes easy,
otherwise it is extremely difficult. Secondly, it is necessary
for the parents themselves to become pious role-models.
Thirdly, it is essential to treat children with love, affection
and mildness. Whilst the occasional rebuke is necessary,
constant nagging produces obstinacy in children.'

Sunnahs Upon Awakening

1) Every time the child awakes, make Salãm to him clearly; as he grows up, teach him to initiate Salãm to his parents, fellow siblings and every Muslim he meets.

2) Gently rub both hands over his face whereby the effects of sleep disappears.   *(Tirmizi)*

3) Recite the First Kaleemah to him/her:

لَآ اِلٰهَ اِلَّا اللّٰهُ مُحَمَّدُ الرَّسُوْلُ اللّٰه

'There is none worthy of worship besides Allah and, Muhammad ﷺ is the Messenger of Allah.'

4) Thereafter, recite اَلْحَمْدُ لِلّٰه (All Praises are due to Allah) three times and then read the following du'aa to him:

اَلْحَمْدُ لِلّٰهِ الَّذِىْ اَحْيَانَا بَعْدَ مَا اَمَاتَنَا وَ اِلَيْهِ النُّشُوْرُ

'All Praises are due to Allah Who gave us life after taking it away and, to Him is our return.'   *(Bukhāri)*

Sunnahs of Istinjã (Visiting the toilet)

5) Even during infancy, when changing clothing and nappies, remove the left sleeve and left foot first; and when dressing, wear the right sleeve and right leg first.

6) When 'toilet-training' the child, make him enter the toilet with the head covered; wearing (correct-sized) slippers and with the left foot first reciting the du'aa:

بِسْمِ اللّٰهِ اللّٰهُمَّ اِنِّىْ اَعُوْذُ بِكَ مِنَ الْخُبُثِ وَ الْخَبَائِثِ

'With the Name of Allah; O Allah! I seek Your protection from the male and female devil.'   *(Mishkhāt)*

7) Teach the child to urinate sitting down and not whilst standing. Stress the importance of avoiding splashing urine because the majority of punishment in the grave is because of carelessness in this area.

8) Whilst in the toilet, train the child not to talk unnecessarily or recite anything but maintain silence.

9) When washing the private-areas, use the left hand.

10) Train the child to always wash the private areas and both hands thoroughly after the call of nature.

11) When leaving the toilet, leave with the right foot and then recite the du'aa,

غُفْرَانَكَ اَلْحَمْدُ لله الَّذِى اَذْهَبَ عَنِّى الْأَذْى وَ عَافَانِى

'O Allah! I seek your pardon. All praises are due to Allah who has taken away from me discomfort and granted me relief.' *(Mishkhāt)*

Sunnahs of Ghusl (Bathing)

12) Even in bathing the infant child, follow the Sunnah method from the beginning:

   i) Make niyyat (intention) of dispelling impurity;

   ii) Wash both hands unto the wrists;

   ii) Wash the pubic areas thoroughly;

   iii) Perform wudhu (ablution);

   iv) Pour water (gently & carefully) over the body thrice.

Sunnahs of Miswāk

13) As soon as the child's teeth are formed, gently clean the teeth with a soft *miswāk* at least 120 mm long. Brush the teeth before and after eating and sleeping.

Sunnahs of Dressing

14) At time of dressing the child, recite to him the du'aa:

$$\text{اَلْحَمْدُ لله الَّذِىْ كَسَانِىْ هٰذَا وَ رَزَقَنِيه}$$

$$\text{مِنْ غَيْرِ حَوْلٍ مِّنِّىْ وَ لاَ قُوَّةٍ}$$

'All praises are for Allah, Who has enwrapped and endowed me in these (clothes) without any effort or toil on my part.'   (Mishkhāt)

15) When wearing any item of clothing, wear the **right** side first. When undressing, recite *Bismillah* and remove the **left** side first.

16) For boys, ensure their trousers and kurta are above the ankles.

17) Constantly remind boys that Allah ﷻ becomes unhappy when clothing overhangs the ankles. Our Nabee ﷺ stated, 'Allah will not look with Mercy at the person whose (clothing) dangles over the ankles...and to whichever length the (clothing) protrudes beyond the ankles...such portion will be burnt in Hell.'

18) Whenever the child wears a new garment, read:

$$\text{اَلْحَمْدُ لله الَّذِىْ كَسَانِىْ مَا أُوَارِىْ بِه عَوْرَتِى}$$

$$\text{وَ اتجَمَّلُ بِه فِىْ حَيَاتِىْ}$$

'All praises are for Allah, Who has enwrapped me in clothes with which I cover my shameful (portions) and through which my life becomes beautiful.'   (Mishkhāt)

Sunnahs of Hair Care

19) When combing the hair, start from the right. For boys, hair should be one length and there is no need to ever cut the hair of a girl after the shave on the seventh day.

Sunnahs of Eating & Drinking

20) Every time the child drinks milk, recite the du'aa:

اَللّٰهُمَّ بَارِكْ لَنَا فِيْهِ و زِدْنَا مِنْهُ

21) Before eating, spread a dining-cloth on the floor and train the child not to walk/place his feet on this cloth.

22) Train the child to wash both hands thoroughly before and after eating and to recite the du'aa:

بِسْمِ اللّٰه و عَلَى بَرَكَة اللّٰه

'With the Name of Allah and with the barakat of Allah I begin to eat.'

23) Instruct the child to eat and drink only with the right hand and to pick up, clean and eat any morsel that falls. Train the child to eat without leaning and not to pick faults with the food and to meticulously clean the plate and cup. The cleaned plate then makes du'aa of forgiveness.

24) After eating recite the du'aa:

اَلْحَمْدُ للّٰه الَّذِىْ اَطْعَمَنَا و سَقَانَا و جَعَلَنَا مِن الْمُسْلِمِيْن

'All praise is due to Allah Who gave us food and drink and made us Muslims.'

Sunnahs of Trimming Nails

25) When trimming the nails of the hand; start with the index finger of the right hand, then the largest, middle and small finger but leave the thumb until the end. When trimming the left hand, start from the small finger and work your way towards the thumb. Finally, trim the thumb of the right hand.

26) When trimming nails of the feet, start with the small toe nail on the right and work your way across (anti clockwise) towards the small toe of the left foot. (Mishkhāt)

Sunnahs of Azān

27) When the Azān is heard, instruct the child to stop all activities (as far as possible) and reply to the Azān.

28) After the Azān, instruct the child to recite Durood and the following du'aa:

اَللّٰهُمَّ رَبَّ هٰذِهِ الدَّعْوَةِ التَّامَّةِ وَ الصَّلٰوةِ الْقَائِمَةِ آتِ مُحَـمَّـدَ الْوَسِيْلَةَ وَ الْفَضِيْلَةَ وَ ابْعَثْهُ مَقَامًا مَّحْمُوْدَنِ الَّذِىْ وَعَدتَهُ، اِنَّـکَ لَاتُخْلِفُ الْمِيْعَادَ

'O Allah! The Creator of this perfect call and the Creator of the Salāh to follow; grant medium and virtues to Muhammad ﷺ and bestow and elevate him unto the Station of Mahmood which you had promised him; for undoubtedly You do not break promises.' (Mirqaat)

Sunnahs of Leaving/Entering the Home & Travel

29) Whenever leaving the home, recite the du'aa:

بِسْمِ اللهِ تَوَكَّلْتُ عَلَى اللهِ وَ لَاحَوْلَ وَ لَاقُوَّةَ اِلَّا بِاللهِ

'With the name of Allah I leave; I have placed my trust in Allah; moreover the ability to refrain from sin and the strength to make 'ibaadah only comes from Allah.'   (Tirmidhi)

It appears in hadeeth that whomsoever recites this du'aa at the time of departing from home, then Shaytãn is unable to harm or mislead him.

30) When entering the home, make Salãm and recite the du'aa:

اَللّٰهُمَّ اِنِّیْ اَسْئَلُکَ خَیْرَ الْمَوْلَجِ و خَیْرَ الْمَخْرَجِ بِسْمِ اللهِ وَلَجْنَا وَ بِسْمِ اللهِ خَرَجْنَا وَ عَلَی اللهِ رَبِّنَا تَوَکَّلْنَا

'O Allah! I ask You the blessings of entering the home and the blessings of leaving. With the Name of Allah we leave and enter the house and upon Allah, our Sustainer, we rely and depend.'

31) Teach the child that it is improper to enter another's house (even the parent's bedroom) without permission.

Sunnahs of Travelling

32) When boarding any vehicle, recite to the child: بِسْمِ اللهِ

33) When seating the child, recite to the child: اَلْحَمْدُ للهِ

34) Thereafter, recite the du'aa:

سُبْحَانَ الَّذِیْ سَخَّرَ لَنَا هٰذَا وَ مَا کُنَّا لَهُ مُقْرِنِیْنَ، وَ اِنَّا اِلَی رَبِّنَا لَمُنْقَلِبُوْنَ، سُبْحَانَ اللهِ، اَلْحَمْدُ للهِ، اَللهُ اَکْبَرُ، لَاۤ اِلٰهَ اِلَّا اللهُ

'Purity belongs to Allah, Who has brought this conveyance under our control, although we were unable to do this. Surely, we are to return to our Lord; All Glory to Allah. All Praise to Allah; for Allah is the Greatest. There is none worthy of worship but Allah!'

Sunnahs of Climbing & Descending

35) From infancy, when taking the child upstairs (or climbing a hill; whether on foot or by vehicle) say اَللهُ اَكْبَر (Allah is Great). When descending recite: سُبْحَانَ اللهِ (Purity belongs to Allah).

Sunnahs of Sneezing

36) When the child sneezes, train him to use a handkerchief with his left hand and to recite, اَلْحَمْدُ للهِ

37) The listener to this du'aa should reply يَرْحَمُكَ اللهُ

The sneezer should respond with يَهْدِيْكُمُ اللهُ وَ يُصْلِحْ بَالَكُمْ

Sunnah of Observing the Face in the Mirror

38) Train the child to recite the du'aa,

$$اَللّٰهُمَّ اَحْسَنْتَ خَلْقِىْ فَاَحْسِنْ خُلُقِىْ$$

'O Allah! You have beautified by physique, therefore make my character good (also).'

Sunnah Du'aa at the Time of Thunder & Lightning

39) During times of thunder and lightening, instead of scaring the child about demons, teach him to recite,

$$اَللّٰهُمَّ لَاتَقْتُلْنَا بِغَضَبِكَ وَ لَا تُهْلِكْنَا بِعَذَابِكَ وَ عَافِنَا قَبْلَ ذٰلِكَ$$

'O Allah! Do not kill us through Your Anger and do not destroy us through Your Punishment and grant us safety before this happens.'

Sunnah Du'aa When Bidding Farewell to Someone

اَسْتَوْدِعُ اللّٰہ دِیْنَکَ وَ اَمَانَتَکَ وَ خَوَاتِیْمَ عَمَلِکَ

40) *'I give in Allah's Trust your religion, your belongings and the result of your deeds.'* *(Tirmidhi)*

Sunnahs of Sleeping

41) Before sleeping the child, dust the bedding three time's.

42) To change the child into different (sleeping) clothes (pyjamas) is also a sunnah.

43) It is advisable to sleep the child on a separate bed/cot but in the same room as a responsible elder.

44) If possible, when the child is able to, sleep him/her on it's right side with the feet pointing away from the qiblah.

45) Recite the following to the child from the Glorious Qu'rãn: Ãyatul Qursi; Surah Kãfiroon, Surah Ikhlãs, Surah Falaq and Surah Naas. Finally, recite the du'aa:

اَللّٰھُمَّ بِاسْمِکَ اَمُوْتُ وَ اَحْیٰی

'O Allah! With your name I die and live.' *(Bukhãri)*

Thereafter blow upon one's palms and rub them over the child's body.

සාව

Anecdote

Shaykh Abul Hasan 'Ali Nadwee ۞ comments, 'The great Sultan Nizãmuddeen Awliya ۞ of Balkh (636-725 AH ~ 1234-1325 CE) was only five years old when his father passed-away. His widowed mother, who was an extremely pious lady took upon herself the Deeni upbringing of this orphaned child with such vigour and determination that the day soon arrived when the young Nizãmuddeen came home and said, 'My tutors have commanded me to wear a turban for graduation...but where shall we get a turban from?' His mother replied, 'Darling, keep calm, I shall arrange something.' Accordingly, she purchased some cotton and soon sewed a turban.

It was the habit of Sultan Nizãmuddeen ۞ upon observing the crescent of the new moon to go to his mother and sit at her feet and congratulate her upon arrival of the new Islãmic Month. Once, according to habit he visited her, when she replied, 'Whose feet will you sit at next month?' Instantly Nizãmuddeen ۞ understood that she was hinting at her impending death and began to cry, 'Mother! To whom are you leaving this destitute?' His mother replied, 'I shall reply to your question in due course but for the moment go and spend tonight at the residence of Shaykh Najeebuddeen ۞.'

Next morning, a servant arrived to summon him, 'Quickly, your mother is calling you!' When he visited her, she spoke,

'Yesterday, you posed a question for which I promised a reply. Now I shall answer you, listen carefully! Which is your right hand?' Nizãmuddeen ☀ presented his right-hand. Holding his hand with her right-hand she said, 'O Allah ﷻ! I entrust him to You!' So saying she passed-away. Sultan Nizãmuddeen ☀ thanked Allah ﷻ for this priceless naseehat and thought, 'If my beloved mother had left me a house full of diamonds and pearls then it would not have caused me as much joy as this advice.' (p246, Mothers of the Awliya)

Shaykh Ashraf 'Ali Thãnwi ☀ narrates, 'Be concerned and spend all your energy and resources in making your children truly pious, for then Mercy and Guidance from Allah ﷻ will always be with them (even after you have departed from this world).'

And our final plea is to Allah ﷻ the Sovereign of the Universe. Peace and Blessings be upon His Final Prophet Muhammad ﷺ...

'O Allah! Bestow on us from our wives and children the comfort of our eyes, and make us leaders of the Muttaqûn (pious).' (Glorious Qur'ãn, 25:74)

Dear Reader, if you have found this Kitab informative would you kindly recite Surah Ikhlãs or Durood three times and bestow its reward as esal-e-thawãb to Prophet Muhammad ﷺ; his Companions ☀, those Scholars whose works have been quoted from; the editor and his team at Ashraf's Amãnat and all Muslims (deceased as well as those living).

Jazaai'khair, Was-salam,

ၷჟ

Other Ashraf's Amānat Titles

Ashraf's Amānat©
PO Box 12, Dewsbury, West Yorkshire, UK, WF12 9YX
Tel: (01924) 488929 ~ email:info@ashrafsamanat.org